100
Semesters

100 Semesters

My adventures as student, professor, and university president, and what I learned along the way

WILLIAM M. CHACE

PRINCETON UNIVERSITY PRESS

PRINCETON AND OXFORD

Library of Congress Cataloging-in-Publication Data

Chace, William M.
One hundred semesters : my adventures as student, professor, and university
president, and what I learned along the way / William M. Chace.
p. cm.
Includes index.
ISBN-13: 978-0-691-12725-5 (hardcover : alk. paper)
ISBN-10: 0-691-12725-5
1. Education, Higher—United States.   2. Universities and colleges—
United States.   I. Title.
LA227.3.C455 2007
378.73—dc22
2006000727

British Library Cataloging-in-Publication Data is available

This book has been composed in 11/14 Sabon

Printed on acid-free paper. ∞

pup.princeton.edu

Printed in the United States of America

3   5   7   9   10   8   6   4   2

To
Grace Murdough Chace
Who, with Love, Taught Me the Best Questions

CONTENTS

ACKNOWLEDGMENTS

Here I thank many people who helped me with this book. Not one of them is responsible for any of its errors or missteps:

The invaluable Murray Sperber, who said I could do it; Bill Wyman, who said I should do it; David M. Kennedy and Luke Johnson, who said I had done it.

At Haverford College: Tom Tritton, Diana Peterson, Robert Kieft, Tom Tredway, and John Douglas. At the University of California at Berkeley: Carol Soc, Judy Siu, and Lee Parsons. At Stillman College: Robert Heath. At Stanford University: Margaret J. Kimball and Paddy McGowan. At Wesleyan University: Nathanael Greene, Stewart Gillmor, Suzy Taraba, Dianna S. Hyland, and Greg Waldron. At Emory University: Gary Hauk, Daniel Teodorescu, Nancy Reinhold, Julia Perreault, Frank Stout, and Linda Kesselring.

And: Joanne Creighton at Mount Holyoke College, William Adams at Colby College, Merrill Schwartz at the Association of Governing Boards, Judith McLaughlin at the Graduate School of Education at Harvard University, Robert Birnbaum at the University of Maryland, Amy Elizabeth Schmidt at the College Board, and Aurora D'Amico at the United States Department of Education.

I know I could never have written what is here without the counsel, encouragement, and bracing wisdom and love of my wife—JoAn.

Introduction

Most people do not stay in school for a long time. For them, the world after and beyond school is more attractive than the academic enclosure. For them, the ladder of education—kindergarten, elementary school, middle school, high school, and college—is climbed once and then laid aside. They go on to "real life" and obtain jobs, establish careers, and look back on formal education as a moment, just a moment, that happened when they were young. Their youth ending, their formal education ends too.

But school never stopped for me—that is the subject of this book. My continuing education on six different campuses defined how I came to terms, year after year, with classrooms, with teachers, and then with the institutions of learning themselves. Briefly describing the years before college, the book mainly focuses on the time thereafter: at Haverford College, where I was an undergraduate; the University of California at Berkeley, where I was a graduate student; Stillman College in Alabama, where I taught for a year; Stanford University, where I taught for twenty; and Wesleyan University and Emory University, two campuses where I was president for six and nine years respectively. I have been in school—inside the campus gates—for half a century, one hundred semesters—and my faculty life continues today.

That is a long time, but this is not a long book. It would be longer were I to tell about my life when higher education did not mark my days or fill up my emotions. My wife, JoAn, and our children, Will and Katie, are only faint presences in what I have written here. Their considerable importance to me rests securely outside these pages. I have sought to tell only the part of the story that can be found in the customs, manners, and procedures of American higher education and the way those things have figured in my life.

I have worried about these confessions becoming a selfish account, even a self-indulgent one. I hope that the stories I tell here, the information I give, and the spectacle of success and absurdity I portray, will move the center of attention away from me and onto the landscape of higher education. In any case, what I have seen in school makes up these pages.

My beginning assumption is a simple one: going to a college or university never turns out to be, for anyone who has done it, a trivial step. If you have been to college, even only briefly, you don't forget it. Memories of who you were then and what you did surge up to please or embarrass you; certain moments of time are fixed indelibly in your mind. That is because college puts you on your own, often before you are ready to stand by yourself. Your strengths and vulnerabilities are on display and you can surprise yourself by how ready you are to do some things and how ill prepared you are to do others. That which surrounds you, the distinctive landscape known as "the campus," is at once reassuring and yet foreign, your home for a while but a mysterious location of studies, pursuits, and preoccupations unknown to you and carried on by countless others. It is bigger than you and retains a power over you. Because of its mysteries and its strengths, you will always remember how it looked, smelled, and felt to the touch.

Going to my first campus, Haverford College, in the fall of 1956, I acquired an interest in what such places do. Now, never having lost that interest, I write about what I saw on that campus and five others. The terrain and culture of each is different: Haverford, a small liberal arts college near Philadelphia founded by Quakers; the University of California at Berkeley, a large and powerful public university; Stillman College, a small and poor institution in Alabama established for African-Americans; Stanford, a distinguished private research university; Wesleyan, another small liberal arts college, this one in Connecticut; and Emory, an enterprising private university in Georgia. At all of these places save the first, I taught. At two of them I was a student. At two I was the president. Taken together, these six schools provide a mirror of much, but not all, of higher education in this country for the last half-century.

Given my experience, none of the rooms where the work of a college or university occurs is now a secret to me; I have been inside all of them: laboratory, seminar room, library stacks, classroom, stadium, student residence, treasurer's office, operating room, training facility, power plant, dean's office, recycling center, lecture hall, presidential suite, board room, and professorial office. These places have made up my world.

As a student, I studied in library carrels. As a professor, I read countless student essays. As a president, I watched the payroll office issue monthly checks to thousands of employees. When students killed themselves, I called their parents and grieved with them and with fellow students; when commencement day came, I congratulated and hugged the graduates. I had the honor of appointing scores of people to administrative positions and the discomfort of dismissing others. For what I did over the years, I received both praise and blame. The praise, I learned, is often no more appropriate than the blame.

A witness of higher education for that half-century, I continue to find the American campus an attractive and even a good place. Most informed people believe that American higher education is the best the world has to offer. They are right. Our colleges and universities might also be the best of America's achievements. Inventive, responsive, energetic, and endlessly productive, they are the cynosure of the world and a tribute to the possibilities of the human mind. I champion them and, in this book, offer an enthusiastic defense of them. But I also find, and report on, things about them to lament.

In this report, I ask one basic question about our colleges and universities: what sustains and fortifies them? What makes a collection of people congregate in a special place, pursue difficult studies, share understanding, wrangle over matters both crucial and insignificant, invest prodigious amounts of money in abstruse investigations, maintain high standards of excellence, for the most part treat each other decently, and come back, year after year, for more of the same? Without the consolation of yearly profits, often in the face of public ridicule or censure, and aware of the massive infusions of money required to keep them solvent, what allows these institutions to survive, indeed to prosper? Put it another way: if we did not have them, would we know how to invent them? Indeed, would we want to invent them? Given their expense, and given also the ways they do and do not comfortably exist within the prejudices and pressures of American life, would a sufficient number of the nation's people want them to dot so handsomely, as they now do, the nation's landscape?

But my question is only "academic." We know that our universities and colleges are not going to disappear. They have become part of the fabric of the lives of many young people, their parents, and alumni, as well as the great number of others whose livelihood depends on their continuing existence. Part centers of learning, part businesses, part havens for the young, and part the places where millions of our fellow citizens are employed, they are central to what we are as a nation. Characterized by their profitless behavior within a profit-making culture, and representing a dedication to intellectual excellence in a country that historically has been ambivalent about such excellence, they are at once admirable, unique, troubling, and permanent. Here I write about them.

My praise is mixed with descriptions of some tough problems they face. The best schools are too expensive, and only a tiny fraction of the young people who could benefit from them even apply to them, much less gain admission to them. Those who arrive on most campuses do not now find what once was the mission of America's best colleges and universities: a commitment to the kind of moral development that produces an informed and responsible citizenry. That kind of education, to which I was introduced decades ago at little Haverford College, is now in danger of being lost. It is sinking beneath the waves of faculty neglect, administrative busyness, preprofessional frenzy on the part of students, and the depressing uncertainty on almost every campus about what moral development might even mean. But it is what some parents want their children to have, and it is a realm of learning that no other entity in the country is prepared to provide. That the nation's best schools cannot, or will not, provide it is profoundly lamentable.

Over the years, many of the leaders of these schools—whose extravagant compensation, I argue, should be reduced to levels closer to that of the faculty—have joined with others to permit, witlessly, the growth of irrelevant entertainments and amusements for students. Chief among them is big-time athletics. On many campuses, it now diverts attention from, and even undercuts, the academic pursuits that are the schools' fundamental reason for being. Not classrooms or libraries, but football stadiums and basketball arenas become the focus of student attention. The climax of the week becomes Saturday afternoon.

In addition, many schools have become overly concerned with marketing, "branding," and the competitive commercialization of the life of the mind. Colleges and universities should combine their strengths rather than wasting energy in emphasizing the small differences between them. And, most distressing to me as an English professor, America's colleges and universities have witnessed a decline in the force and relevance of the humanities, once a source of delight and wisdom to students and graduates, and now, for many people within and outside the academy, an arid, unattractive, and inaccessible subject.

I would not write about these institutions as I do if I did not cherish them. My respect is mixed with anxiety; my affection is tempered by misgivings. But about their importance to this country I have no doubt. As a nation, we have invested a large share of our hopes and dreams in our colleges and universities. As a student, teacher, and president, I have seen for five decades the extraordinary dividends of that investment. In the pages of this book, I show what living so close to higher education for so long has meant to me.

1

I Knew Exactly What I Was Doing

When it came to college, I knew exactly what I was doing. I was going to West Point. The year was 1954 and I was a high school junior in Bethesda, Maryland. Many of my classmates were seeking an NROTC college scholarship, for with it the cost of college would be defrayed, provided you agreed to serve in the Navy upon graduation. This sounded good to me, but West Point sounded even better. Patriotism was in the air. The "police action" in Korea was still in the news, the armistice having been signed in 1953. West Point—the United States Military Academy—would be a way for me to serve my country, save my parents the cost of college, and give me a good engineering education. Since I knew I wanted to be an astrophysicist, I thought engineering would be the way to get there. I also nurtured visions of military heroism. I would join the Long Gray Line.

Knowing that admission to West Point would be tough, I trained hard for months: push-ups, sit-ups, rope-climbing, running distances. All this I did myself, for mine was a wholly private ambition. My parents—my father was a public relations officer in a downtown Washington trade association and my mother was busy raising four boys, I being the eldest—knew what I was up to, but found it all puzzling. My father, a Princeton graduate with a doctorate in history from the University of North Carolina who had left academic life, had never served in the military, and my mother, a Simmons College graduate, feared the very idea of war and what it might do to her boys. But my parents let me be. So there I was—out in the backyard with the climbing rope. My father, on what would be our one and only stop on "the college tour," took me to West Point while on a business trip and a journey to see his reclusive sister, an artist who lived with her husband in Nyack, New York. When we got to our goal, my father and I stood together and looked down upon the broad expanse of the Hudson River. Then we turned to see the cadets in formation and were told about the heroes who had been trained there, the men who had fought the battles and won the victories and saved the nation. He was, I am sure, puzzled about what I was up to, but I knew for sure—the United States Military Academy was what I knew it would be: stonily austere, weighty with history, uncompromising in its dedication to ritual, and for all these reasons, thrilling.

In high school in Maryland, I loved all the science courses and did well in them. My greatest pleasures were in math: algebra, plane geometry, and trigonometry. I grew happily lost in the problems set before us and then emerged, giddy with delight, when I could find their solutions. As for English, I was only an average student, being required to read with annoyance both *Romeo and Juliet* and *Macbeth*, taught as they were by a teacher who periodically removed herself to the ladies restroom only to return smelling of alcohol. We would begin a reading of the play and make some small progress. But after she came back, with her memory blighted, we would return to just where we had started: Act One, Scene One. Later I was to learn that Aristotle saw drama as having three parts: beginning, middle, and end. In her course, we had only beginning. Although I secretly wrote poetry, I was not a particularly good student, and I was never among the students placed each year in advanced English courses with better teachers.

Being in those days shy and inward, I participated in no clubs, played no sports save those required in phys ed, and went to only one dance in four years, the Senior Prom, for which all-important event I trained by attending dance classes at Arthur Murray. I was unknown to many of my classmates. Today I would be grouped with the geeks. But when it came time for the West Point tests (at nearby Walter Reed Army Hospital), I was ready. I bunked for three days with other young men striving to do their best to win appointments, for if you passed those tests, that was the way you got to the United States Military Academy—along with a nomination from one's senator or congressman. I vividly recall my fellow candidates as uniformly immense and highly, if not obsessively, focused. Most of them were high school athletes, as I certainly was not. One of them told me he had 52 football scholarship offers to colleges and universities. That made sense to me; he was the largest human I had ever seen in person. He said he was worried that he might not have strong enough SAT scores to get into West Point and he told me the cut-off point was a total, on the math and verbal, of 950.

For those three days, we ate together, were closely examined by a battery of doctors, ran races against each other, did those sit-ups and push-ups (I was ready), and were examined again by other doctors. Nobody in my high school knew I was doing this. Mine, as I say, was a private quest.

After a couple of months, I ripped open a letter from the Department of the Army notifying me that I had passed all the tests and was "qualified" to be a candidate. But merely passing the tests was not enough. I still needed that nomination to West Point. Despite discovering that one of the two Maryland senators, J. Glenn Beall, had already given his to someone else that year, I wrote to him about myself. By return mail, he graciously nominated me as his "first alternate," a category useful in light of the fact that many first-year West Point students (the "cadets") washed out. That was not enough, however, to get me what I wanted—admission. I still had no nomination in hand. But given the happy proximity of our house in the Maryland suburbs to the United States Congress, I was able to spend several days walking the corridors of the office buildings housing congressmen, trying to find one who had not made a nomination because his district had no "qualified" candidates. I knocked on many doors and saw administrative assistant after administrative assistant. One of them, working for a Wyoming congressman and willing to be helpful, asked if my family had any relations living in Wyoming or if we owned property in the state; the man for whom he worked would be glad, I gathered, to make me his candidate. But we had no Wyoming connections.

After knocking on those many doors to no effect, my West Point ambitions and dreams came to an end. I was not to gain an appointment. It was all too late. The class of "cadets" was being formed. I was not to march in the Long Gray Line; I was not to serve my country; I was not to spare my parents the cost of a college education. I was to go somewhere else.

But where? I knew nothing about colleges. I looked in books; I stared ignorantly at catalogs; I asked my friends what their plans were. In those days, the Kaplan Guide to the Best Colleges in the U.S., the Peterson Guide, the Fiske Guide, the knowledgeable school counselors ready to advise, the private courses promising to add points to your SAT—none of these things, years later to swirl about the head of every applicant to college, existed. I had only names, cloudy impressions, and random remarks about this or that college. All the schools I read about looked far away and imposing; their standards and traditions appeared both noble and impossible ("You will join a community pledged to learning and to the highest moral behavior"); everything emphasized the serious and the hallowed.

One day, my mother told me about Haverford College. I had never heard of it. But a friend in the neighborhood, a Quaker, told her it was a "good" school, one founded by the Religious Society of Friends. I knew nothing about Quakers either. I looked the school up, discovered it was small, was single-sex (like many private schools of the time), and didn't have fraternities. About them, I was worried, for I was under the impression that fraternities were tony and sophisticated (years later I got to know them better). I had only limited social skills and did not relish the thought of having to develop any more. And the school was outside Philadelphia, not so far from home. Moreover, the name "Haverford" seemed prestigious. I applied. I did so as someone, I later learned, who fitted neatly the profile of most college applicants in the 1950s: I was white, male, native-born, not yet twenty-one, Protestant, from a family with a father in professional or managerial work who earned more than the national average.[1] The Haverford application cost my father ten dollars. I submitted my SAT scores (600 in the verbal section, 727 in the math, and, as I thought about it, more than good enough for West Point). I also applied to other schools, knowing little more about them (Lehigh,

Princeton, the University of Virginia, Tufts) than I knew about Haverford, with ten dollars for each of them coming from my father. And then I waited. I had never seen Haverford; I had not seen any of the other schools. The West Point trip was the only time I had ever been on a "college" campus.

Haverford wrote back a short letter: I had been admitted. Without much more knowledge about the place than what I already had, I decided to go. Why? Among the schools to which I applied, it had the highest average SAT scores of entering students, and while I did not think of myself as an "intellectual" (and would not have known anything about the connotations of the word), I knew from high school that, all in all, it was more interesting to be with smart people. And the college was near home. No fraternities. Small. Henceforth Haverford was to be the center of my life—an intense and confused life—for the next five years.

In embarrassing sum, here was my situation: I had wanted to go either to a military academy that would teach me the skills I would need to wage war and direct others to kill people or to a small private school founded by Quakers that would inspire me to admire pacifism. Out of such certainty and self-knowledge, off I went to start my education. There was no way of knowing then that education would define the rest of my life.

ENDNOTE

1. See Seymour Harris, *A Statistical Portrait of Higher Education* (New York: McGraw-Hill Book Co., 1972), pp. 7–8.

2

Haverford—the Guilty Reminder

When I applied to Haverford in 1955, I was one of about 450 young men to do so. Of those admitted—about 240—120 chose to enroll, and those young men—boys, in fact—constituted the Class of 1960. The aim of the College was to have a total student body numbering 460. In the language of present-day admission officers, that means that for the Class of 1960, Haverford had a 53 percent admission rate and a 50 percent yield rate. The aim of every admission officer at so-called "elite" colleges and universities today is to reduce the admission rate ("we are hard to get into") and to increase the yield rate ("anyone lucky enough to be admitted will be eager to show up"). If that aim is realized, that officer and that school will have done well indeed, for the school can then truly and proudly proclaim to be "highly selective." It is not beyond the capabilities of some institutions to encourage more and more applications, for such an abundance of candidates, most of whom will be rejected, will help to mark those institutions as "highly selective." Only a few schools today are, in fact, genuinely selective, even though many would like to be and quite a few pretend to be. As the *Atlantic Monthly* reports, of the nearly three million people who finish American high schools each year, two million seek additional education. Of these, the magazine says, about "250,000, less than one tenth of all graduates, are involved in the struggle for places in the most selective schools."[1] While there are approximately 4,100 institutions of higher education in the United States, of which more than 2,300 are four-year colleges and universities, it is only a handful of these that make up the inner circle of schools for which there is genuine competition for admission. Nonetheless, among these schools, that competition is fierce—among the students who want to get in and among the schools that are admitting them (or, to put it more accurately, rejecting most of them). Applications (or "apps," as they are known in the admissions trade) from that relatively small sub-group of young men and women (about a quarter of a million of them) flood admission offices. They come in via the postal service, FedEx, UPS, courier, and on-line. The result is a situation described by the *Atlantic Monthly* as "chaotic and unpredictable . . . corporate and marketized . . . [and] hysterical."[2] Admissions officers have to work harder each year to keep up with an increased workload of applications because more and more young people want to attend the same small and hot cluster of schools; more and more parents act as zealous advocates for their children in the process; more and more secondary schools see their prestige rise and fall by virtue of the success of their students in getting into the right schools; and the schools themselves, looking at the admission rate vs. the yield rate, want to make sure that they have admitted not only those students worthy of admission but exactly those who will actually show up in the fall.

Questions at the schools abound: What is the most efficient way to allocate the limited resources of financial aid to help bring about the desired outcome of an excellent class comprising just the right students? How much "merit aid" should be provided—and to which students—to make sure that the incoming class will be adorned with very gifted youngsters (for whom lots of schools are competing) but whose collective presence will not bleed dry the admissions budget? Which applicants are genuinely interested in the school and which see it as only a form of backup insurance? By the same token, which students are to be placed on the "wait-list" as a form of insurance for the school? And, at the end of the process, how can the admission officers "shape" the class to bring about the right balance of men and women, minority and non-minority students, those who can pay the full costs and those who will receive financial aid?

In 1955, things were different. Only slightly less than a quarter-million high school graduates entered selective private schools then. In 2001, more than twice that number, 508,000, did so. The numbers of those entering public institutions, then and now, are more dramatic. In 1955, some 283,000 high-school students enrolled at public institutions, but in 2001, 867,000 did so.[3] Private education has, with respect to all the numbers, been eclipsed in extraordinary ways.

As all studies show, the magnitude of everything about colleges and universities—students enrolled, tuition costs, buildings built, administrative personnel hired, research activity generated, size of libraries developed, and all the rest—has dramatically increased in the last half century. One telling example: in 2005, 1,251,312 college-bound seniors sat for the Scholastic Aptitude Test (SAT), but in 1955, that number was 208,600.[4] A few other stunning parts of the landscape of higher education to consider:

- In 1956, the total value of the physical foundation of higher education (land, buildings, and equipment) was some $60 billion in current dollars; today, it is $220 billion.
- At the close of the 1960s, the endowment market value of all accredited universities and colleges stood at some $27 billion in current dollars; in 2004 (the last year for which there are reliable records) it stood at more than $267 billion.[5]
- In the last year of the 1960s, voluntary support to higher education (alumni giving, corporation giving, the giving of foundations and friends) came in at $3.8 billion in current dollars; in 2000–01, such generosity totaled $24 billion.[6]

Higher education has been a boom "industry" for as long as most Americans can remember. So central to our thinking and our dreaming is the prospect of college, and what it will cost, and the way it is alleged to determine all the rest of life's choices, higher education in all its ramifications now shapes a large part of American family life, particularly for the middle class. Parents prepare for it, save for it, and worry about it; children are drilled as to its significance and the consequences of not going to the right school; tutoring businesses (now bringing in more than $1 billion per year), and now even summer camps where young people are trained to take the SAT exams and write applications, flourish by virtue of their promises to position young men and women in exactly the best place to gain admission to colleges and universities.

So as to be ready, even seventh and eighth graders can take a version of the SAT. And about one in twelve high-schoolers and their parents make use of professional consultants as they fill out the applications; such consultants can charge up to $10,000 for their services.[7]

But when I applied, and when I was admitted those several decades ago, I did so as a befuddled innocent (West Point or Haverford?), and the schools that accepted me were themselves going about their work with simplicity and innocence. The industry was only beginning to stir. In applying to Haverford, as I so naively did in the mid-1950s, and when I thereafter entered the world of so-called "private" higher education, that sector comprised some 996 schools. And here again is the exception to the pattern of immense growth. While everything else has been on the upswing, the founding of liberal arts colleges has not kept the pace. What was once one of the glories of the eighteenth and nineteenth centuries—the building of new liberal arts institutions—has slowed considerably. While, in 1956, there were 1,878 institutions of higher education in the United States and Haverford was one of the 996 privates, today there are more than 4,100 schools, and only 1,713 of these are four-year liberal arts colleges that are not part of universities.[8] And with respect to the total number of students it enrolls, the private sector is every year dwarfed by the numbers enrolled in institutions of public higher education. To take one telling example: the University of Texas, largest in the nation, now enrolls slightly more than 47,000 students. And Arizona State University intends to grow 61 percent, to 92,000 students, and to become a "nationally recognized research university," it says, by 2020.[9]

When I enrolled at Haverford in the fall of 1956, it had 454 students, all male, six short of the school's goal. It would have been very hard to be smaller. Today, after much study by the College's trustee leadership, it has more than doubled its size—to 1,100 students, with women (their admittance an innovation in 1978) now slightly outnumbering men. In my class, there were two African-Americans; today almost six percent of the students are black. This growth at Haverford in the number of women students and the number of racial and ethnic minorities, including African-Americans, is in keeping with national figures. Across the great spectrum of higher education, women outnumber men 56 to 44 percent, and students coming from minority categories (the uniformly recognized ones being African-American, Hispanic/ Latino, Asian and Asian-American, and Native American) today represent about one-quarter of all those in attendance. At Haverford today, the figure is 26 percent.

The Haverford that admitted me was more than small. It was also narrow in the backgrounds—ethnically, culturally, economically— of the students it brought to the campus; it was, moreover, geo- graphically provincial, with most of my classmates coming from comfortable middle-class homes on the Eastern seaboard. Today, more than twice the size it was fifty years ago (but still very small), it has a much greater percentage of students from other parts of the United States and even other parts of the world. It has thus mirrored the large demographic shifts in enrollment in higher edu- cation: more women, more students from ethnic and cultural minority populations, and thus, to employ the most shopworn term of the day, much greater "diversity."

But the Haverfords of the world are yielding the larger demo- graphic shifts to public institutions. As that public sector, main- taining its responsiveness to population growth and civic demand within the respective states, continues to expand, it seems— ironically enough—to be well on its way to becoming less "pub- lic." Schools once defined as "state-supported" now describe them- selves as "state-assisted" or "state-noted," and the presidents of some schools have even remarked, in a stoic and melancholy way, that they really are no more than "state-neglected." Ambitious fund-raising campaigns now mark the atmosphere of many "pub- lic" campuses, with alumni and other allies of the institutions being solicited for the kind of support once drawn from state cof- fers.[10] Relative tuition costs, once the great marker distinguishing "private" and "public" schools, now draw closer to each other. For instance, in the fall of 2003 the University of Maryland charged $6,759 tuition plus mandatory fees for full-time undergraduate students from the state of Maryland and $17,433 for nonresident students. Those were increases, from the previous year, of 14.6 percent and 15.5 percent respectively. The university had to ratchet up its tuition charges because the state could not, or would not, continue to shoulder the burden of supporting the institution in the manner to which it had become accustomed.

The result is a landscape of higher education with "private" higher education, led by great research institutions such as Stanford, Harvard, MIT, and Johns Hopkins, becoming more "public" because of the amount of federally sponsored research grants those schools pull in, and "public" higher education becoming more "private" because of attenuated state support. As the two sectors converge, American higher education gradually assumes a new identity.

In this larger and confusing world, my alma mater continues to play its small and noble part. It now serves, as it served a half-century ago, as a marker, even a guilty reminder, of what a certain form of education has been in this country. This has consistently been the role of places like Haverford: to draw attention, by their example, to the importance of small classrooms, intellectual seriousness, intense individual tutelage, and a strong honor code emphasizing personal responsibility.

When I applied, the routine was standard and simple: ten dollars to move the application along, submission of the high-school grades and the SAT scores, a visit to the campus, and the expectation that one's parents would be paying the stipulated tuition, room, and board. Financial aid was then called "a scholarship" and was determined in a rather informal way, case by case, by the institution, according to what it saw as the student's particular situation. For the academic year 1956–57, my parents were asked to pay tuition to the tune of $850, a board fee of $470, a room fee of $250, and a "unit fee" of $85. The total: $1,655. I was given a scholarship of $600. Today things are entirely different at Haverford, as everywhere else. For 2005–06, the tuition is $31,466, fees for room and board come to $9,840, and the student activity fee at $294 brings the total to $41,600. This stunning figure, a twenty-five-fold increase in half a century,[11] is in keeping with what other "highly selective" colleges and universities charge, and the differences in prices among those "highly selective" private institutions turn out to be very small (each of the schools watches what the others did in the previous year and plan accordingly). The "sticker price" for 2005–06, up to $43,000 at some top schools, was an amount equal to about two-thirds of the median income for a family of four.[12] The extraordinary shock of this "sticker price" is lessened for those families who ask for, and are awarded, financial aid. This difference between the stated price and the sums families qualified for financial aid actually pay is known as the "discount rate." A great many families receive such aid, but some do not. Painfully enough, some families with annual incomes of more than $100,000 might not qualify for financial aid, even though they cannot afford the full tuition and other costs. Their children will likely go to less expensive schools.

With many institutions dramatically discounting the advertised tuition rate, there is often a yawning gap between what the school fixes as its tuition and what some parents actually wind up paying. Application fees typically come to between $50 and $80 per school. One can apply "early decision" (which means that the applicant makes a moral commitment to attend the given school and no other if admitted) or "regular." Parents or guardians hoping for financial aid (no longer called "a scholarship") submit personal financial disclosure forms as complicated and probing as IRS documents (and just as likely to promote a certain amount of hide-and-seek about assets and liabilities). Some applicants, in order to cover all their bets, will apply to a dozen or more schools. Campus visits are an opportunity for the schools to show off their many attractions, not all of them bearing directly on the purity of traditional academic pursuits: playing fields, bowling alleys, entertainment centers, rock-climbing walls, saunas, elaborate computing centers, stadiums, and weight rooms. And applicants can seek to make their visits opportunities to exhibit their personal virtues and achievements to admission personnel.

The result at the most elite schools is an enormous, and labor-intensive, process involving hundreds of thousands of applicants, miles of files, thousands of people to process the application folders and make intelligent decisions about whom to admit, whom to reject, and whom, as the parlance goes, to let "swim" for a while in the great pool of the undecideds.[13] Woven into that process are considerations of those applicants who would give geographical balance, those who are children of alumni (the so-called "legacies"), those whose presence would bring racial and ethnic character to the entering class (now a consideration under the vigilant eye of all those concerned, for whatever reason, with "affirmative action"), those whose athletic or artistic or debating or chess skills would stud the class with victory or variegation, and those with such promise all around that they are deemed at some schools deserving of that old-fashioned honor, a "scholarship" or financial aid—"merit aid"—irrespective of their ability to furnish the quoted tuition.

At the largest schools, most of them public, this labor-intensive process has to be radically foreshortened. Numbers, and only numbers, can count: SAT and ACT scores, high-school grade-point averages, rank in class. The volume of applicants is too great to do more than run the numbers through the computers and classify the results: admit, deny, "swim." At some schools, as everyone knows from following the history of affirmative action court decisions, race and ethnicity can count in substantial ways to shape the class. The "weight" of race is factored into the admit/reject calculation (although the degree to which it can be given importance depends on the state or the court district, and even more court decisions could again change, or even end, affirmative action). But the careful consideration of individual cases, considered one by one, is now deemed too expensive in time and personnel.

No one should think, however, that even with large amounts of institutional money being allocated to financial aid at the colleges and universities with the greatest prestige, almost all of them proclaiming their belief in "diversity," their student bodies reflect actual social or "class" diversity. After all the financial aid has been given out, and after all the qualified minority students have been admitted, and after all other considerations have been observed, the "best" institutions remain, by and large, what they have always been: home to the well-to-do. The title of a recent book about Harvard—*Privilege*—sums up the admission procedures there. "Meritocracy is the ideological veneer, but social and economic stratification is the reality," says its author, Ross Gregory Douthat.[14] The *New York Times* has reported that

> In 2000, about 55 percent of freshmen at the nation's 250 most selective colleges, public and private, were from the highest-earning fourth of households, compared with 46 percent in 1985. . . . The number from the bottom fourth dipped slightly over that period, while those from the middle 50 percent fell sharply. In many cases, the less wealthy students went to less selective schools, including lower-ranked campuses of state universities.[15]

In sum, only a handful of college students go to the prestigious institutions. The rest, in huge numbers, go everywhere else, to places large and small, old and new, urban and suburban, where everything from animal husbandry to forestry to restaurant management to ancient history, Shakespeare, and the history of Vietnam is taught. The world of higher education has indeed changed in the last fifty years. What was once smaller, less expensive, less inclusive, less complex, and less ambitious has taken on massive dimensions and importance and has become centrally involved in the lives of millions of people, Americans and others. In 1956, when I entered college, I was one of some three million in attendance; today the total enrollment of college and university students is more than sixteen million.[16] For those millions, the universities and colleges of the United States serve to inspire hope, escalate the possibilities of social and professional advancement, centralize and codify learning in myriad spheres of knowledge, and employ a vast legion of teachers, administrators, and service workers.

But the industry of today did not seem industrial in 1956. And, in coming to Haverford in the fall of that year, I came to nothing that seemed a part of any industry at all. How could a campus of 204 acres, a student body of 454, and a faculty of 70 appear to be anything but what I saw: a place for an eighteen-year-old boy to become the astrophysicist he thought he wanted to be?

ENDNOTES

1. James Fallows, "The New College Chaos," *Atlantic Monthly,*
November 2003, p. 106.
2. Ibid., p. 108.
3. Table 183, "Total First-time Freshmen Enrolled in Degree-granting
Institutions, by Attendance Status, Sex of Student, and Type and Control
of Institution: Fall 1955 to Fall 2001," *Digest of Education Statistics
2003* (National Center for Education Statistics, 2004, http://nces.ed.gov/).
4. Figures courtesy of the College Board.
5. See the 2004 NACUBO (National Association of College and
University Business Officers) Endowment Study (http://www.nacubo.
org/x2321.xml). This study surveys institutions with endowments
greater than $1 million.
6. See table 352, "Voluntary Support for Degree-Granting Institutions,
by Source and Purpose of Support: Selected Years, 1959–60 to
2003–04," National Center for Education Statistics, http://nces.ed.gov/.
7. See the survey conducted by the Independent Educational Consultants
Association, as cited by the web publication *Inside Higher Ed*
(http://www.insidehighered.com/) (August 9, 2005).
8. Table 246, "Degree-Granting Institutions, by Control and Type of
Institution: 1949–50 to 2002–03," National Center for Education
Statistics (http://nces.ed.gov/).
9. Michael Arnone, "Arizona State U. Plans to Build Additional Campus,
to Help Accommodate 92,000 Students by 2020," *Chronicle of
Higher Education,* April 9, 2004 (http://chronicle.com/daily/2004/04/
2004040904n.htm).
10. State funding for state institutions dwindles with each year. As Ami
Zusman has noted, ever since the economic recession of the early 1990s,
higher education has had to compete (unfavorably) with other state services, particularly K–12 education, Medicaid, and prisons. "Issues
Facing Higher Education in the Twenty-First Century," in *American
Higher Education in the Twenty-First Century,* ed. by Philip G. Altbach,
Robert O. Berdahl, and Patricia J. Gumport (Baltimore and London:
Johns Hopkins University Press, 1999), p. 110. And one former president
of the University of Michigan reports that in thirty years, state appropri-
ations to that institution have dwindled from more than 60 percent of its

operating budget to some 10 percent (see James J. Duderstadt, *A University for the 21st Century* [Ann Arbor: University of Michigan Press, 2000], p. 311). For further evidence of declining state support of public higher education, see Sam Dillon, "At Public Universities, Warnings of Privatization," *New York Times*, October 16, 2005, p. 12.

11. Corrected for inflation, that 1956 figure of $1,655 would be equivalent, in 2005 dollars, to $12,096, only a seven-fold increase.

12. See U.S. Census Bureau, "Median Income for 4-Person Families," http://www.census.gov/hhes/www/income/4person.html, 2005. The exact figure is $62,732.

13. See *Atlantic Monthly,* November 2003, for several informative essays on the admissions process.

14. Ross Gregory Douthat, *Privilege: Harvard and the Education of the Ruling Class* (New York: Hyperion, 2005), p. 9.

15. David Leonhardt, "As Wealthy Fill Top Colleges, New Efforts to Level the Field," *New York Times,* April 22, 2004, p. 1.

16. Table 174, "Total Fall Enrollment in Degree-Granting Institutions, by Attendance Status, Sex of Student, and Control of Institution: 1947 to 2001," National Center for Education Statistics (http://nces.ed.gov/).

3

And All Will Be Well

In the early fall of 1956, my father and I set out for Haverford. He drove our family car, a green two-door 1950 Ford, bought used, to New York for a business trip and he took me with him. With me went a suitcase with several shirts and trousers, underwear, toiletries, socks, and a second pair of shoes. I wore my only sports jacket. In addition, I had with me a portable manual typewriter, a dictionary, and a thesaurus.

We successfully made our way toward Philadelphia and out onto the Main Line, Route 30, to the site of the College. By night-fall, we reached what the map said was our destination, but we found no Haverford, said to be between Ardmore and Bryn Mawr. Nor did we find any signs for the College. (Only later did I learn that the Quaker sensibility giving Haverford its character was not much interested in anything so ostentatious as a sign noting the location of the College). The night was getting darker and my father, never at ease with night-time driving, was worried about getting on to New York. At last, thanks to information provided at a gas station, we found our way down a long drive into the College. It was about ten o'clock. All lights, save one coming from a distant building, had been extinguished. My father and I agreed that I would proceed alone and ask at that building for further instructions. We both could see just how odd our situation was. To comfort me, and (I think) to cheer himself up as he left his eldest son on a dark campus neither of us had ever seen before, he said, "Don't worry about a thing, Bill. All will be well." And so, bidding each other good night (and, in a way unspoken but nonetheless felt by both of us, goodbye for a while), I was on my own.

With my modest belongings I walked toward the distant light. It illuminated the front door of a large and imposing, almost baronial, building. I knocked once, knocked twice, and then was greeted by a very large young man not dissimilar in appearance from the young man with whom I had bunked when trying out for West Point. He looked at me and said: "Football or soccer?" This was a disconcerting question. While I had been preparing myself for difficult challenges in college, this particular inquiry put me wholly at a loss. But he waited, and I knew I had to stand and deliver. Remembering that I had played soccer in high school and had even, on a fluke, once scored a goal, I responded "soccer." And he said, "OK, over there; here's your stuff. Good night." My stuff consisted of running shorts, a tee shirt, and an athletic supporter. The direction he gave me was to a cot surrounded by other cots on which scores of young men were sleeping.

By then, it was late. And so to sleep, in strange surroundings, with surprising procedures, I went. My father's words, "All will be well," echoed in my mind. They were to echo there for a long time.

At five-thirty the next morning, I was awakened by the sound of everyone dressing in their shorts, putting on their running shoes (I was given a pair), and gulping down breakfasts of juice and cereal and milk. And then, in the early dawn, I found myself running across the playing fields of Haverford. It took me several hours, and several artful questions posed to my running mates, to discover that I was with Haverford's soccer and football teams, there for early training. My father and I had misread the freshman schedule, and we had driven to college a week ahead of time. My classmates, those of the Class of 1960, had not yet arrived. All indeed would be well, but not for a while.

The Haverford that was my home for the next five years was then an institution of 70 faculty members, an administrative staff of a dozen, an annual operating budget of $985,000, an endowment of $15 million, and a strong dedication to Quaker principles. Of the 454 students, half came from public secondary schools and half from private. About one in eight students were Quakers (or, more formally, members of the Religious Society of Friends), as were a number of the senior administrators and the faculty.

I lived that first year in Barclay Hall, an imposing granite building of four stories that had, over the years, weathered not only the somber winters of Pennsylvania but also the living habits of thousands of young and active boys. Barclay was apparently the least desirable place to be, and so most of the 120 freshmen ("Rhinies" as we were mysteriously known) found themselves there. Where I lived was called a "suite": I had a room, my roommate had a room, and there was an unfurnished "living" room between us. In each room were a bed, a chair, a small table, a bureau, a study lamp, and a desk (that is where the typewriter went). The College supplied these items. The bathroom—dank and lit by fluorescent bulbs—was down the hall. One pay phone was in the entry to the building; three others were on the three landings of the floors above; no student had a phone in his room.

The other accommodations were just as plain and straightforward. Twenty meals were served per week; there was no breakfast on Sunday, but Sunday dinner—at noon—was the best meal of the week. All 454 students ate together at designated hours; at dinner we were served by other students whose jobs helped them pay for their schooling; at lunch and breakfast we served ourselves, buffet-style. The food was nourishing but no more; in time, it was to become tiresome, and, as a result, we now and again erupted in lively food fights, the cost of repairing the damage they caused promptly pro-rated among us all. In what was soon no longer to be a tradition, each of us was given a thorough physical examination by the College doctor. That, and the test to determine if we could swim the width of the rather small College pool, was abandoned by the time I was to graduate.

Almost at once I learned that two realities lay at the heart of Haverford. The first was its moral seriousness; the second was the intensity of its academic challenge. The fact that we all lived together in Spartan surroundings, with limited access to the world beyond the campus, gave force to these realities. Some students (but no freshmen) had cars; the suburban train, a commuter operation, ran into Philadelphia, a city which we had few skills or means to enjoy; Bryn Mawr College was only a mile or so away, but that mile brought one to severe Gothic architecture, strict parietal rules common to women's colleges in the 1950s, and an atmosphere of academic rigor no less challenging than that of Haverford. For all freshman students, the simple fact of the first year was that it was spent almost entirely, save for vacation breaks, on the campus. On that plot of ground, long ago designed by an English gardener of considerable skill and vision, we got to know each other, and we learned what was then thought by the College right to learn.

The curriculum, designed with our best interests at heart, was lean and offered no escapes. Everyone in the freshman class took five courses, including a science course, a course in a foreign language, a course in the social sciences, and English 11–12, "Reading and Writing on Human Values." Brought into existence in 1950 by the prompting of the then president and a grant from the Carnegie Foundation, this last course was designed by three professors in English to challenge the minds of young men and to provoke them into classroom discussion. It was central to what Haverford thought of itself and its students. In the academic year 1956–57, it was taught by six professors in six different sections of twenty students apiece. And so, in that first week of September, we met, the twenty of us, to talk, first about Emerson's essays, and then about Sherwood Anderson's *Winesburg, Ohio*, and thereafter *The Catcher in the Rye*, and, by December, the poetry of W. B. Yeats. These encounters were followed by tutorial sessions, one per week, during which we met with the professor in groups of just four to discuss the reading more deeply. And to these hour-long sessions, held in the professor's small office in the library, we brought, each of us, a 500-word essay—to be read aloud, discussed, and most likely, torn apart.

My classmates in these sessions were Fred Schulze, Paul Sinclair, and Dick Teitlebaum. Fred, a Quaker, was from the Philadelphia area; Paul, one of the two African-Americans in the Class of 1960, was from Jersey City, where his father was a physician and the Hudson County coroner; Dick, one of a handful of Jews in the class, was from New York and devoted to musical composition and performance. Our teacher was Alfred Satterthwaite, an assistant professor trained at Harvard and just appointed to the faculty.

Thanks to him, thanks to the College, and thanks to everything about me that was still adolescent, this was to prove the most important college course I ever took. It efficiently demolished, one by one, most of the inchoate certainties about the world I had brought, along with my few physical possessions, to Haverford. And while it did not provide me with certainties any stronger, it did give me an urge to question, on a weekly basis, those offered by others, particularly those coming from Schulze, Sinclair, or Teitlebaum.

The nature of literary analysis has changed greatly over the last fifty years; looking back, I note that "Reading and Writing on Human Values" was strikingly moral in its scope, its diction, and its intentions. We pondered these questions: Is it possible truly to lead a life of self-reliance, as Emerson urged we do? Was Holden Caulfield right in his rejection of all that is phony in the world? What should we make of the lives led by those forlorn characters set before us by Sherwood Anderson? Little time was devoted to the complexities of literary technique, nor did we attempt to place the author in a racial, gender, or class "context." We engaged no theories, nor did we doubt the possibility of, at some point, assigning coherent meaning to all we read and discussed. And over the year, prodded by the anxiety about what our tutorial colleagues and Professor Satterthwaite said about our 500-word essays, we did learn to write better.

My other courses—SocSci 11–12, introduction to social science, German I, Chemistry I, and Math I—seemed less relevant to the theme resounding that year for me everywhere on the campus: that a moral life, lived honestly and simply in full accord with a sympathy for the integrity of the lives of all others in the community, was what mattered. Polling statistics, German irregular verbs, and the calculus did not speak to the moral life; but the books we read under the scrutiny of Professor Satterthwaite and the way we used them to question each other did.

In that first month, the 120 of us, the Class of 1960, were informed about "The Haverford College Honor System." That deepened our sense of the seriousness for which Haverford stood. Brought together in a room one night early in the fall by several upperclassmen elected to leadership positions, we were told that the honor system had been established for two reasons: to make college life "pleasant and responsible" and to "preserve the standing of the College in the eyes of others." In particular, the system, which students themselves maintained, implemented and enforced standards of behavior in two specific areas: scholastic work and the "entertainment of women guests." About the first, the rules could not have been more clearly stated, even though we were later, out of self-interest, to spend many hours parsing their inner complexities and possible self-contradictions: first, that "no student shall give or receive aid" during examinations; second, that "a student shall never represent another person's ideas or scholarship as his own;" and third, that "in the preparation of written home-work and laboratory reports . . . students may work together, provided that each member of the group understands the work being done."

The second area, that devoted to the "entertainment of women guests," read: "Any act which, if it became public, would damage the reputation of the College, the student and/or the woman guest involved, shall be considered a violation of the Honor System." Our eyes fastened on these several words. About intellectual honesty, the emphasis had been placed entirely on the student himself and his duty to do his own work. But about "women guests," another force—the force of "reputation"—presented itself. If we committed certain acts, "the standing of the College" could be hurt; the woman guest could be hurt; even the offending student could be hurt. And lest the imaginative or reckless freshman have wayward thoughts about the possible flexibility of the phrase "any act," the language was unambiguous: "sexual intercourse is . . . interpreted to be a violation of the Honor System because it would obviously damage the reputation of the College." Just as specific were the parameters defining the courtly term "entertainment." They stated that "a student may entertain women guests on the campus at any time except between 2:00 a.m. and 7:30 a.m. Monday through Friday morning and between 3:30 a.m. and 7:30 a.m. Saturday and Sunday mornings."

These were the rules. But what was to bind us together and give fiber to the moral life of the College was yet another injunction.

Not only were we to be scrupulous about our scholastic work and beyond reproach from any quarter about our entertainment of women, we also had to report on ourselves if we violated the policy and we had to report on others if we thought them in violation: "any student who discovers a possible violation of the Honor System shall immediately tell the alleged offender to report himself. . . . in case the alleged offender does not do so within a week, the student who discovered the alleged violation shall immediately report it." Immediately we understood that beyond primary responsibility for our own actions, there existed secondary responsibilities for the actions of others. But what, some of us began to think, about "tertiary" responsibility? What should we do if we heard that a given student, observed to be in violation of the policy, was asked by another to report himself and refused to do so and the second student then did nothing? Did the "third" student have a duty stemming from the "first" student's failings and the "second" student's passivity? What, in its fullest dimensions and possibilities, did a moral life mean? What did we owe to others while being aware of what we owed to ourselves at our best? With such complexities our young minds then wrestled.

In time, I learned much more about the Honor System in a direct and painful way. But that hard lesson did not come until my sophomore year.

"Reputation" alerted us to the fact that, while the campus was small and seemingly self-enclosed, a world beyond—made up of people who thought about us and would judge us—did exist. Haverford's existence elsewhere was affirmed in our eyes as the year went on. The *Chicago Sunday Tribune*, foreshadowing what *U. S. News and World Report* was later to do with its rankings of colleges and universities, announced that Haverford was "first among men's colleges by an overwhelming majority of scholars and scientists consulted by the *Tribune*." The paper also said that "compared with even the greatest universities, with an undergraduate enrollment many times its size, Haverford's superiority for general education at the college level is unchallengeable."

One might think these happy tidings from afar ("first among men's colleges" and "unchallengeable" superiority!) would have caused great elation on the campus. But the editorial in the student newspaper (*The Haverford News*) commented only that "we don't think that the publicity attendant to the release of these ratings will begin a flood of admission applications to the College," and the acting president of the time, the revered Archibald MacIntosh, after returning from a trip to the Midwest, said, in his customarily laconic and understated way, that "the rating in the *Chicago Tribune* hasn't done us a bit of harm." Other administrative voices were not so sure about that. Fearing bad things on the horizon, they warned that the College might face a flood of applicants and be obliged to hire more people to consider them. What may have created delight on other campuses of the time (and today would have prompted schoolwide celebrations and public relations bonanzas) prompted at Haverford only a Quakerly apprehension that the world might be encroaching upon the campus and its concerns.

Let Haverford's uneasiness about such favorable attention serve as a reminder that institutions of higher education in this country have not always been devoted to enhancing their reputations. Today, "marketing" and "brand-name recognition" have become the specific missions of well-paid administrative officers at hundreds of colleges and universities. These men and women operate offices designed to latch on to local institutional particularities (and sometimes peculiarities—"we have the most sunshine of any school in the Midwest") that can be imagined to be attractive to prospective students and their parents. They formulate strategies meant to wrest *this* likely student from *that* other school. They design handsome brochures, folders, postcards, and DVDs that show the institution in the most favorable light. Rare is the school that does not somewhere feature in its advertising arsenal a photograph (taken on a beautiful fall or spring day) of undergraduate students gathered in happy diversity (men and women, blacks, Hispanics, Asian-Americans, and whites) around a fountain, on an age-worn bench, beneath the school flag, or at the welcoming campus gates. For such marketing officers, little time indeed is spent worrying about the question of whether higher education is a business. That question has been answered: of course it is, and

the competitive practices and tactics of business must be employed
to attract the best students, the most welcome attention of the
media, and the most favorable regard from civic and professional
leaders. Who at Haverford in the late 1950s could have imagined
that some four decades later about one-third of America's colleges
and universities would spend, on average, $2,200 to attract and
enroll each entering student? And who could then have imagined
that, at these same schools, some $3,000–5,000 per student would
be invested in the kind of consumer attractions (recreation centers,
dining arenas, and living quarters) designed to persuade such a
student that Institution X was vastly preferable to Institution Y?[1]

   Haverford was Quaker, and that explains something about its
shyness at the time. It knew what it had, was calmly proud of its
ability to teach and to fashion a certain kind of moral awareness
in its graduates, and did not think it seemly to trumpet its virtues.
The school's attractions would be recognized in sensible ways—by
word of mouth, by the accomplishments of its alumni, and by
what its teachers would say to other teachers and to the public.
Anything more would be alien to the refusal to proselytize that is
so much a part of Quakerism itself. But such shyness was not
unique to Haverford. No school at the time thought of itself as a
business operation—tuition in and graduates out, consumers to be
satisfied and rankings to be improved, reputation exalted and the
competition belittled. Such commercialism was yet to thrust itself
on academic life.

   That the school was Quaker in its identity was brought to the
attention of everyone on a weekly basis. On each Thursday ("Fifth
Day") we all walked the three-tenths of a mile from the campus
proper, past a small Quaker graveyard, to the local meetinghouse
of the Religious Society of Friends. Attendance was mandatory,
our names being checked off by fellow students. The room in
which we met was a plain rectangle, windowless, untouched by
religious iconography or decoration of any kind, the only accommodations being one small set of wooden benches occupied by
senior Quakers of the College and community that faced the
larger set of benches occupied by students. No liturgy. No music.
No one presiding. The only sounds breaking the silence of those

one-hour meetings were the voices of those who, being prompted by an "inner light," offered observations about matters they deemed important. Should the light move us, any one of us could speak; the senior Quakers could (and often did) speak. Amid the prevailing silence, we were brought home to our selves, our very small community, our thoughts individual and shared. In ways that were only implied, we were being taught by the traditions of Quakerism that the individual is often alone, yet important, and always in the company of others who are separate and yet near. We were also being taught that what we were experiencing, as students, was extraordinary in its moral seriousness and in its separation, if for only four years, from the rest of the world.

But the insularity of the campus was, in fact, penetrated often. In that first Haverford year, a long list of distinguished scholars, diplomats, scientists, and writers came to speak, most notably at "Collection," a regular Tuesday morning event that all students attended in the largest campus auditorium. There we heard, among others, the photographer Edward Steichen, the novelist Wright Morris, Norman Rockwell, Bayard Rustin, Branch Rickey, and Norman Thomas. Other eminent people—the psychologists Gordon Allport and B. F. Skinner, the historian Henry Steele Commager, Senator Paul Douglas from Illinois, the physicist Polykarp Kusch, and the sociologist Robert Merton—also came to campus. In later years, the visitors included Jacob Bronowski, Alan Bullock, Alfred Knopf, Al Capp, Thurgood Marshall, Hans Morgenthau, Sir Charles Snow, the Juilliard Quartet, Richmond Lattimore, Robert Lowell, C. V. Wedgwood, and Glenway Westcott. They were there for us, all for us. It was a dividend of our education that, at the time, we did not know how to assimilate. But it served in some vague but glorious way as a reminder of the world "out there," a world lying beyond both the gates of the campus and our youthful understanding.

In that year began a struggle within the campus that, in keeping with the principles of patient understanding to which the Quaker college was devoted, took many months to resolve. It reflected what the College was and what the temptations and realities elsewhere were. In the autumn, three professors in the natural sciences asked if the College would sponsor their applications for research funding from the Department of Defense. An open hearing on the matter was held on the campus, and both students and faculty members spoke at it. A committee was formed to study the matter. Letters from many members of the College community were written. While, on the one hand, certain Quaker principles of pacifism suggested that Haverford would not, could not, enter into any relationship with the military, other Quaker principles, namely those that stressed the inviolable integrity of each and every person, suggested that the scientists seeking sponsorship should not, could not, easily be turned aside. In the end, after a year of study, the Board of Managers decided not to sponsor the applications, but it also decided to create a fund of $10 million for scientific research on campus. And thus was sounded, but not in ways that I then could fully grasp, my first acquaintance with that immensely complicated issue, soon to dominate many campuses, of sponsored research.

Measured against the concerns that today erupt from college campuses, those arising from students in that freshman year were touchingly modest—even deferential. A report from a visiting committee of the Board of Managers noted that the students "think that someone they respect should more often say 'do this,' 'don't do that'" and that they "would like to have more understanding of what the Administration is doing. For instance, they [are] much concerned about the felling of campus trees, and would have liked an earlier and fuller explanation of the Dutch Elm Disease." And the same report noted what was then, is now, and perhaps shall ever be a declaration of distress from college students: "The students feel that many of the most important things that Haverford is giving them are derived from the smallness of the College. Nevertheless, they feel that even the relatively small student body is fragmented and without much unity. The students feel the need for better communication with other members of the Haverford community." Even with only 454 students and 70 faculty members—a little population that was together daily on a campus of a few hundred acres—we somehow believed that we did not know each other. The report closed with an observation that is, for every university, timeless: "Students are debating among themselves the comparative values of faculty research and teaching ability and are concerned with the importance of having the right balance between research and teaching."[2]

By midyear, I knew I was not to be an astrophysicist. That ambition simply vanished one evening while I was writing one of the essays for Professor Satterthwaite. Everything came to a delicious stop for me and I found myself alone with words, seemingly forever happy with what I saw I could set before myself on paper. I came up with metaphors, rearranged sentences and paragraphs, maneuvered words this way and that, and saw what language could do. By the very nature of things, the essay was a modest achievement. But it was mine. After that, I knew I wanted to write, that's all I wanted to do. I did acceptably well in the math course, but nothing like several of my classmates who did exceptionally well (one went on to win a Nobel Prize in physics). A course in the natural sciences was yet to come, but it promised— whatever it might be—little interest. I slogged, as others slogged, through the banal introduction to the social sciences (we were informed that empirical studies had revealed—surprise—that "people behave differently in groups than when they consider themselves acting alone"). The German course was taught well by a gentle and patient Quaker, but the daily class routines, untroubled by any intellectual concerns, since the course was wholly introductory, prompted me to think even then that the United States is odd in the degree to which its finest colleges and universities have committed themselves to teaching elementary language courses. Much money is spent in doing this and no small amount of professional friction and even unpleasantness arises from the fact that those teaching such courses never attain the prestige of faculty in many other departments. But learn a little bit of German I did, as well as a number of banal sociological truisms, and some math; still, my mind was on English.

By the end of the year, a year that passed with stunning rapidity for me, I had passed my courses, but had done no better than that. My highest grade was in English; I received only modest grades in three others, and in Chemistry, about which I wasn't diligent or interested, I came close to failing. Haverford gave no letter grades, only numbers from 1 to 100, and my average that year was 78.3. This was fair grading, untouched by either inflation or indulgence from my teachers, and I knew the score when I went home in June. The year had been both exhilarating and sobering. When my parents and my brothers asked if college was hard, I told them that it was.

What I did not tell them, and could not at the time, was that I had learned that college—by which I meant a campus set somewhat apart from the world, a set of serious intellectual and moral provocations, a vocabulary of rules and tradition, a system of pedagogical authority and youthful curiosity—was a way of living. In the end, it proved the only way of living I would thenceforth experience, but how was I to know that at the time? What I knew was that Haverford, which I did not doubt for a moment was the most important place in my life until then, had given me something precious. But what I did not know that summer was that I was unready to meet its further demands or answer it in kind. The sophomore year was soon to come; I was soon to fail.

ENDNOTES

1. Jonathan B. Weinbach, "College: Luxury Learning," *Wall Street Journal,* November 10, 2000, p. W1.
2. "Report of the Visiting Committee's Meeting with the Undergraduates, 4-19-57," in the Haverford College Library, Special Collections.

4

The Readiness Is All

The Haverford to which I returned in the fall of 1957 was a place for which I was not ready at all. From the start everything seemed wrong. For my sophomore year, I had chosen to live "off-campus," by which I meant to sound a dissident note. With a roommate, I occupied a second-floor room in a large house, the first floor of which was occupied by a distinguished professor of economics and his family. The remaining two floors above were given over to some fifteen students. The choice of living in such a place—"Scull House"—sent a message to all other students: we are different, we do not fit in, nor do we wish to do so. Each of us affected a posture we thought culturally advanced, the evidence of which was that (1) on our small (monaural) record players we played jazz (Charlie Parker, Thelonious Monk, John Coltrane, Horace Silver) or "folk music" (Leadbelly, Brownie McGhee, and Sonny Terry, and the first album by Joan Baez); (2) we invited girls from Bryn Mawr to our rooms with our own non-Quaker understanding of "entertainment"; and (3) we adorned those rooms with certain signs—a copy of Flaubert's *Education sentimentale*, say, or a matchbook from a New York City jazz club—denoting the level of our sophistication. We also saw to it that the faculty family below did not rest easy. Out of one of our windows we now and again lowered a speaker and from it we played into their living room "Sounds of Sebring," a recording of autos endlessly racing around a track. To thumb our noses at "authority," we surreptitiously wired the public pay phone on the second floor to give us, without a coin, a dial tone to the outside world. When we could, we ate at a nearby diner so as not to be seen consorting with our classmates. Thus Haverford's avant-garde in the late 1950s.

Our little mutinies were untouched by anything ideological or well thought out. We nonetheless pushed ourselves to believe that we were on to something remarkable because we saw that others thought us odd and were apparently embarrassed by our behavior. Much of the time, however, we were simply unhappy. I grew what I hoped would become a beard, but it turned out to be only oddly protuberant tufts and wisps. And, as the semester went on, my grades steadily went down: 60 in Intermediate German and only 77 in "The Literature of the English Renaissance." My highest grade was in Humanities 21–22, taught by Mr. Michael Shaw, M.A., an itinerant part-timer from nearby Swarthmore College. That course included James Joyce's *Portrait of the Artist as a Young Man,* and I knew instantly upon reading it that I *was* Stephen Dedalus and that his insurgence, his ardor for the things beyond his time and place, his swooning love for the unreachable girl, and his superior air (which I did not recognize then as puerile) were my own. For Mr. Shaw I wrote an essay that was to reveal to the world (or at least to him) the affinity I had with Joyce. It was concocted in a style that dispensed with logic and saturated itself with my home-cooked version of Joycean diction. Mr. Shaw promptly returned the paper to me with the reasonable comment that he could not grade it because he could not understand it. That paper was the high point of my academic life that year. All the rest was confusion and tumult. I knew I was drowning, but the giddiness of that knowledge only prompted me to sink deeper into the waves. The swagger of adolescence, the peculiar sense of superiority stemming from the fact that I alone was the captain of my disorder, the gleeful fatalism—all pushed me further into irresponsibility.

The academic year 1957–58 ended abruptly and painfully for me before the second semester came to an end. Two other students, one of them my freshman year tutorial partner Paul Sinclair, and I drew up a plan to steal all the silverware in the dining hall. We would do so on a Saturday night and therefore no one would be able to enjoy the favorite Sunday midday dinner. We acquired a key to the dining hall, filled several pillowcases with the sacred utensils, and gave the stash to girls we knew at Bryn Mawr. Then we went to bed with keen anticipation of the trouble we would delight in witnessing the next day. But there was no trouble. The College—with scrupulous Quaker foresight—had a backup supply of silver, and we entered the dining hall to find everyone happily eating the chicken, mashed potatoes, green beans, and apple pie so much a part of Sunday at Haverford.

And, in short order after a quick and probably not counter-intuitive investigation by one of the deans, the acting president, Archibald MacIntosh, summoned me to his office. We did not discuss my guilt in the matter, nor could I, in his presence, even imagine denying it. He told me that I was suspended indefinitely from the College, that I was to return home in one hour, that he had already called my parents, and that everyone was ashamed of me. He told me that my partners in the escapade would also be disciplined, but that he would be dealing with us one by one in Quaker fashion. Never first the group, always first the individual. I summoned up enough strength to ask him if I could ever come back to Haverford. He said that he would consider the matter but that under no condition could I return without fully supplying him with evidence that I could better manage my affairs. I thanked him, shook his hand, and that evening was back in Chevy Chase. My father could not bring himself to speak to me; my mother hugged me but said nothing; my brothers seemed astonished and puzzled. I was miserable.

I had done poorly in my courses; more importantly, I had abused my parents' trust and had squandered their money; Mr. Shaw, seeing me walk to the train station on the day I left, said: "Chace, you have made an ass of yourself." So I had. Later in my life, I was to hear many times that "education is wasted on the young." It certainly had been wasted on me that sophomore year. Haverford had entrusted me with some clear moral responsibilities. I had defaulted on most of them. I had known from the first day I was there that my courses were only part of what I was to study. I was also to study how to behave in a world that was given to me to share. Of course, since I was ignorant and had much to learn, I had obvious duties to myself. I was encouraged to be as ambitious as I could be—to learn, to comprehend, and to begin a mastery of a few topics. But my ambition could not be the whole story. To others I had duties—to defer, to help, and to honor. I went home having abused those duties.

In time, I was to become abundantly aware of how much education is indeed wasted on young people who, for various reasons, do not take advantage of what colleges give them. The schools I was to learn about in the years to come—the University of California at Berkeley, Stillman, Stanford, Wesleyan, and Emory are campuses where, at any given moment, a notable percentage of the students are wasting money and time and opportunity. As I had failed, so now are they failing.

In 1958, with only three complete semesters of college behind me, I was almost twenty years old, home again with my parents, haunted by my sense of shame, and uncertain where I was to go in the world. I knew I had to work; I knew I had to leave the house, where I was a reminder of family embarrassment. My experience with work until that point had consisted of six years of delivering the *Evening Star*, Washington's afternoon newspaper, setting pins in the local bowling alley, and caddying at one of the local country clubs. I had never worked hard.

That changed when my mother spoke to her brother, a civil engineer with a Boston firm, Metcalf and Eddy. He was supervising the construction of a municipal refuse incinerator in White Plains, New York, and said that if I could get to the job site, he could arrange work for me as a common laborer. I left home the next day.

The work was hard and dirty and I had to deal with the fact that my uncle, pulling strings, got me the job by seeing to it that another person—a real laborer—had been discharged. About that I could do nothing, and so to work I went. I lived by myself in a rented room, read Dostoevsky's *Crime and Punishment* (not a random choice of novels), saw almost no one, and joined the union—the International Hod Carriers', Building and Common Laborers' Union of America. I lifted things, carried things, dug trenches, mopped and swept. At summer's end, the job was done and I went home, but this time with at least a union card in hand. With it I went to the Washington union local and found jobs, some of them lasting one day and some longer. I was one of the few white members of the local and worked with young black men, most of them recent immigrants from Southern states, many of them illiterate, all of them much stronger and tougher than I would ever be. The pay was $2.50 an hour, $100 for the forty-hour week. The high point of that year—1958–59—was a long stretch of employment by a concrete construction outfit. We poured decks for new buildings in Washington, and I, working with a crew of others, pushed a "Georgia buggy," a steel wagon on large rubber wheels that carried hundreds of pounds of wet concrete along wooden ramps to waiting rakers and smoothers. It was demanding, dangerous, and exhilarating labor and after months of it—day after day—I gained muscle and endurance. I also gained respect for those with whom I worked. They were strong and were likely to remain laborers for as long as they lived. I, on the other hand, had "prospects"—what they were I did not know—somewhere else.

Archibald MacIntosh had told me that I should keep the College informed about what I was doing during my suspension. I believed that the only way I could keep that suspension from becoming an expulsion was to ask my various bosses to write letters to those at Haverford about my diligence and hard work. This was best done, I soon learned, by drafting the letters myself and having the bosses—very few of whom were given to composing letters—sign them.

One such letter read, in part: "I found this man to be a very willing worker able to be given a task to accomplish, and carry same out with the minimum of supervision. He seemed to be able to grasp a situation easily and often made many worthwhile suggestions that assisted in expediting the completion of the work that the personnel he was working with were engaged in doing. It has been a pleasure to find a person of his age that is so very willing to work diligently, for today it is the exception rather than the rule to find such people. This is a credit to him and to the institution of learning that he is attending, for they certainly appear to endeavor to bring out the best in their students." In seeing to the creation of this letter, I thought it appropriate that my boss at the time lavish the College with praise.

After several such letters, all of them similarly formal, coming from job sites in Washington, MacIntosh informed me that no further letters were necessary. I do not know if he harbored suspicions about their authenticity, but I can imagine that he had grown tired of the sameness of their praise of this "very willing worker." And then, in the late spring of 1958, he wrote me that I could be readmitted to the College, pending a final interview with him. So one spring day, full of hope mixed with anxiety, I went back to Haverford and he greeted me in his kind but austere way. I told him that my parents, for good reason, were no longer supporting me. He asked me how much money I had saved. I told him: $1,600. He then informed me that tuition and board that year was $2,500 and that the College would give me a scholarship of $900 to make up the difference, but on two conditions: that, to save money, I live off-campus in a small apartment owned by a woman with two small children who would need my baby-sitting services, and that I "go out for football."

This last condition was disconcerting; I had never played football but he brought our conversation to an end by saying, "you must now be tough as nails." With a sense of gratitude, I agreed to his conditions (I would have agreed to any conditions) and knew I had been given a second chance at something of immense value—an education at Haverford. I could return.

As for the football, I did "go out," but the coach knew more about my football skills than did Archibald MacIntosh. I went to every practice and suited up for every game in the 1959 Haverford season. But I never played in a game, not even one. This fact put me in an unusual position, for that year the Haverford squad lost five games, tied one, and won one. In our little league of small liberal arts colleges in the Philadelphia area, we could not have done much worse. Elementary logic therefore suggests that I must have been one of the worst college football players in the nation that year. Having established such an identity, at least in my own mind, I did not "go out" the next year and Archibald MacIntosh never again brought up his unusual condition. That was OK with me and, I think, OK with him. Thanks to his patient understanding of who I might get to be, I was back in school.

I returned to find that Mr. MacIntosh would be leaving the post as acting president and that the College had found a new president—a scholar from Columbia, Hugh Borton, whose expertise was in Asian history and politics. Small, quiet, unassuming, and reflective of Quaker values, he accepted Haverford's leadership in a wholly unflamboyant manner. Most students did not know him, nor did they think that knowledge of the president, or indeed of anyone in the administration, was important. What administrators did was, to students, an entirely inconsequential mystery. That fact dates my time at Haverford. Not until the latter part of the 1960s did "the administration" at America's colleges and universities emerge as a presence—and then as a malign creature—in the student bestiary. Nor did we have any clear idea of what our professors thought of President Borton. Faculty did not talk to students about such things. The records show, however, that the College wanted the distance between the president and the faculty kept very short, at least with respect to compensation. In 1959–60, the highest paid professor, Howard Teaf, an eminent economist, was paid $15,750. President Borton was paid exactly $250 more: $16,000. Thus Haverford demonstrated an admirable community of effort, with the president enjoying only a very small privilege by virtue of his office. No one at that time would have called Hugh Borton a "CEO," nor could anyone have imagined that, in just a few years, presidential salaries would skyrocket far beyond what any professor (outside a university's medical school) could dream of making. The Haverford president was thought necessary and even important in his own way. But he was not exalted, nor was he expected to have a unique "vision" that would both spur the institution to fame and justify his compensation. I believe Borton's idea of the College was modest yet powerful: assemble a fine faculty and fill small classrooms with students as intelligent as the admissions staff could find. Presidents with "visions" more complicated than this were known (Robert Maynard Hutchins at Chicago, for example) but they were rare. Most were ordinary men (and a very few women) reputed to be "reasonable" and "faithful" to the school. The need for presidential "visions," for "branding" a school, and for "marketing the product" was to come later.

Thanks to my year away and what it taught me, I did better with my academic work. I met two teachers—Ralph Sargent and Guy Davenport—whose ways of teaching were very different from each other but whose attitudes to books gave me much of the mental flooring on which I was to stand for all my teaching life. Sargent taught a course on William Faulkner, and he patiently led us on, from difficult book to yet more difficult book—from *As I Lay Dying* to *Light in August* to "The Bear" and then on to *Absalom, Absalom*—with the operating instruction that the difficulty of the books itself was the point. It was the medium through which we were to understand the world of the South and then the country and, at last, modernity. Yes, he told us, the books were hard going, but worth everything we could give them. The reward would be our recognition that life itself was just as complex, ironic, and strangely twisted as Faulkner's world of passion, memory, and guilt. But while Sargent saw the books as inexhaustible in their implications, he never thought they could mean just anything we might make up. He began with the implied assumption that they were, after all, much better in some sense than we were or ever would be. That was why we read them—to see them as extraordinary human achievements. But in reading them and trying to understand them, we needed to see them for what they were. Yes, they could be understood, but their meaning was not infinitely elastic. We should come to them not as conquerors but as supplicants; we did not impose meaning on them but drew meaning out.

Davenport was the oddest teacher I have ever known and the only one to whom the term "genius" could fairly be applied. He had dropped out of high school, was nonetheless later admitted to Duke, became a Rhodes Scholar, had ambitions to be a painter and was inflexibly opposed to conventional interpretations of anything, did not drive a car, and daily fed himself exclusively on fried bologna sandwiches and Snickers bars. He acquired a Ph.D. at Harvard and came to Haverford on a visiting appointment. He took me on for a one-person seminar my senior year. We studied the works, all of them, of Ezra Pound, whom he knew and had visited when the poet was incarcerated in St. Elizabeths Hospital.

I first asked if he would conduct such a seminar on the poetry of W. H. Auden, but he told me, with exasperation in his voice, that Auden was only "a stale imitator of Pound." So, twice a week, week after week, he sat cross-legged on the floor opposite me and told me everything about Pound. Where Sargent had been gently solicitous of his students and patient with their intellectual naïveté, Davenport was imperious. His mind, stocked with information that was literary, archeological, historical, musical, biblical, geographical, and architectural, fired information at me, hour after hour. Any question I could pose in my efforts to keep up only revealed to him my profound ignorance. As we moved into Pound's *Cantos*, I could no longer even ask him questions. I simply sat and listened. The immense poem sprawled before me, but to Davenport it was compact, of a piece, superbly coherent. When it was left to me to write a senior thesis about Pound, all I could do was provide a weak imitation of what I had heard from him. I rode behind his draft. But I learned from him something important: how much I did not know and how precariously thin my intellectual capital was.

What Sargent and Davenport taught, and what then I came to believe, is that we study literature to learn from it and to appreciate its superiority to a great deal of the rest of human endeavor. Given all that human beings have done—good and bad—over the centuries, the achievements of literature are valuable in their very slenderness. Acknowledging that fact, we study and teach books. I was later to learn that this unassuming and yet decent credo could be, and would be, subjected to withering analysis. But at the time, it was wholly sustaining.

At the end of that senior year, our class (1961) sat for our "comprehensive examinations" in our major subject. The exams lasted three hours on a morning in May. In English, we were held responsible for a rudimentary working knowledge of English and American literature from the time of Chaucer to the time of Samuel Beckett and Arthur Miller. The exam included such questions as "Point out what kind of literature (ideas, attitudes, style, forms) each of the following authors reacted against and rejected; then show what new achievement in literature each

accomplished: Ben Jonson, Dryden, Fielding, Wordsworth" and
"Outline briefly Wordsworth's poetic theory, and state in how far
[sic] and in what way it is a criticism of Pope's poetic theory." This
exam arose, I now can see, from an assumption on the part of my
teachers (and on the part of those from whom they themselves had
learned) that English literature was a coherent and delimited
field of discourse, a "discipline" that made sense in its own terms,
and that it was bound together by a historical chain of cause
and effect. The questions we were asked were straightforward and
exacting. They presumed that the responses we could make
would fall within a narrow range of "true," "not so true," and
"false." This was a test of objective knowledge. We had to know
the works to which we referred and we had to know them well.
And what we knew of those works was not meant to be a
platform from which we were to launch either theoretical or self-
regarding flights of prose (no more sophomoric rhapsodies about
James Joyce). In sum, the exam was based on the proposition that
to know what were unapologetically believed to be the "best"
works of English (and American) literature was to know a great
deal. To master that knowledge would be for us graduating seniors a considerable accomplishment. At the time we could have
had no way of imagining that our interests—the interests of both
Haverford student and Haverford teacher—could be seen, and
ultimately would be seen, as culturally narrow and naive. What
knew we then of literary theory, of "male hegemony," or of the
allegedly parochial insufficiencies of so many literary works?
What knew we then of the ways in which the "canon" would be
exposed and execrated for the exclusive, narrow, and bigoted
thing it was? What knew we then of the possibility that, to some
in the profession, the books we praised were to be mere grist for
the mills of "advanced thought"?

We knew as little about the extraordinary changes that the
study of English and American literature would soon undergo as
we knew of the social changes the coming years would bring. But
there were hints. Just before the academic year came to an end,
several Haverford and Bryn Mawr students joined in a sidewalk
picket against the local F. W. Woolworth department store. They

marched in protest against what they alleged were unfair employment practices—against black people—on the part of Woolworth's nationwide. The local store did employ Negroes, but that, the students said, was irrelevant. Woolworth stores elsewhere, it was believed, did not. Nor would those other stores allow Negroes to sit at their lunch counters. What mattered was "racism," a term few of us were accustomed to using. The protest was polite and modest, Quakerly in its demeanor. It ended as the school year ended. But it marked the opening of a new decade. The '60s had begun.

My grade average for 1959–60 was 83.7; in my senior year, it was 87.3. In the English courses I was given grades in the high 80s or low 90s. And, at Commencement on June 9, 1961, when our speaker was the British historian Arnold Toynbee, I shared with another senior the Newton Prize in English Literature, each of us winning a check for $25. My parents were happy about that prize, for I had put them through a lot. In addition, I had been granted "Honors" in English. As we sat and listened to Toynbee, we heard him tell us that we had a duty "to criticize [the] government's acts and to try to keep them under control." To do otherwise, to believe that "the government knows better than I do," is, Toynbee told us, to be guilty of "high treason." Toynbee could not have predicted how soon the cries of protest against the government would characterize life in the academy for many members of my generation.

And thus my years at Haverford ended. I had been awarded a Woodrow Wilson Fellowship ($1,500) to study English at the University of California at Berkeley. And to bring my college career to rest on an appropriately callow tone, I wrote a poem for the College literary review. Its verses capture the pose of wisdom and worldly fatigue that was mine by the time of graduation:

GAIT

I have lost my sight
In these hanging vines.
I have wept in long forests
And have clotted my breath
With love.

High above me
An eagle tumbles
Lost in a pocket
Free of air.

I have walked beyond
The last good farm.
The fine, rich mud
Sings with my thirst.

I now hear nothing
But the past.
My son has grown
To sear the land,
To curse it.

High above me
An eagle tumbles
Lost in a pocket
Free of air.

I was to go on to Berkeley, but without either the imaginary son or the imaginary farm. I was to leave Haverford, but the College was never to leave me. To it, I owed whatever firm grounding I had in what a college education could be. It gave me the beginnings of intellectual passion. It taught me about teaching, and when it was good (Alfred Satterthwaite, Ralph Sargent, Guy Davenport) and when it was not. It told me about the trust an older person (MacIntosh) can have in a younger one. It gave me standards of behavior and maturity that first I failed and then honored. I learned there that an unassuming, modest, and very small place could be as large and powerful as anything in the world.

I now thought I was ready for what was next to come: Berkeley. Wrong again.

5

Berkeley: Thoroughly Unready

Hindsight gives me some understanding of who I was at Haverford and why I behaved there as I did. Some understanding, but not enough. I know now that I was part of the "silent generation," and that my peers and I had been submerged in the politically and socially somnolent 1950s. One of those peers, the novelist Frank Conroy (Haverford, '58), later said of the time that "We had no leaders, no programs, no sense of our own power, and no culture exclusively our own."[1] Call it, as some have, a "transitional generation" or a "middle generation," our impoverished moment came after a successful war that consolidated American power and confidence, and before the eruptions of the 1960s. The music was yet to change, the sexual mores were yet to change, the drugs and their dark glamour were yet to appear, and the drama of the civil rights struggle was only in its first stages. We were wedged between "the get-it-done G.I. and the self-absorbed Boom." Yet the insularity of that time and our innocence of much of the world beyond the campus were not protected by a perfect seal. We at Haverford showed surprise that one of our classmates was actually thinking of going into something so crass as "advertising" after graduation. We registered astonishment that the best student to attend the College in generations, the singularly brilliant Anthony Amsterdam, decided to go to law school rather than to further his stellar achievements as a student of French literature. How, we thought, could anyone desert the world of high-minded morality and seriousness that Haverford represented? Nonetheless, we knew that something was happening "out there." We reluctantly had to come to terms with the fact that the world of business and the world of law were real enough. Not everything would fit beneath the benign shelter of Quaker morality and academic sobriety. There were other signs of transformation too, signs of things to come. One of us, later to become a distinguished religious thinker at the University of Chicago, boasted that he consumed peyote and was exultant about its powers; another began a seventeen-year struggle (ultimately successful) with heroin; and the jazz we listened to was being supplanted by the folk music and then the rock 'n' roll soon to dominate popular culture. That last fall at Haverford, we gathered to see John F. Kennedy debate Richard Nixon on television, some of us doing so on the Bryn Mawr campus, which now seemed friendlier and warmer, and the girls apparently closer and more amenable to our entreaties. We cheered Kennedy on and thought Nixon a hopelessly rigid square. Politics was changing and its romance with images and sex appeal was beginning.

Now we can proclaim that we were present at an immense generational shift. But to say that such a shift could explain my own situation is too facile. Even if the generation was confused and at a loss for an identity, I do not see myself as representative of any national picture. Large patterns cannot wholly explain individual derelictions. Even in an odd time, I was a bit odd. I had been thrown out of college and my classmates had not. I had taken five years to complete Haverford; most others had taken the traditional four. I consign myself to a separate and very small compartment in the pattern of generational change. I seemed to be out of step with a time that was itself disoriented.

But none of us was ready for what was to happen next: the 1960s in America. And the place to be thoroughly unready—and that includes almost everyone who happened to be there—was the University of California at Berkeley during that decade. Berkeley was the one and only school to which I applied for graduate study. Why? At Haverford, I heard that Berkeley was a very exciting place to be. Not all predictions come true; some do. This one burst with truth itself.

In the early fall of 1961, I drove across the country, bringing with me to California my Haverford legacy—a small stockpile of knowledge, some modest confidence, and unsettled academic ambitions. As I instantly found out, Berkeley—immense, imposing, brilliantly sunny, surging with people and importance—was everything that Haverford was not. The little school on Philadelphia's Main Line bestowed solicitude on its students, each and every one; Berkeley, with some 24,000 enrolled students, had no interest in being solicitous of anyone.[2] Haverford stressed moral development; Berkeley stressed professional accomplishment. The horizons of Haverford stopped with undergraduate life; Berkeley's horizons seemed limitless, for it was at the center of *research*, with teams of graduate students and professors working on projects of apparently great magnitude and importance. The university had been one of the national leaders in vital research for a very long time. It was then, and still is, the flagship of the greatest system of public learning the world has ever seen, with its research capabilities rivaled by only a few universities, public or private: Harvard, MIT, the University of Michigan among them. And the University of California system was then headed by the most influential prophet of what the American academy could be and was becoming: Clark Kerr. Less than two years after I arrived at Berkeley, Kerr gave the Godkin Lectures at Harvard, which became his book, *Uses of the University*. Those lectures set the terms of debate for years about what the American university was to be.

Kerr's description was objective and clear, even at times tough-minded. Later, despite the fame the lectures brought him, he regretted ever giving them. Attacked from both the left and the right, he became for many people the symbol of what had gone terribly wrong in American higher education. The fame of the book perhaps cost him his job, for when newly elected Governor Ronald Reagan took office in 1967, he immediately worked to eject Kerr from the job he had held for nine years (Kerr dryly remarked that he was leaving in the same way he had arrived at the presidency—"fired with enthusiasm"). But the book deserved its fame both then and now, for it was the product of extraordinary analytical judgment and candor about the research university. Much more right than wrong, it saw the modern research university for what it was: a wholly new entity in the cultural and economic life of the nation.

Kerr wrote that the university—the modern research university—was not the place that Cardinal Newman had imagined in the nineteenth century when he envisioned a citadel aimed "at raising the intellectual tone of society, at cultivating the public mind, at purifying the national taste, at supplying true principles to popular aspirations, at giving enlargement and sobriety to the ideas of the age, at facilitating the exercise of political powers, and refining the intercourse of private life." Aloof from the world, judging it but never becoming one with it, Newman's university, Kerr said, represented a "beautiful world," but one that was "being shattered forever even as it was being so beautifully portrayed."[3] It had been supplanted by another idealized version, that projected by Abraham Flexner, who in 1930 said that the university "is not outside, but inside the general social fabric of a given era. . . . It is not something apart, something historic, something that leads as little as possible to forces and influences that are more or less new. It is on the contrary . . . an expression of the age, as well as an influence operating upon both present and future."[4] Cardinal Newman saw the university transcending the transient and merely worldly; Flexner saw it as the place where specialized expertise of the highest order could be brought to bear on the toughest problems the world faced. But just as Cardinal Newman's vision had been overtaken by events, so had Flexner's. Where Newman did not anticipate the degree to which the modern university simply could not and would not immunize itself from all the infections of the world, Flexner did not grasp just how much of the world the university would want to absorb, study, explore, and serve. Indeed, the university had become, much to Flexner's displeasure, omnivorous, even gluttonous, in its interests. For that reason, he was unhappy with it and scorned even Harvard, which, he said, was devoting no more than a fraction of its resources to "the *central* university disciplines at the level at which a university ought to be conducted" and was wasting those resources on things as foolish as a business school.[5]

Kerr believed the views of both Newman and Flexner to be obsolete. He announced the arrival of the "multiversity"—an entity responsive to every intellectual, research, social, and civic demand. It absorbed the energies of what gave life to the ideas of Newman and Flexner but went beyond their self-limiting formulas. Enormously expansive, the "multiversity" would become just what the University of California, with all its campuses, had become by the time of Kerr's lectures, a place with

> operating expenditures from all sources of nearly half a billion dollars, with almost another 100 million for construction; a total employment of over 40,000 people, more than IBM and in a far greater variety of endeavors; operations in over a hundred locations, counting campuses, experiment stations, agricultural and urban extension centers, and projects abroad involving more than fifty countries; nearly 10,000 courses in its catalogues; some form of contact with nearly every industry, nearly every level of government, nearly every person in its region. Vast amounts of expensive equipment were serviced and maintained. Over 4,000 babies were born in its hospitals. It is the world's largest purveyor of white mice. It will soon have the world's largest primate colony. It will soon also have 100,000 students—30,000 of them at the graduate level; yet much less than one third of its expenditures are directly related to teaching.[6]

This was the institution on whose flagship campus I arrived that fall. Kerr might have said that I came as an immigrant from a world—Haverford—constructed on the Newman model; that I, as an immigrant, would be happy to see that Berkeley had preserved, say, a department of classics with small classes and almost monastic scholars. In that limited sense, Newman's spirit had been preserved at Berkeley. And he might have remarked that I could observe all around me the remnants of the Flexner model—the many research institutes and high-level theoretical enclaves studding the campus. But what I would really witness as an immigrant was the full constellation of all that Berkeley had become as a multiversity. I would be dwarfed by what I could see, but everyone else would be dwarfed too. No one could dominate such a landscape nor comprehend its magnitude; no single individual or even set of individuals had caused it to come into being; its interests were myriad and it was in no position to deny responsiveness to any of them; it would grow exactly as muscles grow and become ever stronger—by being used.

In seeking to describe what held it together, Kerr himself seemed as puzzled as anyone, and everywhere in his writings can be detected a note of passivity as he witnessed the spectacle surrounding him. He could not stand against the flow; nor could anyone else. In defining the university he saw, he could suggest only a variety of formulations that mixed bureaucratic formalism with his own laconic wit: "a mechanism held together by administrative rules and powered by money," or "a series of individual faculty entrepreneurs held together by a common grievance over parking,"[7] or something—the university in its entirety—that "can aim no higher than to be as British as possible for the sake of the undergraduates, as German as possible for the sake of the public at large—and as confused as possible for the preservation of the whole uneasy balance."[8]

He did not ignore what he knew were the liabilities of the multiversity: undergraduate teaching would be slighted; introductory classes would likely be large and the instructor remote; faculty would be more loyal to their academic disciplines than to the institution, particularly as the temptations of off-campus funding made professors compete for national recognition; the university president could not imagine himself to be a visionary "giant," but was, by necessity, only a mediator juggling myriad conflicting constituencies on the campus and beyond; the campus, once a more or less homogeneous "community," would fragment into scores of isolated subgroups; and the students, both undergraduate and graduate, would form a new kind of restless educational "proletariat" that would want to turn the university "into a fortress from which they can sally forth with impunity to make their attacks on society." Kerr proved to be right on every count. In particular, he was prophetically right about what undergraduates would confront at places like Berkeley:

Recent changes in the American university have done them little good—lower teaching loads for the faculty, larger classes, the use of substitute teachers for the regular faculty, the choice of faculty members based on research accomplishments rather than instructional capacity, the fragmentation of knowledge into endless subdivisions. There is an incipient revolt of undergraduate students against the faculty; the revolt that used to be against the faculty *in loco parentis* is now against the faculty *in absentia*. The students find themselves under a blanket of impersonal rules for admissions, for scholarships, for examinations, for degrees. It is interesting to watch how a faculty intent on few rules for itself can fashion such a plethora of them for the students. The students also want to be treated as distinct individuals.[9]

Kerr's observations, coming as they did from someone who had graduated from Swarthmore College, a school rooted in the same Quaker traditions as Haverford, now appear almost calculated to portray institutions such as the University of California as the antithesis of everything for which Haverford and Swarthmore stood. Of this he must have been aware, and perhaps his knowledge of Swarthmore, on whose Board of Trustees he served, gave him the means to describe so unerringly the weaknesses, soon to fuel campus-wide insurgencies, of the teaching at Berkeley.

For Kerr, the undergraduates presented one of the most problematic issues facing the new kind of university. It was the undergraduates, he later acknowledged, who had turned against what they found at the campus he oversaw. One can read in the tone of his analysis the kind of adversary relationship soon to dominate the Berkeley campus and others like it. In his view, the responsibility for the problems students faced was the faculty's: it was they, he unfairly implied, who had created the large classes, transferred teaching duties to TAs, emphasized research over teaching, and, above all, heaped up the endless rules and regulations under which students would suffer. His analysis held administrators—vice presidents, deans, or himself—guiltless of any of these corruptions of pedagogy. But just as the undergraduates, in only a few years, would turn against their own school, so the faculty would soon scorn the administration as uninterested in the plight of teaching. The professors became thoroughly unsympathetic about the problems the administrators faced, and they did not blame themselves for the situation the students faced. Lines were thus drawn in those early years of the '60s—between students and school, between students and faculty, and between administrators and faculty—and they would not for years be erased—at Berkeley or anywhere else in higher education.

The '60s in Berkeley are now remembered (celebrated in some places while regretted in others) for their days—many of them—of political upheaval: student arrests, sit-ins, jailings, protest against whatever the "administration" stood for, and the abiding sense that "youth" was right and the "older generation" had lost all authority. Someone, either Jerry Rubin or Jack Weinberg, was responsible for the "Kilroy was here" of the time: "Don't trust anyone over thirty." That is how the '60s are recalled. But that history is wrong. The real lesson for higher education in the '60s was that while youth was on its way, in fact, to winning very little, centralized authority—larger campuses, more money put into research, large classes replacing small ones, publication trumping teaching in importance, and the entire educational effort becoming less local and more national and international—was on its way to immense triumphs.

Kerr suffered defeat at the hands of the Berkeley students of the day. But this defeat masks the larger victory that was his: the large campus, fueled by research grants, structured as a semi-corporate organization administered by professionals, responsive to the national imperatives of the state, unsentimental about the yearnings and postadolescent confusions of undergraduates, and tough-minded about the sources of money needed to keep the huge enterprise afloat, was to be the research campus of the future—in California and everywhere else in the United States. Not only would the small liberal arts colleges stay small in number and remain virtually constant in how many students they educated, but they would have almost nothing to say about what higher education was to be for the rest of America's young people. The universities that were to make the difference were on their way to becoming ivyless and more corporate, less standoffish about the social structure surrounding them and more ambitious about the impact they could have on the functioning of the nation. Not through the isolated impulses of private learning in small and sequestered classrooms, but through large accommodating reactions to public need would the "knowledge production and consumption" (Kerr's phrase) of the modern university connect with the emerging knowledge-based economy.

Central to his thinking—and thus the thinking of others at the time who were influenced by his vision of the future of higher education—was a borrowing from James Burnham's *Managerial Revolution* (1941): the new elites—people like Kerr—would, in the public interest, direct and allocate federal and private resources. Such a formula gave less weight to the faculty, an entity earlier believed to be at the heart of the educational venture. Professors would become "tenants rather than owners" of the institutions where they worked; their loyalties would increasingly lie not with their "home" institutions but with their various scholarly or research disciplines. Management and not debate, efficiency and not the messiness of quarreling professors, would define the new American university.

Despite the claims of the students to the contrary, Kerr's ideas were "liberal," but they issued from a liberalism he helped to redefine. Under his strangely passive guidance, the liberalism of democratic involvement yielded to the liberalism of bureaucratic management and administrative rationality. Both forms of liberalism sought to favor the public good—a more informed and enlightened citizenry and a more progressive social order—but the older faculty-driven sensibility gave way to the systematic top-down control of the organization. The faculty did not supervise the institution, but the institution made faculty life itself possible. A further development was that once teaching, the activity traditionally considered the heart of higher education, began to lose its centrality in the larger enterprise, any liberal arts conception of that task was in jeopardy.

The loss was considerable. In the 1850s, John Henry Cardinal Newman identified liberal learning as the necessary process for "the cultivation of the intellect." The Berkeley on whose campus I arrived in the late summer of 1961 would have considered such cultivation, if it had been mentioned at all, as a charmingly quaint remnant of attitudes and sentiments best left in the attic of American memory. The "multiversity" could not be detained by such pedagogical nostalgia. It was on its way to a full participation in the American economy broadly conceived, an economy that utilized brainpower for what it could do, the material differences it could make, and not the private introspection once held, by Newman and others, to be the essential aim of education.

I was a long way from Haverford.

ENDNOTES

1. As quoted in William Strauss and Neil Howe, *Generations: The History of America's Future, 1584 to 2069* (New York: William Morrow and Company, Inc., 1991), p. 279.
2. Student enrollment at Berkeley was scheduled to reach a maximum of 27,500 by the end of the '60s. From 1960 to 1964, that enrollment grew from 18,728 to 25,454. See W. J. Rorabaugh, *Berkeley at War: The 1960s* (New York and Oxford: Oxford University Press, 1989), p. 12.
3. As quoted in Clark Kerr, *The Uses of the University* (4th ed., Cambridge, MA, and London: Harvard University Press, 1995), pp. 2–3.
4. As quoted in ibid., p. 3.
5. As quoted in ibid., p. 5.
6. Ibid., p. 6.
7. Ibid., p. 15.
8. As reported by John H. Fenton, "The Emerging U.S. University Is Called a Model," *New York Times,* April 26, 1963, p. 18.
9. Kerr, *Uses of the University*, p. 78.

6

The Discipline of Literature

But of all these matters the cohort of graduate students entering Berkeley in English that fall was innocent. We knew nothing about Kerr or his ideas. Numbering 120, the same number of my original class at Haverford, we were preoccupied with where we were and what we had to do. We came from everywhere—the Ivy League, the Big Ten, small liberal arts colleges, public schools and privates. We all had done well with English in our college years and now, we thought, we could advance to the next stage—whatever that might be. In some dim way we knew that the graduate study of English would be different from what we had known earlier. And while we assumed we would some day become professors, we possessed only shaky knowledge of what was expected of professors and did not yet really see ourselves joining their ranks. Students still, the one place where we felt comfortable was the classroom, for it had been the scene of our earlier victories. Without those conquests, we would not have been admitted to Berkeley. So to the classroom we trooped.

An entering cohort of 120 graduate students in English at any university is today inconceivable. Perhaps a dozen or so now typically enter Berkeley, Stanford, Harvard, or other such schools to study English. Those graduating from colleges and universities with a B.A. know better than to sign up for six or seven years of graduate study that will likely lead nowhere. Teaching jobs are few, many are part-time, and many others come with no prospect whatever of a tenured professorship. But 1961 was different. English was still "hot," and neither law school nor business school had assumed the glamour or security they were to possess in the decades to come. We had read good books in college, had written what we thought were worthy essays about those books, and we were now ready to do more of the same.

My Woodrow Wilson Fellowship, with its stipend of $1,500, was enough to defray the $250 tuition for out-of-state students. I knew, moreover, that in one year I could qualify for "state resident" status, which would bring the tuition and fees down to the grand total of $136.50 for a full year. I found an apartment, appropriately squalid but near the campus, for $60 a month. I bought my books. I enrolled in my classes, three of them: an introduction to bibliographical study, Chaucer, and a survey of the English Renaissance. Thus my entry, lost in a sea of thousands, into the multiversity.

I could not have known it at the time, but the English department, looming so large and important to me that fall, hardly figured in Kerr's world of high-level sponsored research and the fusion of university activities with state and federal agencies. His Godkin lectures had noted in passing the less advantaged status of the humanities in general—true then, truer today. Its professors drew smaller salaries, had fewer secretarial services, could not avail themselves of supplemental summer financial support, and could garner no prestigious grants from federal sources. Their faculty colleagues in the natural sciences and some of the social sciences had been deemed, post-Sputnik, part of the collective national effort to generate the kind of intellectual and research inventory that would oppose the Soviet menace. Washington, with its many agencies, would underwrite work on nuclear energy, physics, statistics, nation-building and area studies. It would give no money to studies of Wordsworth.

However, my fellow graduate students and I detected in our professors neither economic impoverishment nor status envy. They seemed utterly confident and self-possessed. To me, they were just what Haverford professors were not: professionals, authors of important books, even "stars."

The faculty of the department numbered 53. Some of the full professors were indeed scholars or writers of considerable distinction: Bertrand Bronson, James D. Hart, Charles Muscatine, Mark Schorer, Henry Nash Smith, and Ian Watt. Of the younger professors were several who would go on to considerable distinction: Frederick Crews, Thomas Flanagan, Thom Gunn, Ralph Rader,

Stephen Orgel, and Larzer Ziff. Three women were members of that faculty; no racial minority was represented at all. The morale of those teachers, whom we held in awe mixed with the cool detachment of young people toward their elders, was high. They knew they were in a good place, one of the best, and they all saw the study of English, as we did, as a high and exclusive calling. Each, with his elaborate and time-consuming research project, had "his work" to do, and the idea conveyed to us was that we should do "our work" too.

That work was to become, in one way or another, like them: scholars. As we learned in the first few months at Berkeley, the presiding ethic for the graduate students in the department was not one of individual self-improvement or moral illumination. It was to learn the books set before us, to be accurate in all we said about them, to explore the complex networks of historical cause and effect that bound them together in a received "canon." That "canon" was English and American literature from 1350 to the present, for which we would—amazingly—be held "responsible." That was the arrangement: we had been given a discipline, coherent and self-enclosed. It would be ours to comprehend and then to transmit. We had to know what we were talking about. We had thus entered the world of literary expertise; the time of inner exploration through literature was over. To bring home that point to us, we were told that the stages of our study would be marked by examinations: at the end of three semesters, an oral exam with three professors asking questions of each of us for ninety minutes about all of English and American literature; during that same period, a reading exam in French; then, when we had been approved for entry into the Ph.D. program proper, a reading exam in German and one in either Latin or ancient Greek, and then, toward the end if we had made it that far, a written exam on a foreign or ancient literature. Lastly came the Big Event: an oral exam lasting three hours during which six professors would examine us in six historical periods of English and American literature. Should we pass that last exam, we would be "free" to write a doctoral dissertation.

The stern laws of attrition, as we discovered as time went on, governed this process. The university certainly was not dependent on our small tuition payments. So the English department, under no compunction to keep graduate students around for financial reasons, was free to maintain its standards of achievement, officiate over the several exams, and witness the fallout as the semesters went along. What our teachers saw was not unlike what military officers see in the worst of battles: many soldiers begin the struggle but few finish it. In the fall of 1961, 412 graduate students enrolled to study English; by the spring, that number had dropped to 374 (an attrition of almost ten percent). In that first year we contended with feelings of fear and doubt, for the gossip surrounding us was that attrition in the department had historically been very high. Indeed, that year, 1961–62, saw only fifteen graduate students being awarded the Ph.D. Those who fell by the wayside had failed to clear one hurdle or another: the language exams, or the oral exams, or ways to find the money for rent and groceries, or the seeming eternity between entering as a grad student and actually becoming "free" to write a dissertation. Later, our cohort followed suit: of the 120 with whom I started, only a dozen ever earned the Ph.D.

Were the faculty even to worry about that kind of attrition, they would have written off such outcomes as the appropriate consequence of high standards, those standards themselves being regarded as immutable. Hence the protocol regulating our progress was straightforward. It went like this: English and American literature, by its very nature, has generated a number of difficult issues, many of them as yet unresolved, all of which must to be addressed by learned professionals in an exacting manner. This is very hard work. Most people, in fact, cannot do it; the attrition figures say so. But a few can. Those few are to be warranted with a degree permitting them to maintain the standards and sustain the protocol. The others will disappear. As Kerr himself had noted about the modern university in general, "the casualty rate is high. The walking wounded are many."[1]

The attitude that few would survive and many would fail grew out of a belief that the teaching of English was more than a profession: it was a *calling*. Graduate students were being considered for membership in a secular priesthood. The failure rate itself was proof enough that the standards for such a priesthood were being preserved. This approach to what they were doing and what we were doing explained why our professors never offered us courses in how to teach, even though we had come to Berkeley to become teachers. When letting us know that our primary aim as graduate students was to train to be like them, our professors seemed to assume that we would some day teach just as we had been taught. Formal pedagogical courses were not necessary; we acolytes would learn by *mimesis*: listening to lectures, we would know how to give lectures; attending seminars, we would see how to conduct seminars. Pedagogical courses, suggesting we were present to acquire a "trade," would have demeaned our pursuit.

Of course none of this panned out. When we survivors first taught, we had to learn to do so from the beginning, false start by false start, trial and error. But this experience would come to us only in time. First we had to attend our courses, prepare for the language exams, and learn what the study of English at the professional level was all about.

A graduate student beginning in the fall of 1961 and surveying the departmental landscape saw on display a narrow spectrum of approaches to literature. There was the strictly philological: literature is the product of language, and language, in its various historical evolutions, can be studied with scientific precision; there was the *generic*: literature comes to us in a variety of forms—epic, the lyric, satire, etc.—and these forms can be described and compared; the *biographical*: literature is the product of writers, and the lives of those writers can be recovered and given shape and form; the *historical-cultural*: literature grows out of a time and place in the development of a locale or nation and to get at the literature one studies the roots from which it has grown; the purely *belles-lettristic* and aesthetic: literature is "studied" (that is, relished) because it is, after all, good, true, and precious.

If there was an approach that could be called "theoretical," only one enjoyed widespread currency: the "New Criticism." Hardly new by then at Berkeley or anywhere else, it first appeared in the 1920s and was spurred on by John Crowe Ransom's *The New Criticism* (1941) and W. K. Wimsatt's and Robert Penn Warren's *Understanding Poetry* (1938). This approach still carried with it an aura of the mysterious and sacerdotal, and fitted perfectly with the semi-priestly atmosphere of the department. A poem did not necessarily mean what it seemed to mean; it had to be deftly taken apart by trained hands in order to reveal it as an ingenious mechanism of parts held in tension by "irony." A trained "New Critical" adept could cast aside the "obvious" meaning of the poem and expose it as a tissue of ambiguities, some of them irreconcilable. The New Criticism thus suggested that literature was accessible only to a select few and was not, at its most serious levels, meant for the common reader. Apparently flourishing as a wholly apolitical procedure, the New Criticism had, in fact, a political posture. It favored the hierarchy, the knowing vs. the unknowing, the learned vs. the unwashed. This was the politics of intellectual stratification, and it fitted in perfectly with the departmental atmosphere of priestly calling mixed with military attrition.

Apart from the New Criticism, theory was not much in evidence when Berkeley opened its classrooms and seminars to my classmates and me in the fall of 1961. Literature itself was the object of attention, whatever the approach, but the approach was always secondary. Had it wanted formally to go on record about what it was doing, the department could have seconded T. S. Eliot's remark that "No exponent of criticism . . . has, I presume, ever made the preposterous assumption that criticism is an autotelic activity."[2] Few Berkeley professors or graduate students in 1961 would have disagreed; no one could have imagined that, in a few years, a revolution in criticism would upend the basic presupposition about what was primary and what was secondary in literary studies.

The three courses I took that first semester were, in order, good, poor, and useless. Thomas Flanagan, newly recruited to the department from Columbia University, taught the introduction to bibliographical study. He was to become in time a wonderful friend and one of the persons most loyal to the ethic of friendship

I ever knew, but that fall he appeared to me as a very unlikely combination of raconteur, ironist, formalist, and cynic. As for his duties to bibliography, he subsumed that dry discipline within class sessions which he devoted to long, running accounts of a famous literary forgery, a nineteenth-century slave rebellion in the Caribbean, certain idiosyncratic episodes of Victorian manners, and excursions into the byways of Irish history, all of which he narrated from memory. Then a chain-smoker, he awkwardly perched himself on a desk and spoke to us as if we were an audience of bumpkins such as Oscar Wilde might have encountered while on tour in backwoods America. On occasion he would throw out a question, and seemed amused if someone could give an answer even remotely sensitive to the excellence of its phrasing. Once he made a classmate quietly cry in her seat by asking her the same question again and again, never satisfied by any response she could give. When it came to our writing—a series of essays with topics largely of our own devising but offering deference to the topic of bibliography—he responded with what I came to expect from every professor at Berkeley: short remarks as if he were paying Western Union by the word, followed by a letter grade. But of one thing I was never in doubt: this man loved writing, lived it, talked about it incessantly, and had formed a life around it. From 1961 on, he was never to leave my consciousness.

The poor course was taught by a man who, I now think, had been drafted into teaching Chaucer, a topic that he may have loved, but for which he had little aptitude. He, George Stewart, had achieved some local and national luster by writing, quickly and deftly, a series of books about natural or man-made disasters of the time, and he knew a great deal about California history. *Time* magazine said at the time, "he writes inanimate prose about inanimate objects." About courtly love, versification in the fourteenth century, the *fabliau*, Boccaccio's *Decameron*, and the religious controversies surrounding John Wycliffe, he knew, day by day, a bit more than we did, but the gap between his knowledge of the topics at hand and ours at times was razor-thin. Some days we seemed to be gaining on him. At one meeting a student was asked to explain a turn in the plot of "The Pardoner's Tale," and answered by saying that it was a matter of "reverse psychology." With admirable candor, Professor Stewart responded by saying he was unfamiliar with the term. After that, whatever pedagogical authority he may have possessed vanished.

The useless course was the survey of the English Renaissance, and its inadequacy was rooted in the unfortunate circumstance that the professor—James Cline—kindly, generous, and perfectly old-fashioned, brought to the enterprise little more than his love of the poems he read aloud to us in class. Some of them made him weep, and this he did with a gentility of manner that came close to embarrassing both him and us, but he was redeemed in our eyes by the evident love he had for the material he had cherished for so long. To those of us who watched him, however, the real lesson he imparted was nothing he had intended: we learned that mere affection for literature would not prove sufficient for what we would someday be: professors. We had come to Berkeley. The work was intellectually demanding. We had years ahead of us to prepare, to know, to think hard, and to transmit to others all we had learned. There was little time for showing affection for what we read.

When the second semester came, I enrolled in three more courses: another one by Flanagan, one on Middle English, and a third pursuing more of the Renaissance. Flanagan's topic was W. B. Yeats and it consisted simply of a reading, day by day, of all his major poems, with questions succinctly put by Flanagan to a small group of students who were, by turns, puzzled, awed, and intimidated by him. But what made the experience exciting to me was that he never made any concessions about the kind of intelligence necessary to understand Yeats. The poet, Flanagan implied, had written at the highest level of his capacity. We the readers must bring ourselves to that same level for our interpretations to count for anything. He thus conveyed the truth that literature does not arise from classrooms nor is its natural home to be found there. He taught us, then, as if he were not a teacher but a writer, as someone in league with Yeats. A decade later he wrote three brilliant historical novels about nineteenth- and twentieth-century Ireland and proved his point.

The Middle English course was taught by one of the three women in the department—Dorothee Metlitzki Finkelstein. She, like Flanagan, had reserves of knowledge and character that were the products of a life outside the academy. Involved in the founding of the State of Israel, she knew several languages, and had lived in Russia and Europe. A medievalist, she had written *The Matter of Araby in Medieval England,* and she was also busy with a book about Herman Melville. Stern, demanding, and intellectually self-possessed, she arranged for her class to meet at 8 a.m. and, despite the time, was always ready for us. Now and again we were ready for her. She was what even many of the most scholarly faculty members were not: an intellectual. I performed only adequately in her course but admired her energy and devotion to what she proposed to do: teach young people about a literature and a culture written six hundred years ago.

The third course was everything the earlier Renaissance course had not been. In a large lecture room crowded with undergraduates and dominated by a man with a stentorian voice—Wayne Shumaker—sentimental affection for literature was driven aside and replaced by dates, nomenclature, generic distinctions, snap quizzes, and a stern regimental atmosphere. We all, undergraduates and graduate students, learned a lot quickly and then as quickly forgot. Surrounded by students younger by a few years than myself, I thought about the privileges I had been given at Haverford. I now was face to face with a form of education shorn of the personal, the intimate, and the moral. But it was what many students around me were used to. Haverford's form of education—intellectual in the first place but intensely moral in the second—was wholly absent from the way things were done in Berkeley's cavernous classrooms. No one had the time, the means, the interest, or the ability to say anything to its thousands of students about their moral responsibilities. Against the surge of those students, against their vast numbers, and against the powerful urgencies of the research agenda of the campus, it would have been quixotic for anyone even to try. The students learned their civic lessons by coping with the bureaucracy they found. In time, some of those students confronted that bureaucracy with all the passion that neglect and resentment could fuel. Many others, however, simply dropped out of Berkeley. In the 1960s, only slightly more than a third of those entering as freshmen graduated in four years; more telling is the fact that those who ever graduated were only half of every entering class.[3] Those who remained, some of them, fought what they found.

Before that semester and those classes ended, however, I received a letter from the Selective Service Administration ordering me to appear for a "pre-induction physical examination" at the Oakland Induction Center. The war in Vietnam was, for American troops, in full fury. My oldest friend, Byard Peake, had just enlisted in the Army Air Corps and was training at Fort Rucker, Alabama. He later would become an "advisor" to South Vietnamese pilots. My card, which I faithfully carried in my wallet, listed me as "1-A" and therefore eminently draftable.

I presented myself, along with hundreds of other young men, at the center, and spent the entire day being examined: blood, urine, vision, hearing, muscle tone, and with all orifices of my body inspected. Perhaps it was an off day in Oakland, but I was surrounded by men my age all of whom seemed to have been in jail or to be planning theft of automobiles or attacks on women. The talk was violent, rapacious, and enthusiastic. Oakland seemed a thousand miles away from Berkeley. The urine tests consisted of peeing into tall and narrow glass cylinders, which were then placed on a large table with identifying numbers. One of our group was too terrified to do this and was told by an officer to come back when his other tests were finished. When he did, he saw that his cylinder was filled. The officer said to him: "I couldn't wait for you, buddy, so I pissed in it myself."

At the end of the day, we were given our "results" and a sergeant told me that I had passed. "Mister, you are going to be in the Army in two weeks." I told him that I didn't think so and that I would receive a student deferment. He told me that wouldn't happen: "Two weeks, Mister." I did, of course, receive the deferment.

No one who was deferred from that war can rest easy with his conscience. I did not go and I lived. But more than 58,000 Americans went and died. It is hard not to think that someone was killed in my place. The war showed that if you were from a working class background, you went. If you came from an educated, middle-class background, as I did, you did not. Only a few years earlier, I had dreamt of attending West Point and becoming an Army officer. Had I graduated from West Point, certainly I would have gone to Vietnam. And perhaps I would have been killed when there, as some West Point officers were, some by their own men in rebellious "fragging" events. But now I deplored what the United States was doing in Vietnam and was glad to have my deferment and the safety it guaranteed. Those men who talked of stolen cars and cornered women served.

By June 1973, the last man to be inducted entered the Army and the draft was over. The war in Vietnam had come to an end in January, five months earlier. One legacy of the '60s was the decision on the part of Congress and the Selective Service that a conscripted army, such as the one that fought in Vietnam, was all too likely to be a source of morale and disciplinary problems. Better a mercenary or volunteer military force than one infested with drugs and violent malaise. For college students thereafter, there was to be no need of deferments. They could be assured of never fighting a war. What had separated me from those of my generation who did fight became a fixture of the world of higher education. From the '70s onward, a solid wedge stood between those privileged to go to universities and those who, given their situations, saw military service as an attractive option. As the century came to an end, few families with comfortable incomes saw their children sign up for military service. And few families in rural areas or in poor urban surroundings made much use of the tutoring companies promising to enhance SAT scores or the counseling services guiding young men and women to the right college or university. Higher education had increasingly become a reflection of that most secret and powerful of American realities: social class. In the years to come, class differences provided, unmistakably, the structure of the college and university world.

ENDNOTES

1. Kerr, *Uses of the University*, p. 32.

2. T. S. Eliot, "The Function of Criticism," in *Selected Essays of T. S. Eliot* (New York: Harcourt, Brace & World, Inc., 1960), p. 13.

3. See Martin Trow, "Bell, Book and Berkeley," in *The State of the University: Authority and Change*, ed. by Carlos E. Kruytbosch and Sheldon L. Messinger (Beverly Hills, CA: Sage Publications, 1970), p. 306.

A New Kind of Proletariat

In 1963, when Clark Kerr said that the students, both undergraduate and graduate, would form a new kind of restless educational "proletariat" that would want to turn the university "into a fortress from which they can sally forth with impunity to make their attacks on society,"[1] he was both right and wrong in ways that even he couldn't have imagined. The Berkeley campus, along with the campuses of Columbia, the University of Wisconsin, San Francisco State University, Harvard, and others, did not become "fortresses." But they did become centers of political activity and symbols of youthful antagonism to virtually every kind of adult authority. National and international causes—the civil rights struggle, the war in Vietnam, the relaxation of sexual mores, the easy availability of mind-altering drugs, the changes in music and dress, the changes in the attitudes of young people elsewhere (France, Italy, Japan, and Germany) underlay this transformation in the thinking of young people on a number of campuses. If those "in charge" defended it, that was reason enough for the young to attack it. When Johnny, the motorcycle leader played by Marlon Brando in *The Wild One* (1954), is asked what he's rebelling against, he answers, "Whaddya got?"

But national and international realities, as urgent as they were, do not fully explain what happened at Berkeley. Local circumstances made the difference. Although most of us naively proceeding toward a Ph.D. had no way of knowing this, the campus to which we came that fall of 1961 was primed for dramatic change. First of all, history: Berkeley as both a university and a city had long been recognized as home to left-wing and progressive causes. And the Bay Area in general had been for decades the scene of labor protests, strikes, and an unruly, bohemian social fabric. Moreover, the faculty of the "little red schoolhouse," as Berkeley was known, had recently undergone a traumatic ordeal that brought politics to everyone's attention, on the campus and elsewhere. Twelve years before, in the era of McCarthyism and anticommunist "spy trials," the "loyalty oath" controversy erupted. With university president Robert Gordon Sproul leading the charge, the Board of Regents adopted an anticommunist oath for all University of California employees to sign. But both faculty and staff quickly declared principled objections to a political test as a condition of employment. Some regents saw that kind of resistance as a challenge to their authority. Other regents sided with the faculty against the oath. Those who refused to sign, faculty as well as teaching assistants, student employees and staff, lost their jobs. Some of the thirty-one fired faculty members later sued, were victorious in state court, and eventually got their jobs back. This struggle left many bitter memories in its wake.

It made up part of the Berkeley story, one moment among many that rendered the conflict between state authority and the individual, between left and right, emblematic of the time. And that moment had its successors: in the late 1950s, a group of Berkeley students, joined by others, invaded the showrooms of automobile dealers on San Francisco's Van Ness Avenue to protest the fact that few Negroes were employed as part of the sales force, although many were new car buyers. That event was followed by a more serious and more violent protest in 1960 by students and others at San Francisco's City Hall, occasioned by the appearance of the House Committee on Un-American Activities at that site. Met by police with fire hoses, some of those protesting were washed down the steps of City Hall. Back in Berkeley itself, students made dramatic protests against Lucky grocery stores and the Bank of America (particularly the one on Telegraph Avenue) on the grounds that neither the grocery chain nor the bank had any appreciable number of Negro employees.

That was part of the equation that generated the Berkeley rebellion. Location—the ambience of the city itself—was also crucial. Telegraph Avenue was everything the university was not, and yet the two opposing Berkeley presences—campus and street—were fused in the minds of every student and faculty member. The campus was intricately complex, immense, prestigious, and managed by trained experts; it spoke officially to California, to the rest of the country, and to interests around the world. The Avenue was informal, shabby, lively, insular, and rich with color. Most of its stores catered to students, and young people worked in them. Telegraph's identity was its record stores, cheap restaurants and clothing stores, bookstores, news dealers, and a prominent coffee shop—the Mediterranean—and two small movie houses (the Guild and the Studio), run by longtime Berkeleyite Pauline Kael, that showed foreign and avant-garde films. Its population, moving on foot, was made up of students, those thinking of being students, those who once had been students, visiting professors, foreigners passing through, beatniks and then hippies, girls in jeans and girls with navy blue pea coats from the Salvation Army, young men with beards and older men with berets.

A quick stroll from the campus gates down the Avenue put you in two worlds, close but strikingly different. You stepped off the campus with students going to classes, using the library, working in labs, playing in the gym, coming from or going to fraternities and sororities, and eating in the Student Union, and you entered a zone characterized by folk and rock music coming from the record stores, street preachers, newspapers and journals featuring dissident political voices, itinerant intellectuals discussing existentialism in coffee shops, and the louche ferment that inevitably arises from free-floating intellectual life. On the campus were smartly dressed "coeds" (the term soon to expire of embarrassment) and young men wearing athletic sweater-jackets; on the Avenue were young women and men discussing Zen Buddhism. UC Berkeley had a football team called "Cal," but a graduate student in English who had come to study at "Berkeley" knew nothing of "Cal." It was something for Saturday afternoons in the fall, when alumni boosters came to see a football game.

In crossing over to Telegraph Avenue, that graduate student in English momentarily left an intense and closed world of scholarly endeavor patterned after traditions at Harvard and Columbia, a world focused on an established canon of literary works and a

ritual of formidable examinations, and entered a world of turbu-
lent energies that seemed both irresponsible and enticing. In turning toward Telegraph Avenue, that student first passed Sproul
Hall, a huge edifice housing the central administrative offices
of the campus. It dominated the southern sector of the campus,
overlooking the Student Union and reminding everyone near it
that one had come to a place where administration itself—authority,
power, and control—played a central role. The Avenue was
otherwise.

The undergraduates of the time gained admission to Berkeley
because they were among the top one-eighth of academic achievers
in California's high schools. As members of an academic meritocracy, they could go to classes at a first-rate university for a tuition
amounting to almost nothing. Yet, for many of them, the place at
which they arrived was not unlike the big high schools from which
they came. Their new place of learning was immense, and each
of them was small. Their numbers were breathtaking: three or four
thousand in each new arriving class. They attended large lectures,
particularly when freshmen or sophomores, and were taught, many
of them, by teaching assistants rather than by professors. The ratio
of students to teachers was 28 to 1, with more than 30 percent of
all undergraduate courses being taught by TAs. In the first two years
of instruction, TAs taught more than 40 percent of the courses; and
in small classes, where one might want the intimacy and wisdom
drawn from seniority, TAs taught almost two-thirds of the courses.[2]
Often existing as numbers rather than as names, the students took
many true-false or multiple-choice exams. Writing about them at
the time, Andrew Hacker noted that undergraduate students at all
large universities such as Berkeley "find they must spend more and
more time dealing with an expanding bureaucracy. Regular visits
must be paid to administrative purlieus to fill in forms in triplicate,
to be photographed in duplicate (face and lungs), to appeal, to
petition, to ask permission. They must not fold, mutilate, staple or
spindle the I.B.M. cards representing their studenthood."[3] Without
any particular adult supervision and with little or no direct contact
with the faculty, they lived either in charmless dormitories, in sororities and fraternities, or in cheap co-ops or rooms off-campus. They

were what Kerr said they were, the casualties of a "lack of faculty concern for teaching, endless rules and requirements, and impersonality."[4] They picked up the phrase "do not fold, mutilate, staple or spindle" and asked that they be treated with at least that minimal kindness. We grad students got to know them for the simple reason that there were not enough graduate courses for us to take in English, so we found ourselves taking undergraduate courses. While in the presence of those slightly younger people, I had a shorthand way of reminding myself of Haverford: it was, again, the very antithesis of the Berkeley way of being an undergraduate.

For those undergraduates coming to a campus to which they had gained admission as an elite group of young men and women but on which they were treated as part of a mass, or for those coming to such a campus only to discover that the ideal academic community they may have believed would protect them did not, in fact, exist—for those students the step toward hostility to the institution was a short one. No community; no community loyalty. No solicitude from the institution; no consideration for it. Rendered faceless, the one became the many and the many ultimately became "the proletariat" whose creation Kerr had accurately foreseen. In 1961, it was slowly forming but not yet ready to act. That had to await the fall of 1964, the year of the Free Speech Movement.

Such student disenchantment was also prompted by the tension that forever fuels youthful resentment: the contrast between what the world promises and what the world is able to give. The collision is always painful and it is forever a part of growing up. After learning at some early point in one's college career that American foreign policy or racial relationships or a fair distribution of wealth or the workings of democracy are not precisely what one imagined they could be, the next step in a young person's educational drama is likely to be a fierce questioning of all the other values, political and otherwise—the newly embarrassing legacies of home and secondary school—once so innocently accepted. Extravagant hopes, each and every one, are then extravagantly dashed. At Berkeley, this paradigm of youthful disappointment and resentment brought a number of students into conflict with the very institution, including its professors, that earlier welcomed them as an elite. Kerr could see it coming:

> There are more of them; they are more activist; they have more grievances against the campus and against society; and they are making gains, and they may make more. For the first time, they are challenging the inner sanctum of the campus where the faculty and the administration have ruled supreme.[5]

Grievances and power, the disappearance of community, activism, the masses against authority, the campus and the street: such were the terms defining Berkeley that graduate students in English, whether they wanted to or not, had to learn. In those first years of the '60s, we studied Chaucer and the finer points of bibliography, but we saw rebellions forming. While it is true that only a small percentage of the Berkeley undergraduates participated directly in the politically insurgent activities of the time, it is also true that in 1962 only a small number of graduate students (and few indeed among those with whom I studied) did anything other than watch. But we observers were forced to think about what our studies meant. How could a rarefied and formalized endeavor such as the study of English and American literature come to terms with the nation as it was changing so dramatically? As with many questions at Berkeley, we were not ready to answer. Nor was the institution ready to respond. But Kerr's "proletariat" was gathering to march. Its marches have now left a legacy—four decades long.

Once the '60s came to an end, and after the sidewalks emptied of the masses of shouting students, and after the boarded-up shops along the way reopened to business once the protestors filed away (some of those shops ultimately becoming boutiques and Starbucks in the '90s), the consequences in the national memory of that extraordinary decade continued to reverberate. They are a part of today's cultural controversies. The geography itself has become iconic. Once providing the avenues of antiwar insurgency, Berkeley and Oakland are today not unlike many urban centers. They mix the poor and the affluent, the gay and straight, black, white, and Hispanic, the young and the old. But they remain freighted with symbolic meaning in the national political consciousness.

A picture is today held in the American memory. It is of protesters, moving as they did from the Berkeley campus down Telegraph Avenue and toward the Oakland Induction Center, carrying signs and Vietcong flags, some smoking pot, some frolicking and others angry, their clothes and costumes of all assemblable sorts, a mass of people anarchic in spirit but molded in some complex way by a blend of every kind of leftist ideology, largely unburdened by leadership and disgusted by everything meant by "Washington." As far as political conservatives are concerned, that spectacle, embedded in today's cultural wars, is about how and where "everything went wrong." From that primal scene of disrespectful rebellion radiates outward the evidence to be used in today's right-wing indictment of the '60s generation. "Antiwar" is linked with marijuana, sexual promiscuity, raucous music, racial anger, and, in general, the breakdown of all traditional forms of conduct.

The ironic result today is that it is not the left, nor the left-liberal sympathizers, who have inherited the '60s. Rather, it is the right, and the neoconservatives, who are the surprising legatees of that moment. No one has made more of the idea of "everything going wrong" than those who enjoy the memory of the '60s for what it can now do to inspire anger against the left, for how it can lend support to "a return to standards," and how it can cultivate enthusiasm for today's Washington leadership. Journals such as *Commentary, The New Criterion,* and *The Weekly Standard,* as well as former Berkeley leftists like David Horowitz, feed on what they see as the derelictions of that decade now long gone. The irony of this has been bittersweet. No one marching then down those streets could have imagined that such protest—so energetic, so determined, so hopeful—would some day be used again and again, and used so profitably, to bash the very idea of insurgent protest itself.

I was later to learn—at Stanford and at Wesleyan—how the legacy of the '60s was to make itself felt on those campuses. That decade provided the language of how one was to talk at those places about the curriculum, the tactics of how students would deal with administrators, the attitude of faculty members as they came to terms with the institution for which they worked, and how administrators themselves understood the nature of their jobs.

But for me at the time, the '60s were just beginning and I had the life of a graduate student to live. The difference between Haverford and Berkeley was enormous and was for me a source of continual discontent. I was not as happy as I thought I should be at an institution so strong and important as the University of California. I knew how the undergraduate students felt: lost in a large place, dwarfed by the vastness of it all, and uncertain about the future. All of us wanted change, and we felt change was in the air. The past and traditional customs bound us, for the moment, in place. Just around the corner, however, an extraordinary transformation awaited everyone.

ENDNOTES

1. Kerr, *Uses of the University,* p. 78.
2. See Martin Trow, "Bell, Book and Berkeley," p. 305.
3. Andrew Hacker, "The College Grad Has Been Short-Changed," *New York Times Magazine,* June 6, 1965, as reprinted in *Beyond Berkeley: A Sourcebook in Student Values*, ed. by Christopher G. Katope and Paul G. Zolbrod (Cleveland and New York: World Publishing Co., 1966), p. 205.
4. Kerr, *Uses of the University,* p. 78.
5. Clark Kerr, "Governance and Functions," in *The Embattled University*, ed. by Stephen R. Graubard and Geno A. Ballotti (New York: G. Braziller, 1970), p. 112.

8

Going South

By the end of that first year at Berkeley, I was not sure that I wanted to go on as a graduate student. I was not alone. By the beginning of the 1962 school year, many faces that I could remember from the previous fall were absent. Attrition had gone about its remorseless work. With mixed feelings about proceeding, I enrolled in two courses—a lecture course on American literature of the nineteenth century and a very small (five students) seminar on Edmund Spenser. The first, though ably taught by Larzer Ziff— intelligent, lucid, and penetrating in his judgments—was not able to convey anything other than a panoramic sense of the books and the culture from which they came. I was beginning to assemble a small inventory of questions about teaching, and this course helped add to them: shouldn't a literature course attempt to return the student to the specific and intimate qualities of the novel, the poem, or the essay in question? Don't survey courses, even as good as this one, falsely suggest that a particular work (a poem by Emily Dickinson, say) is best understood as one part of a grand cavalcade of literature within an historical evolution? What about the unique particularities of the work? Doesn't the retrospective analysis hide or deform such uniqueness? I hoped that I would not be called upon, later in life, to give such a survey. (And of course I was, and then silently thanked Ziff for the model of clarity he gave me).

The course on Spenser was the strangest and most chilly learning experience of my life. The instructor was Robert McNulty— spectral, emaciated—who viewed *The Faerie Queene* as a repository of religious and philosophical truth. By way of contrast, he viewed the world in which he (and we) lived as vulgar and fallen. Could we but return to the word of God as proclaimed by the Church of

England in the time of Queen Elizabeth, could we but replace the democratic license and bad manners of the modern young with the aristocratic splendor of the Court, and could we put aside all the slovenliness so evidently present on, say, Telegraph Avenue, we would exist as we should exist.

Such views created a mood of dramatic confrontation in the small room in the university library where we met twice a week (at the end of the room was a very old printing press, complete with a powerful screw used to leave ink indelibly impressed on paper; its symbolic significance as a crushing instrument grew as the course went on). As Professor McNulty saw things, we five students were part of the decadence from which, by manner and belief, he believed himself absented. While he read Spenser's poem as, among other things, an irrefutable indictment of the modern world and its vulgarity, it was for us a poem—one more poem, albeit a great one—whose inner workings should be understood and interpreted, even criticized. These two approaches worked like a wedge between us. Was *The Faerie Queene* something to question or was it something whose glories should everywhere be proclaimed? The idea that students would propose to lay the poem open to "critical" approaches was, to him, anathema. The only proper way to write about *The Faerie Queene* was, he implied, to spell out its virtues, one by one, in detail, and then to praise them.

Not one day went well in that class. We questioned (politely); he defended (adamantly). Once one of the five of us wore oddly colored sneakers to class and, in addition, recklessly posed the question of why Roman Catholics of Spenser's time were so badly treated through exclusion and legal penalties against them. The combination of such dress and impudence brought from McNulty the supercilious announcement that the sneakered student would be sure "to find happiness in another course." And so he left, never to return. I stayed. The "moral lesson" that Berkeley dispensed was simple and cool: survive, outlast, and endure—endure even those courses that offer their own peculiar form of "moral" instruction. Haverford was now two years and a long distance away.

I thought about not returning after receiving the token M.A. degree the department handed out after the probationary period had been completed. The road to the Ph.D. seemed long and the prospect of passing over the next hurdles—language exams, the oral exam, and the dissertation—seemed remote. More pressing, however, was the concrete reality of what was in the newspapers, on the radio, and in conversation: civil rights struggles in the South, the 13-day standoff between the Soviet Union and the United States over missiles en route to Cuba, and a series of nuclear tests undertaken by the Russians that weakened the prospects for world peace. Less noted was the fact that the United States was then beginning its gradual buildup of "advisory forces" in South Vietnam. The public world pressed its weight into the thinking of everyone I knew; the private world of study was drained of color. I sought, with little success, to imagine myself a professor some day. Such a future seemed improbable at best, and so I thought of law school and, momentarily fancying myself an attorney, took the LSAT exams. But this was only a step to the side, a step taken indifferently, and my interest in being a lawyer evaporated as quickly as it came.

Enter the Woodrow Wilson National Fellowship Foundation. The foundation's announcement in early 1963 that it would sponsor teaching positions at "predominantly Negro colleges" in the South for former awardees was the intervention for which I had vaguely hoped. The idea of the sponsorship was that Woodrow Wilson grad students could discover what teaching was like and could help schools where energy and devotion might count more than proven skill. The prospect made sense to me for another reason: I wanted to know more about the Deep South. I had grown up in Maryland, a border state, and until 1954 had been educated at segregated public schools. But Maryland was not Alabama or Mississippi. That South was the world of James Meredith, just admitted after extraordinary struggle and violence, to the University of Mississippi. That South was the world of civil rights bravery, heroism, and violence. It was where much of the music heard on the sidewalks of Telegraph Avenue came from. That South was also the world of Faulkner. In sum, that

South was mythic and exotic. I immediately applied for one of the teaching positions. And just as immediately I was accepted into the program. I thus became a member of the first Woodrow Wilson class to take much hope and much ambition, as well as almost no teaching skills, South. We soon were to learn that the South itself would be our teacher.

With two years of graduate study behind me, then, I left California. I did so after having passed the ninety-minute oral examination (one professor, the stern Shumaker, noted of me that "Mr. Chace is more intelligent than knowledgeable") and at last having received a minimally passing grade on the French reading test. With my token M.A. in hand, I set off for Tuscaloosa, Alabama, the home of Stillman College, the school to which I had been assigned by the foundation. Leaving, however, was not easy, for I was departing from what had become, and was forever to be, the most valuable presence in my life: I had fallen in love. In just one year, she—JoAn Johnstone—and I were to become married but we did not know that at the time. A lovely girl whom I had once seen wearing one of those Navy pea jackets on Telegraph Avenue, she was also studying English at Berkeley, having graduated from Pomona College. Ahead of me in the progress toward the Ph.D., she gave me hope that one day I might finish Berkeley. She helped me through the French exam and she taught me about movies, hiking, cooking, and many other worlds about which I knew nothing. But for now, we were to separate, she to take up a teaching position at Lehmann College in New York City. Not to be with her would be, I knew, the only regret I had when, slim pedagogical credentials in hand, I would go to Tuscaloosa.

One stop—Washington, DC—would intervene between Berkeley and Alabama. I wanted to be with my parents as I prepared to repeat a journey my father had made some twenty-five years before. In the fall of 1936, he had taken a position at the Hampton Institute and for him, as for me, an academic career had begun at a "predominantly Negro college." Armed with his Princeton degree, he saw the South for the first time. At Hampton, he joined with a colleague, George Ketcham, to raise money for the institution: "Chace and Ketcham," as they got to be called. Now I was following in his footsteps.

Before leaving home, I attended, as did thousands, the March on Washington and there heard the words from Martin Luther King that, as long as the United States has a national memory, will live as *the* speech announcing how life would change for blacks and whites alike in this country. "I Have a Dream" was King at his most eloquent, passionately triumphant, and inspirational. JoAn and I heard him talk about Alabama:

> I have a dream that one day the state of Alabama, whose governor's lips are presently dripping with the words of interposition and nullification, will be transformed into a situation where little black boys and black girls will be able to join hands with little white boys and white girls and walk together as sisters and brothers. I have a dream today. I have a dream that one day every valley shall be exalted, every hill and mountain shall be made low, the rough places will be made plain, and the crooked places will be made straight, and the glory of the Lord shall be revealed, and all flesh shall see it together. This is our hope. This is the faith with which I return to the South.

I carried his words in memory with me to Tuscaloosa. I now hear in them, however, something I did not hear in 1963: a note of hope never to be fulfilled and thus hope made all the more desirable. The world of the future King described that August day is one of perfect justice, equality, and harmony. It is the world that everyone wants to come into being and yet those to whom it would come—both black and white—are those whose present imperfections make up the world as we know it. King's voice seemed to recognize that irony. It was a voice whose undertones reflected a tragic understanding of the fallen nature of humanity as he saw it. That understanding made his evocation of a better world yet to come all the more moving.

I left the talk and moved through the huge crowd, knowing that I would soon be in a part of the country, the Alabama of which he spoke, in which the drama of freedom and justice he had portrayed would be played out in ways I could not imagine. King's dream gave me a reason to travel South; but he was telling me that my destination was a land of rough and crooked places. I left with a sense of soaring excitement mixed with an unwelcome sense of fear.

What was Stillman College, where I was going to teach? In 1874 a group of white Presbyterian ministers headed by Dr. Charles Allen Stillman petitioned the General Assembly of the Presbyterian Church in the United States to establish a training school for black male students, largely illiterate, to become ministers. The school opened its doors in 1876, although it did not receive a charter as a legal corporation from the State of Alabama until 1895. First named Tuscaloosa Institute, and then Stillman Institute, it was, by turns, an academy for ministers, a junior and senior high school, a junior college, the home of a hospital and a nurses' training school, and at last in 1948, Stillman College, a four-year institution. As of my arrival on campus, all of its leaders had been white men. Its enrollment in 1963–64 was some 500 students; its faculty and staff numbered some 50. Its endowment was far short of even a million dollars. The tuition was $240 a year plus an "activities fee" of $35. (Not many years before, some students were admitted when their parents traded a cow or some pigs in lieu of tuition.) I was a long way from Haverford, a long way from Berkeley. On soil new and strange to me, I thought of only one thing: I had come to teach.

My commitment to teaching was reinforced by the College from the start. President Samuel Burney Hay, who had been presiding over Stillman for fifteen years in his comfortable and lordly way, informed me at our first meeting that I would be teaching three courses of freshman English and one course on literature. My first class of the fall 1963 semester would meet at 7:30 a.m. and the three others would follow in order as the day progressed. He disclosed to me my salary for the year: $5000. Never having made anything like that sum, I was elated.

I found a comically small apartment—once the bed had been opened, the "living room" was full—near the other institution of higher learning in the town. The University of Alabama, "the Crimson Tide," was the home of the renowned football coach Paul

"Bear" Bryant, a university whose reputation rested on fraternities and sororities, parties, Homecoming, and the recent memory of Governor George Wallace "standing in the schoolhouse door" to prevent, if he could, the admission of any black students.

Two kinds of Alabama greeted me those early and very hot September days: a black Alabama still poor, ill-educated, marginalized, and at siege; and a white Alabama proud, traditional, and obstinate. In that white Alabama and in Tuscaloosa, I soon learned, could be found the headquarters of the United Klans of America, an umbrella racist organization led by the rabid demagogue Robert Shelton. This was Alabama defiant, Alabama self-conscious, Alabama readying for the worst. But to the racial politics and tension of the time I did not then give my attention. I had come to teach. Civil rights was one thing; my classes, about which I was anxious, were another and more important thing.

That first day of teaching, I walked to the school, some two miles from my apartment. On the way, I thought about what I would say, how I would say it, and how everything I knew about English would now be employed in an environment about which I knew almost nothing. As I immediately found out, my learning curve would be very steep. Those classes gave me an entirely different idea of what education—far away from Berkeley, from Haverford, or from anything I had ever known—could be. In front of the first students I had ever taught, I discovered just how unprepared I was. My four classes, back to back every morning that fall, had to be, I immediately saw, about basic things I had long used but about which I had given little thought: the noun, the verb, the adjective, the adverb, and the complete sentence. Drawing upon my imagination, I drew up lessons about the declarative and the interrogative voice. I elucidated the differences between the colon and the semicolon. I soon discovered that, owing to the educational deprivations my students had suffered, the paragraph in its fullness would lie at the furthest end of my teaching reach. These grammatical issues constituted my pedagogical inventory, four times each morning, five days a week.

And who were my students? I found them sweetly disposed but not easy to get to know. They were deferential to me—a young white man from the North whom they could see was as innocent of Southern things as they were innocent of foreign realities such as California. Many of them came from devout religious families and had grown up in the South, mostly in Alabama. Some came from cities like Birmingham and Huntsville, but most came from rural backgrounds. They all had been taught by family and friends alike about what was expected of them in the presence of whites. Little by little, I discovered that what I first thought of as docility on their part turned out to be attentiveness. In class, they watched me—looking to learn who I was—just as I watched them for the same reason—looking to learn who they were. What could have seemed only a class in basic grammar was, in fact, an intimate drama in which they, only seven or eight years younger than I, were in possession of the culture all around us, while my sole property was a knowledge of the parts of "proper" speech. In every human way, they had the advantage.

As the days and the months went on, the several screens separating us lifted a bit and we got to know each other slightly better. I was asked by the drama teacher to take part in a production of Edward Albee's *The Death of Bessie Smith* and I did so, appearing as the white doctor opposite a strikingly beautiful student who played the part of the nurse. Midway through one of our two performances, I forgot my lines and she, quickly and expertly, fed them to me. Around midyear, the wholly incredible James Brown and the Famous Flames gave an afternoon performance in the school gym and I, never before having seen him sing or dance, was stunned by his performance. Charged by intensely rhythmic patterns of request and answer, punctuated by pleas and surrenders, flamboyantly erotic, the show evoked a part of the black world never in evidence in the classroom. I was sitting behind one of my students and she, suddenly turning to me, mischievously said: "I'll bet you can't do that, Mr. Chace!" Indeed I couldn't and told her so; she gave me a happy smile. She was telling me something about the differences between her world and mine that, I knew, were hard to disclose in any other way. We were not the same, she black and I white. The music—sexually charged, rooted in Africa, the black church, passions suppressed and passions released—told us so.

I learned other things about my students and the South, things hard first to accept and then impossible to forget. One of my students came to me to tell me why he had been late to class. Trying to explain, painfully distressed, he told me the Tuscaloosa police had stopped him while he was walking on a country road the night before. Telling him to sit in the back of the patrol car, they turned a flashlight on him and ordered him to lower his trousers. Confused and terrified, he did so. They then asked him to explain why he had been "fucking sheep." He was speechless with terror. They repeated the question and told him they would have to cut off his penis. He wept in the seat and pled for mercy. Laughing, they stopped the car, let him out, and told him to go home.

When, the previous June, George Wallace had attempted to prevent Vivian Malone and James Hood from being the first black students to enroll at the University of Alabama, they demonstrated considerable bravery as, with U.S. Deputy Attorney General Nicholas Katzenbach leading the way, they forced Wallace aside and enrolled. Once there, however, both were harassed on a daily basis by the Tuscaloosa police, who, citing "danger to them from other students," followed them on roaring motorcycles everywhere on campus, class to class. Needing what she rightly called "R and R," Malone came to the Stillman campus to be with other black students. They took her in "as a sister" and I asked to meet and congratulate her on her courage and tenacity.

As the months went on, I saw with greater clarity the institution to which I had come and to understand better what it had been for almost a hundred years. Its history was a record of what such schools in the deep South had been from their beginnings: poor, academically undistinguished but nonetheless proud in the face of that fact, and founded on the assumption that religious denominations might help where history itself had hurt. In the early 1960s, schools like Stillman stood as evidence of what the combination

of slavery, Reconstruction, piety, poverty, and hope could bring
about. Of them, one observer has written:

> these schools are for the most part small, financially marginal, rel-
> atively unknown, poorly equipped and housed, with poorly pre-
> pared students, and staffed by faculties with a minimum of
> advanced degrees. On the other hand, they also have an unusually
> strong commitment to teaching, undergirded by a nurturing atmo-
> sphere and a special affinity and expertise for awakening untutored
> minds and molding underprepared students into functioning pro-
> fessionals and contributing citizens.[1]

Berkeley had no time to think about how it would prepare its
students to be "contributing citizens." Its research mission rendered such a function naive and antiquated. One was trained at
Berkeley to enter the workforce, add to the economic well-being
of the state and nation, and solidify the status quo. Stillman had
something else in mind (so had Haverford). Stillman wanted to
give its students the foundation, morally and intellectually, with
which they could try to enter the larger world, a world not particularly interested in welcoming them. They needed confidence;
Stillman sought to show them how to find it. The little school outside Philadelphia and the little school on the outskirts of
Tuscaloosa were linked by a common aspiration.

As I taught more, with the weeks stretching into months and
with that first semester and all its challenges—pedagogical and
personal—behind me, and with my sense that I had learned some
crucial things about teaching, I began to understand how narrow
in its own way the world of Berkeley was. Despite its sophistication, its distinguished history, and its assembly of superior
researchers and intellects, it possessed no greater reality than
Alabama. The Southern world all around me had become, in time,
less opaque, less exotic, and more compelling. As it did so, it
became every bit as immediate and complex as California. More
importantly, it was the scene of a powerful drama. Living that
year in the Deep South, I witnessed the latest chapter in a long
American struggle that had begun with chattel slavery, included
the bloodiest war in history, produced Reconstruction and then

Jim Crow, and had lodged the experience of racism's poison deeply within the minds of both black and white people.

That September, shortly after my arrival, four black children were killed when the Sixteenth Street Baptist Church in neighboring Birmingham was bombed; the cousin of one of those girls was in one of my classes. Every passing day brought to me, a privileged young white man, some new awareness of not only how cruel one kind of Alabamian could be to another, but also how the spirit to overcome such cruelty was rising up. The name of Dr. Martin Luther King, Jr., was everywhere in the air—for both blacks and whites. His eloquence, bravery, and charisma spoke of a new day. My students had heard his voice and had seen what he and his followers, particularly young people, could do. So had many white people, and they reacted with suspicion, fear, and bewilderment. No one believed that things would go on as they had. Change was upon us.

ENDNOTE

1. Albert N. Whiting, *Guardians of the Flame: Historically Black Colleges Yesterday, Today and Tomorrow* (Washington, DC: American Association of State Colleges and Universities, 1991), p. 35.

9

Reading in Jail

As I began my second semester at Stillman, it became more difficult, day by day, to keep my growing sense of political and social
realities separate from my teaching. Many of the students I taught
felt the same pressures. By March, some of them began to
approach me—shyly and in a roundabout way—to talk about the
struggle for civil rights. No more than I had they come to Stillman
to protest anything. But they had heard about the sit-ins at lunch
counters by black students at schools such as North Carolina A & T
in Greensboro, North Carolina. On TV they had seen, as had
the entire nation, the protests against segregation in nearby
Birmingham. They knew about "Bull" Connor and his police
dogs. But about the struggle in general they were tentative, unsure,
and concerned that any kind of activism could jeopardize their
education. They did not come from protesting families. They were
Stillman students because they believed that a college degree
would give them some security in their lives. They were studying
because their parents wanted them to have advantages they themselves had been denied. Most of them were the first in their families to attempt a college education. Since some ninety percent of
all black students at that time went to "predominantly Negro
institutions" (now called HBCUs: "historically black colleges and
universities") and since most of those places were in the South,
the insularity of my students was considerable. That kind of insularity gave them protection, nowhere better exemplified than
when a student who had been raised in Alabama took me aside
and, combining local loyalty and parochial innocence, told me
that Mississippi (only an hour away) was a place full of racism.
Somehow she thought, as a proud black Alabamian, that she was
a native of a safe place.

My students' insularity led me to understand better Stillman's value to them. Of course it provided formal education—my elementary classes in grammar, punctuation, and exemplary spelling were a part of that. But Stillman's greater value was to strengthen self-confidence in its students and encourage them to believe that even in a place—Alabama—where indignities and deprivation were commonplace for black people, pride of accomplishment could respond to bigotry. Stillman, like its counterparts, told them they could succeed. It spoke to their timidity and self-doubt, but said that such weaknesses could be replaced by hope. From their beginnings, such schools, almost all of them founded in the years immediately after the Civil War, had become the chief means by which a small middle class of black doctors, dentists, lawyers, judges, army officers, schoolteachers, and ministers emerged in this country.[1]

Stillman had been a part of all these changes in the South. By 1963–64, even more were on the way. The University of Alabama would soon admit a large number of black students, not just one or two, and other previously segregated universities in the South would do the same. By the '70s, affirmative action policies would ensure the presence of black students at virtually every institution of higher education in the United States. Yet the argument for HBCUs now is as strong as it was then. The existence of such institutions is warranted by virtue of the emotional and psychological benefits they can give to their students. Stillman, for instance, continues to provide the same support it has provided for decades, and it is fiscally sounder than when I taught there. What Stillman has given and continues to give is not something my lessons in English gave; rather, it imparts a sense of personal worth. HBCUs are places that offer the chance to develop black identity; they are encouraging places for the ordinary student; and, as one study says, they are "a place for the weak, the timid, and the militant; and a setting for black affirmation."[2]

But even though my students began with timidity, they slowly began to show an interest in that very "black affirmation." And as they became more attentive to civil rights, I became more attentive too. Stillman's administrators were deeply uneasy with those early signs of political restiveness. The school's president took me aside to say: "I will not be happy if you make the mistake of getting involved with the students in what I hear they're up to." In this respect, the Stillman administration wasn't much different from officials at Berkeley. Both were concerned about "reputation," about "what the town would think," about the danger into which the institution could be thrust if the students became active on the streets. In time, they did become active, and as they did, they championed the very values—pride and self-assertion—for which, in fact, Stillman stood. But in 1964, the Stillman administration, like the Berkeley administration, was not willing to recognize any such championship.

As spring came, and as the likelihood of some kind of protest action grew, I began to think about what education can give to the young. The world of Berkeley and the world of Stillman then began to converge, and I could not easily separate them. Stillman and schools like it had students whose self-assurance was lacking, and those places stood ready to offer remedies. But thinking of Stillman made me think of Berkeley: were all its undergraduates, as bright and enterprising as they were in that sunny and prosperous state, truly secure in their psychological well-being? Were not some few "unready"? Were not some, in fact, immature and confused, just as I in my time at Haverford had been? The problems of post-adolescent confusion are evident everywhere in colleges and universities (I was later to learn, at Wesleyan and Emory, much more about the pains of such confusion). While "black" Alabama did not look like "white" Berkeley and Haverford, the element common to all three, and to all higher education, is that it is a world made up of young people. For them, college is both a place to gain prowess in intellectual disciplines and a place (for some, the only place) to find a way to psychological maturity. Some of my students were seeking what I once had sought, and what many students always will seek.

The Stillman students, however, faced what I had never faced and what few Berkeley students would ever confront: the denial of their very beings on racial grounds. They all knew what it was like to be shouldered aside, to be told that they could not enter certain places, do certain things, or entertain certain hopes. They knew what it meant to be considered inadequate, incapable, or just plain worthless. They had all been called "niggers." Some of them, I thought, had decided to live within such demeaning confinements, for they saw no way out of them. Others began to see exits of their own devising and to believe that the ways of Alabama life could not, would not, be sustained forever. In February, one such student came to see me, saying that she would be riding the next day "up front" in one of the city's segregated buses. She asked me if I would come with her. I was astonished, then pleased that she would think of me. I agreed to do so, and off we went—she to dare what few would have dared at the time and I—with nothing to lose but everything to learn—to be with her in her bravery. We boarded the bus and both sat up front. As things turned out, the driver, perhaps wanting to get back to the depot without any problems, simply ignored the two of us. From the back of the bus, however, a group of black women raised their voices and told my student, in stern matriarchal tones, to "get yourself back here, little girl, where you belong." But she sat up very straight, looked back at them only once, and stared proudly ahead. In that brief moment, I was given a lesson—succinctly and efficiently—about generational conflict and difference in the black community. Younger African-Americans would now have their say, and the older women and men, the ones who "knew their place," would see their authority evaporate. My student returned to the campus with victory showing in her face. Her generation would lead the way.

By March, the racial situation in Tuscaloosa had become serious. The immediate cause was the fact that while the city's black leadership, largely made up of ministers, had been promised that the new county courthouse under construction would be built without offensive special bathrooms and drinking fountains traditionally set aside for "colored," those symbols of racism were, in fact, part of the building when it was completed. The leadership was hurt and angry. The Reverend T. Y. Rogers, a minister installed in his church earlier that year by his fellow Baptist, Martin Luther King, Jr., felt betrayed, believing that Governor

George Wallace was behind the installation of the degrading features. With the memory of King's visit in his mind, a visit that had brought to Tuscaloosa hundreds of black people bent on seeing King, hearing King, perhaps even meeting him, Rogers helped to form and lead the Tuscaloosa Community Action Committee (TCAC). He was determined to act against the betrayal of the promise.

Several weeks of planning went into a proposed demonstration against the courthouse, the local officials, and Wallace. TCAC selected April 23 as the day of a march around the new building. Stillman students—at first only a few and then scores of them— put their energies into recruiting others to join the demonstration. Several of them asked if I would be coming along. I hesitated, but at last saw no reason not to be with them; we had been together in class and now we could be together on the sidewalk. And so, on that warm spring morning I found myself the only white in a gathering of some 300 persons. No other faculty members from the college joined us.

Our assembly included the young and the old, the brave and the fearful, some singing and some staring nervously ahead. A few dressed in Sunday finery, as if going to church; others came to march in coveralls. Near to me, a woman prayed quietly and carried a Bible in her trembling hands. Some of the Stillman students, gathered as if one, laughed to cheer themselves up. Tension filled the humid air. The procession began peacefully, but we were all quite aware that our little band, uttering slogans of "No More Racism" and "End Segregation" in unison, was being observed by scores of Tuscaloosa police officers and Alabama state troopers, some on motorcycles with engines running and some high on horseback, as well as by hundreds of town residents, all of them hostile to us. As we chanted our slogans again and again, the townspeople shouted back, "Go home, niggers, go home." I wanted to stare directly ahead, but I caught sight of the menacing faces of the crowd, the impassive look of the troopers, and the steady slow progress of my fellow marchers. Even today, the mixture of fear, pride, and adrenaline coursing through me confuses my memory. I recall in bits and pieces the crowd's growing

hostility, the police both protecting us and yet limiting our movements, the patient labor of our motion, and the sense that we had
to keep moving, forever and forever around the courthouse, lest in
stopping we become isolated and vulnerable. Our marching
seemed to work as a ceremony to shield us. And then, suddenly, I
was on the ground, my arms pinned behind me, my face in the
grass, and an electric cattle prod shoved against my trousers and
pressed tightly against my rectum. With hurtling swiftness, I was
rushed into the courthouse, booked, my pockets emptied, and my
fingerprints and photograph taken.

Those arresting me—four counts: unlawful assembly, resisting
arrest, loitering, and failure to disperse—were at first businesslike
and interrogative. They had arrested only me and so had plenty of
time to focus on who I was. There were four of them, four over-
weight men in plainclothes. Two of them, I saw, did not come
from Tuscaloosa but from Montgomery, the state capital. Later I
found out that they were part of an intelligence operation looking
into "civil rights agitators." Their questions began in a matter-of-
fact tone: Who was I and who had told me to march in the demonstration? What was my association with CORE (the Congress of
Racial Equality) and who had sent me South? Did I know the kind
of danger I had been in, that the police had confiscated scores of
ax handles that were being readied against us? Then they were
hostile: Did I like niggers? Did I sleep with the students on campus? Did I believe in race-mixing? Answering those questions, I
was calm without but frightened within. And then I suddenly was
hustled into yet another part of the jail: solitary confinement.

In pitch-blackness, seated on the concrete floor, with the scent
of urine and tobacco filling the room, I became aware of the
presence of someone else—breathing heavily and smelling of
alcohol. My confinement would not be "solitary." I spoke, giving my name and asking his. He asked why I was there. I told
him what was going on outside. He held a match up to my face
and looked closely at me. I looked at him and saw that he was
black. He asked about the march. I told him what I knew. He
then said that I would be "OK" with him. I asked him what that
meant. He said the police had told him that I would soon be

coming in and that it would be his job to "beat yo' ass up fine." He said he wouldn't. I took a series of long breaths and thanked him. And we sat.

After a few hours, I was removed from that room and spent the night in a cell upstairs in the jail. When asked by an officer if I wanted anything from "home," I reacted instinctively and said I wanted the German book—Thomas Mann's *Tonio Kröger*—I had been studying for the German language exam back in Berkeley. Strangely enough, miraculously enough, the book soon appeared in my cell. So there I was, in an Alabama jail for how long I did not know but with my mind loyally focused on graduate study. My fellow inmates, a couple of cells down, were two women arrested for prostitution. At first I couldn't see them, but after a while one of them, wise to the ways of jail, thrust a small mirror out of her bars, gave me a look at her grainy and angular face, then gave me the mirror and asked me to show her my face. She then said: "You're the one. We heard they were bringing you up here. You're the nigger-lover." The other, reflecting on the realities of Southern life as she had seen it, shot back: "And I'm a nigger-lover too, long as they pay." A tough-looking young trusty came to my cell, stared at me for a long time, and said: "I'm just looking at you, because when you get out and when I get out, I'm going straight ahead kill you."

Thanks to the quick and aggressive intervention of two lawyers from the NAACP Legal Defense and Education Fund, my release came after one day. I walked out and into the arms of the Reverend Rogers and three of his ministerial colleagues. Knowing and fearing things about the South that I did not know, they had waited for me outside the jail all night. They took me to the home of one of them, gave me a shower and some food, and told me that I could never go back to my apartment. Some other place had to be found where I could live, for I was, they said, in danger.

In time, I did find a place to live for the rest of the school year, one of the rooms in the house of the Stillman College Presbyterian chaplain, a lovely woman who saw to my needs in a motherly way. My students welcomed me back. The president wouldn't talk to me. And then the year ended (Stillman was offered another Woodrow Wilson teacher for the next year but declined). Three weeks after I left Tuscaloosa, three civil rights workers, after having been released from jail in Philadelphia, Mississippi, were killed and their bodies buried in an earthen dam in Neshoba County. Philadelphia's jail was some two hours from the Tuscaloosa jail. The ministers had been right. I had not been safe.

What had I learned that Stillman year? That I wanted to be a teacher. I had worked hard on all the courses I taught and saw the time devoted to them rewarding. The one literature course seemed to have gone well—we read American short stories and, at the end, John Steinbeck's *Grapes of Wrath*, a book that surprised many students. One of them, poor himself, told me that he had never known that white people could be so impoverished, hungry, and desperate. I was impressed by how a work of the imagination could strike, in him and others, the chord of sympathy. He and his classmates had much to think about in their own want, but the book let them know that they were hardly alone in deprivation. Teaching books would be a way, I could see, of uniting rather than dividing people. I liked the young men and women I had taught and believed that, here and there, I had helped them. I liked the fit and feel of the classroom, the expectation it sets forward and the gratification it can sometimes give. The drama of teaching—the sudden accelerations of learning, the surprises of thought, the quiet mutual struggle against ignorance—appealed to me. I thought of those who had taught me and considered my own teaching, as amateurish as it had been that year, as an appreciative response to them. I wanted to go back to Berkeley. I now would take it for what it was, a rigorous institution of professional training, a place that would license me to do what I wanted to do: teach.

I had also learned that the distance between the classroom and political reality was shorter than I imagined it to be. I had taught, but I also had tried to stand for something—racial justice—in which I believed. I had seen something about a way of the world that had done huge damage to many people. I had seen it could be addressed and challenged. Never before had I conceived a way both to think and act, to consider important matters and then take steps to change reality. When I went back to Berkeley, I would, I thought, be ready this time.

ENDNOTES

1. See Julian B. Roebuck and Komanduri S. Murty, *Historically Black Colleges and Universities: Their Place in American Higher Education* (Westport, CT: Prager Publishers, 1993), p. 13.
2. Ibid., p. 11.

10

Poetry and Politics

I returned to California a married man. From now on, it was no longer to be "me" but "us." JoAn and I chose our strategy, a distinctly "bourgeois" one: we would live in San Francisco, not in Berkeley. No going back to the place where we had once been unmarried graduate students. Now established as a couple, we would live in a real city (albeit one with a grand bohemian history) where college life did not define everything. Berkeley would be "work" and San Francisco "home." Rounding out this picture of secure domesticity was our purchase of a red Triumph convertible. We thus marked our graduation from Berkeley grunge. Flashily commuting across the Bay, we would complete what we had to do: JoAn to finish her dissertation on the Renaissance poet Edmund Spenser and I to clear the remaining hurdles on the way to a Ph.D. The degree would be my pass to a career. Teaching at Stillman had taught me I wanted to teach.

After our wedding in Roseburg, Oregon, we had a three-day honeymoon along the Northern California coast and then found a small apartment on Telegraph Hill with windows overlooking the Oakland Bay Bridge. It was owned by an Italian-American couple—he a retired carpenter and she a former employee of the Planters Peanut Company—to whom we paid $90 a month. He made his own wine and shared it with us when, on Sundays, he invited us to dinner—pasta and *osso buco*. Settled in, we went about our tasks. Before me stood a few more courses in the English department, two language exams (German, and then Latin or ancient Greek), the three-hour oral exam, and the writing of a dissertation. Thanks perhaps to those additional hours reading *Tonio Kröger* in the Tuscaloosa jail, I quickly passed the

German exam. Knowing neither Greek nor Latin, but having been told that Greek had the better literature, I chose Greek.

The atmosphere on the Berkeley campus to which I returned was charged with an intensity unlike anything I remembered from my earlier time there. I was not the only one returning from the South. Some fifty to sixty students had been in Mississippi, Georgia, and Alabama over the summer to work on voter registration efforts, and some of them had come to decisive positions about other political questions too. Among them was Mario Savio, a twenty-one year old philosophy major from New York City. He immediately got involved in the civil-rights struggle on campus, but also in antiwar activism. Other students established groups that occupied card tables on campus, distributed literature, collected money, and organized activities at both the "old" entrance to the campus at Sather Gate and the "new" entrance at the corner of Bancroft and Telegraph. The latter, a rectangle measuring 26 by 90 feet, was believed at the time to be the property of the City of Berkeley and therefore immune from the restrictions against student "political advocacy" that the Berkeley administration had established.

It did not take long that fall of 1964 for the confrontation between students and administration to erupt. President Kerr and Chancellor Edward W. Strong had earlier declared that students enjoyed no rights to engage in advocacy of off-campus political acts that could be considered illegal. But they soon found out that the university, not the city of Berkeley, owned the "immune" zone. So they immediately prohibited "advocacy" speech there too. The students, on the other hand, believed they had the same rights to speech, including political speech, that every American citizen possessed. Kerr and Strong, nervously sensitive to the negative publicity that the earlier sit-ins in the city of San Francisco had caused, acted to protect the university's nonpartisan political position. They correctly believed that the Regents did not want to wake up in the morning to read in the *San Francisco Chronicle* or the *Los Angeles Times* about yet another "Berkeley event." The students, on the other hand, saw the restrictions against them as not only legally suspect but demeaning, and they took note that those restrictions were tightening day by day. They were offended by the traditional code of *in loco parentis,* by which the university could act in place of parents in supervising their lives. Young people defining their lives in political terms were not about to abide by rules that devalued their passion.

And so, on a sunny day in October, the campus changed, and changed forever. Those changes wrought other changes elsewhere in the nation, on campuses and off. The urgency, confusion, and fervency of that fall on that campus marked virtually everyone who was there. It is not true that "if you can remember the 'sixties, you were not there." Those who were there have some of the events, the sights, and the atmosphere of confusion and excitement, locked forever in their minds. They are locked in mine.

The immediate cause of the change was the astonishing spectacle, on October 1, of a local activist (but not a student), Jack Weinberg, being held for thirty-two hours in a police car on the campus while thousands of students encircled and immobilized it. He had been arrested for refusing to give up a table promoting the Congress of Racial Equality. The table had been placed directly in front of Sproul Hall. On my way back to the Triumph to go home, I stayed to watch, part of the crowd. But I did not stay long. I recall thinking: "This is happening and it's important. But it's not happening to me. I have my work to do." That mixed fascination and diffidence marked the 1960s at Berkeley for me.

The larger cause, to which Weinberg and the car and the astonished police were but supporting actors, was a dramatic change in American higher education. Students infused with the energies and hopes of the civil rights struggle saw the campus as the stage on which they would exercise their moral convictions. Protest, anger, and impromptu activity were their engines of change. If there were campus "wrongs" to be corrected, spontaneous mobilization would respond. If older generations—administrators and faculty alike—could not summon the will to remake the campus, students would. This was a revolution, or so Berkeley students thought, that did away with traditional ideology. It put youth against age, idealism against compromise.

In retrospect, it is easy to see that what the students wanted was not, in fact, revolutionary. Most of them wore jackets and ties, or skirts and blouses, and spoke in respectful terms to administrators when they sat with them at formally arranged meetings to negotiate. When they mounted the police car to speak to the crowd, they first took off their shoes. They did not want to destroy the university, but to change its rules. They did not want to remake society radically, but to make it work in a better way. They brought moral fervor, but not ideological rigor, to how they thought and what they did. Although the newspapers of the day spoke of "Communist influence," thus alarming and confusing the general public about campus events, this was not a time when either the university or society was upended. Although everyone at the time thought that "revolution is in the air," it's now easy to see that it wasn't. But the distribution of power on campus was changed. Students were to assert, as they had never done before, the authority uniquely belonging to them.

As he sat in the police car for those thirty-two hours, urinating in a Coke bottle, surrounded by hundreds of students, Weinberg was making history. History often is created in strange ways, with the participants being aware only of something unusual enveloping them but unsure what it might be called. In this instance, Weinberg's incarceration led to something with a name soon to become notorious—the "Free Speech Movement." And then history moved with great speed. After Weinberg's release from the police car, the university cited seventy students for violating the rules about advocacy. The ante was upped. Quickly thereupon the Berkeley faculty became involved in the issues and, in a packed meeting broadcast to hundreds of students waiting outside Wheeler Auditorium, voted its opposition to the tactics of the administration. No action on the part of Berkeley professors could have been more dramatic or polarizing. Kerr and Strong were one force; the other force was the faculty in all its distinction and luster. Then, on December 3, students and others held an overnight sit-in at Sproul Hall, the main administration building, which led to the arrest of more than 800 of them. The sit-in began with a speech by Savio, by then the acknowledged leader of the student struggle. Standing on the steps of Sproul Hall, dressed in his customary worn leather jacket lined with fleece and looking out across the sea of thousands and thousands of students, he said:

> There is a time when the operation of the machine becomes so odious, makes you so sick at heart, that you can't take part; you can't even passively take part, and you've got to put your bodies upon the gears and upon the wheels, upon the levers, upon all the apparatus, and you've got to make it stop. And you've got to indicate to the people who run it, to the people who own it, that unless you're free, the machine will be prevented from working at all![1]

Savio's speech was one kind of rhetoric; it proved both powerful and persuasive. Others spoke too, most memorably a young philosophy professor, John Searle, who—jacket and tie—aligned himself with the students and denounced the administration in language mixing passion, clarity, and wit. My memory of Savio's language, however, is how much more "adult" it was than the words coming from anyone else. He was, after all, a young man, an undergraduate student, indeed younger than Searle and younger than I. What inner force moved him? Out of what store of historical awareness was he able to gauge so unerringly the mood of his fellow students? His remarkably charismatic gift was to measure out his moral conviction in tones bespeaking tragedy: "There is a time . . . to put your bodies upon the gears and upon the wheels." Implying that the cost for political freedom could be death, he spoke as if he were in touch with ancient prophecy. No one at the time was more compelling.

The sit-in led to no one's death. The result for the arrested students was hours of incarceration at the distant Santa Rita Rehabilitation Center and Prison Farm in Alameda County. The tragic tones of Savio's speech were not heard again; his own celebrity soon slipped away from him. But what he demanded— the right to political advocacy—was soon to come to him and to every Berkeley student. Thereafter they could speak as they wanted. But Berkeley never stopped being Berkeley. While the arrests went on, and while the aftermath of legal hearings proceeded, and while Chancellor Strong was soon fired and a new chancellor, Martin Meyerson, took his place, and even when the FSM later descended into a caricature of itself by becoming the "Filthy Speech Movement," classes continued, research was maintained at its usual pace, and the campus stood. The Cal "Bears" still played against the Stanford "Indians" in the annual Big Game.

Surrounded by this confusion and tumult, I knew that returning to graduate study would be more difficult than I had imagined. I reminded myself when I set foot on campus that I hadn't gone to Alabama as a political activist, nor had I intended to return as one. What happened to me in Tuscaloosa arose not by any intention on my part, but by events themselves. And I came back to Berkeley not to protest anything, but to get the degree that would let me teach. I did not participate in the sit-in, and I was never arrested. But political life at Berkeley was insurgent, and with activism everywhere around me, it seemed imperative that even if I had chosen not to be arrested, I still had to make up my political mind. Savio's rhetoric had touched me as it had touched thousands of others. The way he conveyed the hurt and the hope of his generation—my generation—could not be denied. I had to respond.

But I had to respond to other realities too. Rhetoric and passion come in various forms, and Savio's were not the only ones alive those days at Berkeley. On a campus that large, with almost twenty-five thousand students and with hundreds of academic departments covering every area of learning, nothing could monopolize the attention of everyone. Even the appearance of "revolution" had to take its place amid a host of other campus concerns.

This was brought home to me when, one day, I ran into the professor, Thomas Flanagan, who was to become my dissertation advisor. At noon we looked together out at the broad expanse of asphalt between Wheeler and Dwinelle halls. Hundreds of police officers protected behind heavy plastic shields and bearing long wooden batons stood there in formation. They were once again readying themselves to do battle—truncheons against stones— with a crowd of students protesting the university's involvement in Vietnam. They had done this many times before and would do so again. With his customary droll perspective, Flanagan asked me: "Well, what shall we do? Go to today's riot or have lunch and discuss Yeats?" We chose lunch and Yeats. When we talked over lunch, we talked books, and it was perhaps this poem by Yeats to which we turned, a meditation in which the poet weighs the solace of creation against the exhaustions of violence:

THE STARE'S NEST BY MY WINDOW

The bees build in the crevices
Of loosening masonry, and there
The mother birds bring grubs and flies.
My wall is loosening; honey-bees,
Come build in the empty house of the stare.

We are closed in, and the key is turned
On our uncertainty; somewhere
A man is killed, or a house burned,
Yet no clear fact to be discerned:
Come build in the empty house of the stare.

A barricade of stone or of wood;
Some fourteen days of civil war;
Last night they trundled down the road
That dead young soldier in his blood;
Come build in the empty house of the stare.

We had fed the heart on fantasies,
The heart's grown brutal from the fare;
More substance in our enmities
Than in our love; O honey-bees,
Come build in the empty house of the stare.

What kind of passion—political or poetic—would be my concern as a graduate student who had come back to Berkeley to earn a degree? How would I avoid fantasies, and what would I build? Flanagan knew, and I later came to understand, that universities, all of them, outlive the issues, every one of them—political and otherwise—that momentarily seize the attention of students and others. On a campus, nothing is so transient as a crucial moment. Indeed, everything at a university is transient except what it perpetually does: teach the young, create knowledge, and save what it can of the past. Yeats knew that we all feed our hearts on fantasies. The fall of 1964 was fantasy-rich. And yet, amid all that happened, the creativity of the university was sustained.

As for rhetoric and passion, the classroom showed me a very different kind from that provided by the protests and the Berkeley streets. Two teachers, William Kendrick Pritchard and Ralph Rader, entered my life and helped me understand that if I was not to be politically active, I could put my passions into academic labor. This was a lesson I never forgot. Pritchard was a senior member of the department of Classics and a preeminent expert on epigraphy (the study of inscriptions on vases and other objects). I doubt if he was obliged to teach elementary Greek, but he did, three times a week, 9 a.m., Monday, Wednesday, and Friday. A Southerner (he had been a school classmate of Dean Rusk, President Kennedy's secretary of state, in Atlanta), he brought to the classroom mildness, charm, and quiet decency. He introduced his small class to the precision and intricate delicacies of the ancient language as well as its stunning power. He told us that he would help us do what British schoolboys in the nineteenth century had been taught to do: read Xenophon's *Anabasis* and then excerpts from several Platonic dialogues. He said we would thus be continuing a long tradition by making a connection with the ancient world, a connection many thousands before us had made. He turned our attention to passages in the *Iliad*, showing us how the stern and imperious power of Homer's poetry works. I loved every Greek word and phrase and every rule of grammar I learned. Taking that class reinforced my awareness that a university lives amid the precious things of a culture, that its teachers preserve them, and that its students are witnesses to the moments when that protection takes place.

Ralph Rader, whose course on James Boswell's *Life of Johnson* I took that fall, was the finest teacher I have ever known. A farm boy from Indiana, short, paunchy, energetic and enthusiastic, he arranged for his seminar of twelve students to meet twice a week around a long table in his office. We had only the one book to read, and read it we did—closely, as deeply as we could, admiringly. Our task was to discover how it worked, how readers could derive so much pleasure and instruction from it, and not only how Boswell was able to make Johnson "come alive" but how our understanding of him was created by the language—the rhetoric—he used. The mysterious transformation of words into the plausible semblance of a human being was what Rader wanted us to probe. How was it that we could feel that we "knew" Dr. Johnson better than we knew most living human beings? How could the otherwise reckless and self-indulgent Boswell—chasing after London whores, drinking himself insensible, seeking after the great men of his time with embarrassing boyishness—assemble language to create a presence as imposing and credible as the one in the pages of that book on the table?

But Rader, I began to see, cared not just for the book. He cared for the thoughts, some right and some wrong, we would bring into the discussion. His attention was bifocal. He looked at the book and he looked at us. At the heart of his teaching was an extraordinary triangulation: the book, the students, and his active and steadily responsive mind. Out of that engagement he made the seminar work, but he was always ready to say that *we* made it work, so generous was he about the investments the dozen of us had made in the challenges he placed before us.

In that seminar, the world beyond seemed for a while not to exist. I don't know what Rader thought of political events on the campus, for we never talked about them. I suspect that he, along with many of his colleagues, had little admiration for the administration. Kerr and Strong had behaved in a clumsy way, greatly misjudging the motives and will of the students. About such matters, however, he could do little. What he could do was teach, and he did that with a singular power and sensitivity. I told myself that if I ever were to teach at a university, I would try to teach my students as he had taught us.

I now reflect that it was not only the insulation of these extraordinary courses and my ambition to get to the end of the Ph.D. process that kept me from engaging with the political struggles of the campus. Indeed, I looked down at those who had become politically impassioned as "the students" and I gave myself a standing in some other category. It was "they" who were protesting, and despite the fact that I agreed with them in every respect about the freedoms they should have, I could not link my aspirations with theirs. As a result, I had an odd sensation, one I think many graduate students at Berkeley then shared, of finding myself within a powerful vortex of political passion yet proceeding as if obeying other signals. The "private" world of my mind was separate from the "public" world of social change. Yet I wanted to connect them. How to bring political passion into academic labor? How to unite an interest in political conviction and moral fervor with an academic career? Some answers to that question did, many years later, come to me. But, for now, the immediate tasks at hand filled my days.

Many of my friends in graduate school found it no easier than I to bring together these "private" and "public" worlds, intellectual existence and political passion. Our studies themselves seemed somehow "counterrevolutionary." We knew that our daily routines of reading and research could be held up to ridicule at any moment. How could we occupy ourselves with bygone literary moments when the *real* moment in world history was here, now, all around us?

One friend, Peter Collier, also a member of the class in which the twelve of us learned to read Boswell's *Life of Johnson*, felt this pressure as strongly as anyone I knew. Peter's career from the time of that seminar onward has been fixed in my mind as a parable of the '60s and its power to transform and define the young people who lived through the decade. Impulsive, ambitious, and blessed with a lively mind given to dramatic responses to every moment in our class, Peter's power of emotion first became known to me as I got to understand what he saw as his role in the seminar. He was quick to challenge any other student's disagreement, no matter how slight, with Rader's direction of the discussion. They had known each other since Peter's undergraduate days at Berkeley and this had made the student a passionately loyal devotee of the teacher. Peter was quick to point out to the rest of us that Rader could do no wrong. For him, friendship—or at least the emotional ingredient of friendship—came before everything else. His passions were not, however, found only in the classroom. He had also taught in a black college in Alabama: Miles College in Birmingham. And he had returned from that experience deeply committed, as I was, to the cause of civil rights. We struck up a friendship and I grew to admire the focused energy and power of attention he gave to everything he did. I liked him immensely, and we spent hours together talking about the seminar and the war and the changes in life occurring everywhere around us. On one occasion, aware of the responsibility we would have were we to become fathers, we pledged that if anything happened to any one of our children, our wives, or ourselves, the one of us capable of providing the most help would come to the rescue of the other.

But a fundamental difference between us in time emerged, one that only deepened my awareness of how difficult it was to reconcile what I knew of the classroom and what I knew of campus events beyond the classroom. Peter faced the same tensions that most of us did. He could imagine, as I could, the kind of life graduate school was preparing us for. And he could see what the world of political engagement might, for good and for ill, hold in store for him. We saw the same things, felt the same things, and both of us wanted a way to work out the conflicts we faced. But then he went one way and I another. Long before he was able to finish his work as a graduate student and emerge with his doctorate, he quit graduate school to become a member of the editorial staff of *Ramparts*, a radical leftist magazine in San Francisco. The days of seeking the Ph.D. were, for him, over. And he, with Collier-like dramatic instincts, made his valedictory attitude toward the graduate study of English explicit by one day pacing barefoot through the halls of the department.

With *Ramparts*, Peter found his voice, and his energy found an instrument. He wrote and edited with verve and a sense of radical exhilaration. Along with a colleague, David Horowitz, who had written *Student: The Political Activities of the Berkeley Students* (1962), one of the first defenses of campus radicalism, he helped make *Ramparts* the most vivid and engaged journal of the time.

Encouraged by its volatile editor, Warren Hinckle, he gave to it an apocalyptic tone, for he believed that violent revolution was the only answer to America's problems: "The system cannot be revitalized. It must be overthrown. As humanely as possible, but by any means necessary."[2] He and Horowitz put Eldridge Cleaver on a national platform, and they saw to the composition and publication of his best-selling *Soul on Ice*.

Together Peter and I later were to edit *Justice Denied: The Black Man in White America*, one of the first of many anthologies of writings about the experiences faced by blacks in this country. The work was to teach me much both about Peter's commitment, always absolute, to the cause, whatever the cause might be, and about his editorial skills, always tough-minded and fair. We were much later to produce a classroom text, *An Introduction to Literature*, a book meant to teach students across the nation about fiction, poetry, and drama, and to make us money. I again admired his energy and tenacity in getting the book into publication (despite our best efforts, it failed miserably on both counts). But ultimately his thoroughgoing desire to *believe* met with my disinclination to do so.

And then the '60s ended and Peter underwent a profound rethinking of everything he had believed and said. He had witnessed things in the world of revolutionary action that I had not seen: betrayal, venality, and sordid violence. He came to believe that the Black Panthers, to whom he had given both support and praise, were in fact a criminal organization whose leaders were murderers. Embittered and remorseful about his connections with the left, he moved to the right. He still wanted to fasten upon conviction; I still wanted to take account of ambivalence and irony. For this he held me morally irresponsible; I thought him a zealot. As a result, our friendship inevitably came to a painful end one night at dinner with our teacher Rader. Both of us, I think, deeply regretted the parting. I saw it as a separation on grounds that were not only political and psychological, but of the 1960s, and the way in which that decade drove all belief, all reading of reality, all understanding, to extremes.

Ultimately I found a way, one given to me by the nuances and con-
volutions of literature, to stand at some distance—rightly or
wrongly—from political passion. Peter hungrily seized upon such
passion and made it his identity. In the end, I became what I remain
today in politics: a liberal, that old-fashioned and now much
battered term. Peter became, and now is, a radical, but a radical
of the right. He has over the years moved across the spectrum—
from *Ramparts* to writing speeches for Robert Dole and other
Republicans—and has become an uncompromising conservative,
a publisher of right-wing books, and a devout Roman Catholic. To
me, these apparently startling changes have revealed only how little
he has changed. He remains Peter Collier: passionate and convinced.
And I, for good or for ill, continue to reserve my options and find
wholehearted belief difficult if not impossible. In very different ways,
the 1960s marked us both. Its challenges were so great that its
products in later years are spread out over a wide arc of belief and
nonbelief, passion and passivity, conviction and doubt. It is a decade
that continues to make powerful claims on the present, claims that
are now being answered in a thousand different ways. Peter and I
represent two of those ways.

ENDNOTES

1. Free Speech Movement Archives http://www.fsm-a.org/stacks/
covers/savio_cvr.html.
2. As quoted in "Goodbye to All That," in Peter Collier and David
Horowitz, *Deconstructing the Left: From Vietnam to the Persian Gulf*
(Lanham, MD: Second Thoughts Books and Center for the Study of
Popular Culture, c1991), p. 27.

11

The Storehouse of Knowledge

Upon entering Berkeley in the fall of 1961, we, the newest class of graduate students, were told that the normal time to complete the Ph.D. degree was five years. During that period, we should be able to take a number of courses, make only a minimal number of errors on our three language exams, pass an oral examination on our knowledge of English and American literature, and write a research dissertation that would add to the "storehouse of knowledge."

No one we knew finished in five years. Legends were handed down about various people who had done so, but their identities were shrouded in mystery. We never encountered these champions of progress, and we could only imagine their excellence. On the other hand, students we actually knew had been graduate students in the department for eight, nine, or ten years. And a few students, having assumed another kind of mythic identity, had been on the roster for a dozen or more years. Somehow they soldiered on, finding employment and sustenance here and there in odd corners at Berkeley—as night librarians, research helpers in projects that would last decades, or teaching assistants in Icelandic. They seemed as permanent in their way as the tenured professors. Now and again an administrator in the graduate division would dramatically launch a purge of these veterans, complete with provocative remarks about "malingering," but the old and savvy veterans kept their heads down and survived. They had accumulated more staying power than any vainglorious administrator.

Month by month, and year by year, those originally admitted to study English at the graduate level in 1961 dwindled in number. The language exams proved the barrier for some; for others, the long-term tedium of the progress toward the doctorate made them give up their library card, think about secondary-school teaching, or imagine themselves carpenters. The difference in native ability and intelligence between those who survived and those who dropped by the wayside was irrelevant. Classmates who were clever and learned left Berkeley; others, whose chief virtue was ox-like tenacity, stayed on. "Meritocracy" was the system, and "meritocracy" it pretended to be, but it winnowed wheat and chaff together.

We learned to conquer, or at least to subdue, the cynicism that leaked into all we did. But it wasn't easy to be light of foot as one took the ritualistic steps of learning that dictated our lives. Impersonality, competitiveness, and drudgery were the order of the day, every day. We cheered ourselves up with mordant humor: "What are the five food groups of a graduate student? Caffeine, tobacco, sugar, alcohol, and pizza." As our numbers narrowed, the specific bottlenecks were two: the Ph.D. oral exam and the dissertation. The first was the perfect recipe for existential dread: six professors in the department, joined by a colleague from another department (whose presence was to guarantee an unrigged outcome), would put a set of questions to the candidate for thirty minutes apiece in specific historical areas of English and American literature—*all* of English and American literature from 1350 to the present. The questions could be specifically factual (dates and names), historical (the definition of the Renaissance, the meaning of "Augustan"), causal (influences, trends, and periods), or even speculative (comparative merits of this or that author). No question was off limits; only the peer pressure of faculty colleagues was a curb to outlandish or unfair questions. The procedure was given both safeguards and praise. A distinguished senior member of the department nobly defended it as "the chance for a man [*sic*] to face infinity." Most of us didn't think we would encounter infinity, but we did anticipate impossible questions: "Well, Mr. Smith, I imagine that, as a young scholar, you must have been spending a great deal of time in the library. So I will give you the names of some authors; you will give me their call numbers."

We prepared as if responsible for everything that occurred, in books and out, during that long stretch of time since 1350. We huddled together in study groups, grilled each other in mock exams, and posed intricately complicated questions growing out of the sadism we could imagine dwelling in the hearts of our inter-rogators. And we lived on the stories, passed down over the years, of those who failed and how they failed. One vomited the moment she walked into the room. Another failed because he couldn't resist pointing out, with nervous chuckles, that one of his ques-tioners had nodded off during the proceedings. Another repeat-edly referred to John Milton's *Lost Paradise*.

My own exam was held one spring morning, and things instantly got off to a bad start. One member of the committee overslept and, after several frantic phone calls, had to be fetched from his home in the Berkeley hills. As the minutes passed, quiet embarrassment built up among the other questioners. Waiting, I silently calculated that this mishap could only be to my advantage. I had been on time; he was delinquent. The officiating chair of the procedure, drafted from the Classics department, thumbed a copy of Thucydides and would have asked me to translate from it at sight had not the missing professor at last appeared in the room, with his sports jacket covering his pajama top.

Once the procedure began, I found myself demonstrating a com-mand of certain forms of knowledge that I did not know I possessed (one of the examiners faulted me for taking "speculative flyers," and I am sure he was correct). Now and again the three hours wandered into a "conversation" about the books ("Mr. Chace, if you were going to teach a course on the poetry of W. B. Yeats, what poems would you absolutely want to include?"), but such bliss was punctuated by a return to the more pointed and exact-ing business of facts, citations, and cross-references ("Please give us a brief history of the way in which the King James version of the Bible was composed." "About whom was Milton's elegy *Lycidas* written?" "What is the name of John Keats's only completed play?" "Is *Gulliver's Travels* a novel?"). After scores of questions—some good and some impossible, some that made me rattle off what I had only days before set to memory and others that made me think—the three hours came to an end. An expe-rience that I hoped would never again occur in my life, it had been an odd third-degree during which everything was, for me, absolutely at stake.

I left the room, waiting outside in a corridor where, astoundingly enough, life itself was proceeding as if nothing momentous at all had happened. Yet I knew differently: I had endured and now all hung in the balance. Inside the room the professors conferred. Yet I *had* to pass. One of the professors came out, shook my hand: I *did* pass. Then I found JoAn, who had passed her own exam earlier. We hugged, knew life would never again be the same, and took the tardy professor to the breakfast he had missed and the lunch we thought we deserved.

Thereafter, as with most such tests, much of the knowledge once held in my memory wafted into the ether, never again to be called upon. One hurdle now behind me, the second was in view: the dissertation, by ancient tradition a document of considerable length including footnotes and an extensive bibliography. This work was at once to illuminate and exhaust a strictly delimited zone of research, serving as proof that the young scholar had mastered the techniques of scholarship. It would demonstrate that he or she knew how to ask a respectable question about literature and had the right tools to go about answering it. Its nature has not changed today. Based on the belief that the field of English and American literature is an area of human achievement whose rich complications will forever present questions worth asking and mysteries worth solving, the dissertation is at once a demonstration (the student has control of the tools) and a datum (now we know something we didn't know before).

In practice, however, while the dissertation serves as a demonstration, it only rarely delivers the datum. In most cases, after dissertations are finished, only those who have written them and the professors required to inspect them have read them. If they are edited, reworked, and reconsidered, some few become scholarly monographs in published form. And these—in printing runs of some 1,500 copies or fewer—enjoy only intensely sequestered circulation. They are published by university presses and bought by university and college libraries and by the author for distribution to friends. Most others disappear into an archive at the university where they were written and where they find oblivion. This, then, is the "storehouse of knowledge." Think of it as a building quite remote from the everyday world. Rarely visited, it is the repository of hard work and faithful diligence.

In just the one academic year 1967–68, my own dissertation was one of 977 English literature dissertations completed at universities in the United States, 717 by men and 260 by women.[1] Perhaps it was all for the best that most of them remain where they now are and did not become 977 unread books. The process continues today, based on the same assumptions: there are things yet to be known about English and American literature. Thus far, they have not come to light. The dissertation in question will provide the illumination for which the scholarly world has been in wait. And behind this assumption lies another: that literary study is a "science" of sorts, one that perpetually must press on to explore frontiers of knowledge by means of a process proceeding inexorably into the future. Untested and indeed mightily resisted—then and now—is the possibility that literary study should not be considered a science at all. Many years later, I came to think that it is rather a way of conserving knowledge—of certain poems, plays, novels, and stories—that are a valuable part of our cultural heritage. These works should be read for what they are because they are aesthetically pleasurable and/or because they tell us something important about human nature. To expect, with each new generation of graduate students, that momentous discoveries about these works will abound, as sometimes discoveries in the sciences abound, is to misread the nature of the humanities. But that misreading shows no sign of being discarded today. The prestigious model of the sciences is simply too strong when it comes to the writing of dissertations.

In fact, there were many reasons my peers abandoned their Ph.D. work. Sometimes a combination of forces obstructed—momentarily or permanently—the writing of the dissertation. The lethargy born of several years of a seedy life darkened by the prospect of poverty was the first impediment. A kind of envy was another: of other people our age who went to school and would become doctors or lawyers, to wind up happily living in the suburbs or in townhouses. We seemed to progress only to the next ordeal. And then there was the sheer size of the writing task: we were used to writing essays of 20 or 30 pages, and few of us had experience in handling anything as substantial as a piece of writing of 200 pages or more. Finally, not every graduate student of my own generation was able to believe that he or she had something worth writing up. Many would fall by the wayside at this juncture.

Those surviving were now a handful—not necessarily the brightest but certainly those who had, over the years, achieved victories over anomie and low-level despair. Those of us who finished dissertations did so by writing them page by page, note by note, reference piled upon reference. We steadfastly attended to all the protocols demanding that our "new" piece of research be deferential to all previous scholarship on the given (small) topic.

My dissertation was prompted by an idea articulated by the literary critic Lionel Trilling, who, in one of his essays, said:

> if we name those writers who, by the general consent of the most serious criticism, by consent too of the very class of educated people of which we speak, are to be thought of as the monumental figures of our time, we see that to these writers the liberal ideology has been at best a matter of indifference. Proust, Joyce, Lawrence, Eliot, Yeats, Mann (in his creative work), Kafka, Rilke, Gide—all have their own love of justice and the good life, but in not one of them does it take the form of a love of the ideas and emotions which liberal democracy, as known by our educated class, has declared respectable.[2]

I turned this statement, delivered in Trilling's customary "findings from on high" tone, into the question I intended to answer. Why had so many literary artists of the twentieth century found their political allegiances not with liberal attitudes but with the conservative right? What drew the writers I admired to ideologies so repugnant? That I was thinking politically was caused in part by what was happening on the Berkeley campus and in the surrounding streets. The study of Greek and Boswell's *Life of Johnson* had not insulated me entirely from the furor outside. The complexities of political engagement were inescapable. And so, in the removed and mandarin way of a graduate student, I tried to unite literary concerns with political ones. I again sought a way to join the world of learning to the world of power.

I now see that Trilling's statement, as well as my adoption of it, arose from the periods of political history through which he, and then I, had lived. An unspoken assumption guided us both—he in New York in the '50s, and I at Berkeley in the '60s. That assumption said that liberal, or progressive, or left-leaning political sympathies were the only appropriate ones for intelligent people to have. Hence there was a great deal to explain about the apparent obtuseness of the Eliots, the Manns, the Rilkes, and all the others.

I chose to analyze two such "monumental figures"—T. S. Eliot and Ezra Pound. Both were immensely important to the history of poetry in the century; they were American-born; they were closely associated with each other. Eliot was High-Church Anglican, reactionary, deviously anti-Semitic. Pound, a virulent anti-Semite, broadcast his support of Italian Fascism and Benito Mussolini over Rome radio during the Second World War. And, as poets, they were intentionally difficult, famously so. That difficulty and the intellectual mystique surrounding it drew me to them. I could tell myself (and others) that I wasn't spending my time on the second-rate, the easy, and the conventional. I now look back and recognize that this kind of snob value somehow made my writing a bit easier.

I first read everything I could find on Pound and Eliot—their own writing and everything written about them. I worked in the Berkeley library and in the Library of Congress in Washington. I read about fascism, anti-Semitism, and conservatism. I read Marx to see what the two poets opposed and studied Dante and French poetry of the late nineteenth century to see what they championed. Occasionally I would talk about what I was doing with my three dissertation advisors, but while they proved encouraging, they were not particularly informed about the issues at hand. This did not surprise me; they had their work to do and I had mine. I kept hundreds of 3-by-5 cards on my desk. I wrote as a mason lays bricks. The unit was the paragraph. I assembled paragraphs, each rooted in a piece of evidence, each as solid and sound as I could make it. Those paragraphs soon made pages. As they were placed face down, one atop the other, they began to form a pile. At regular intervals, I would then take this accumulation to a typist (word-processing lay fifteen to twenty years ahead). When it was returned to me, I would rework the typescript and rethink the ideas. Typed up again, my arguments took on firmer shape and I began to imagine that an end was in sight. I came to feel that, increment by increment, I could get to the last page.

But before I did, I knew that I had to find a job teaching English at a college or university. In those halcyon days, a few years before the iron gates clanged shut and the job market for the humanities became the hugely depressing spectacle it is today, many departments were looking to enlarge their rosters of assistant professors. Colleges and universities had money, and the arts and humanities still enjoyed the considerable prestige that today they have seen ebb away. The reasons for this good news had to do with large national patterns. In the 1960s alone college and university enrollments more than doubled, from more than three million to eight million. Those getting Ph.D.s each year tripled; and more faculty were appointed than had been appointed in the earlier three centuries of American higher education. Places like the State University of New York at Buffalo, Indiana University, and even exclusive and insular Yale, were hiring. I wrote to them all and was happy to receive the warm encouragement of the professors— Tom Flanagan, Ralph Rader, Alex Zwerdling, and John Traugott—who had taught me. They wrote recommendations for me and thought my prospects good.

Owing to such support and to the fact that many jobs seemed available in those days, my return mail brought happy tidings. One institution—the University of Virginia—used a string of Edgar Allan Poe stamps on the envelope mailed to me, hoping that I would make the connection between his one-time presence there and the university's devotion to poetry. Yale, in the person of the illustrious scholar and Sterling Professor Maynard Mack, called me on the phone. Few people at the time had a greater reputation in English literary scholarship than Mack. He was an expert on

Shakespeare, and had overseen the Twickenham edition of the poems of Alexander Pope. From New Haven, he announced that a job awaited me at Yale. This appeared to be great news indeed, but I was bold enough to ask, given what I already knew of Yale's pattern of only rarely giving tenure to assistant professors, what my chances of a permanent position there would be. With practiced disingenuousness, he quickly replied: "Oh, Bill, we will always have a place for you." I thanked him but knew better than to believe him. Many years later, Yale would approach me with another kind of job in mind.

Two institutions with offers for me—MIT and Stanford— seemed more attractive than the others. The first had the advantage of being in Cambridge, Massachusetts, had established a wide-ranging department of the "Humanities" rather than just an English department, and had powerful intellectuals like Noam Chomsky on the faculty. The second had a singularly attractive attribute in its favor: it was in the Bay Area, where JoAn and I wanted to remain. But I knew little about the place and, almost to a person, my Berkeley teachers spoke of it with enormous condescension. It was, they said, "the Farm," a school for rich and lazy Californians, a place where nothing political ever happened, an "unreal" university.

But I turned aside all this advice and chose Stanford. The person who interviewed me there, Ian Watt, the distinguished scholar of the novel, the eighteenth century, and Joseph Conrad, had earlier taught at Berkeley. JoAn had been one of his students, and he thought highly of her. He told us that we would be happy at Stanford. He was right. Stanford turned out, over the years, to be good to me and to JoAn. It had no nepotism rule, and she also was given a position as a lecturer in the English department.

In that summer of 1968, I finished my dissertation, stored it away, and we drove down the Peninsula to Stanford with our young son Billy, born that June. We found a rented house nestled in the woods above the university. JoAn took me out to buy my first suit. I would need this, she said, for I had become a "professor." In the formal sense, my education was over. I was thirty years old, married to a wonderful person, had a son, and now had a job, a good job. And while I had much to look forward to, I would be saying goodbye to a way of living, of learning, and of enduring. I was leaving an extraordinary institution of public education, without equal among the assets of the State of California, the most prestigious public university in American history. Tough, demanding, and thoroughly professional, Berkeley set its standards at the graduate level and then stood back to watch how a surviving minority of students would meet them. It had given me a first-rate professional education. It did so without sentimentality of any kind. And so while I left it with regret and with admiration, I left without affection for the place. It did not ask for love of alma mater; and I never thought of extending love to it.

One year before we left for Stanford, the Regents, led by incoming governor Ronald Reagan, had fired the person who had presided over its growing distinction—Clark Kerr. Reagan had targeted Kerr as just the kind of liberal he wanted to dump, thus to affirm his position with his right-wing supporters across the state, the people who resented Berkeley and who had no interest in its intellectual achievements but only its political reputation. Kerr's colleague and friend, Charles Young, the long-term chancellor of the University of California at Los Angeles, summed up how Kerr was dispatched:

> What happened that October 1 [1964], involving the arrest of a former student named Jack Weinberg, a civil-rights activist, his placement in a police car at Sproul Plaza on the Berkeley campus, the surrounding and capture of the police car, and the fiery oratory from atop the car by a young student named Mario Savio, has been told many times. I think of it as the opening scene of a Greek tragedy that would lead to the action taken by the regents 27 months and 20 days later. Clark disagreed with the conduct of the protesters, but resisted the regents' demand that he punish them. Ultimately, after Ronald Reagan became governor, he was forced out.

Such are the ironies of political activism. The '60s changed many things about Berkeley, about higher education, and about young people and their aspirations and hopes. But embedded in those changes was the growth of right-wing hostility against what higher education, at its best, stood for and has always stood for. In time, that hostility emerged in full force. After his triumphs in California, including his sacking of Kerr, Reagan ascended to the American presidency, Mario Savio saw his brief moment of greatness come and go, the war in Vietnam became only more miserable, the dream of a civil rights revolution in which blacks and whites would together find harmony and justice was eclipsed by the rise of Black Power, and in the late 1960s Berkeley descended into aimless protest and prolonged street violence. For me and for others, the era was over. The Chaces were now down at Stanford, "the Farm," peaceful and untroubled, or so we thought. The years ahead would again show me how faulty my expectations could be.

ENDNOTES

1. National Center for Education Statistics' Digest of Education Statistics, http://nces.ed.gov/programs/digest/d98/d98t286.asp, "Earned Degrees in English Language and Literature/Letters Conferred by Degree-Granting Institutions, by Level of Degree and Sex of Student: 1949–50 to 1995–96."
2. Lionel Trilling, "The Function of the Little Magazine," in *The Liberal Imagination: Essays on Literature and Society* (Oxford and Melbourne: Oxford University Press, 1981), p. 94.

12

Unfolding the Origami of Teaching

As we drove to Stanford, our two dissertations went with us, along with a collection of questions and anxieties. What would it be like to teach as a "real" professor? What would the students be like? What would the colleagues be like? And what would Stanford, with its campus between the Bay and the Pacific Ocean, be like? I took with me the memories of what my Berkeley teachers had said about Stanford's placidity. Would the place be as dull and rich as they had said?

A hint of what was to occur that academic year 1968–69 came in the previous April immediately after the assassination of Martin Luther King, Jr. Ian Watt, having become chairman of the Stanford English department, called me at home: "Yes, Bill, Ian here. Yesterday a large group of Negro students marched on the President's office here. They have made demands. One of them is that we teach Black literature. You taught at a black school in the South some years ago. You will be taking this course on." "Well, yes, Ian. Thank you. But, you know, I really don't know anything at all about the topic. I simply don't." And he, having served in the British army and having been a prisoner-of-war of the Japanese near the bridge on the river Kwai, responded with military crispness, "Read up. That will be it." I pleaded, "But we have just had our first child, and I'm preparing my other courses." And he said, "Just attend to the task at hand. You are the person we need. One deals with necessities. Cheers."

And that was that. I was to teach "Black Literature" in the spring of 1969, the first time Stanford offered such a course. The university had begun to experience the intensities of the civil rights movement. I also was to teach an introduction to poetry and a couple of courses in freshman English. I was to find out, in time, a great deal about what was not placid at all about Stanford in 1968. And I thus began to sort out, in a preliminary way, a sense of the place to which I had come to work. When I had first seen it in 1961 on a visit to a Haverford classmate studying medicine there, it was what my Berkeley professors said it was: something of an undergraduate country club, populated largely by California students from wealthy families, and blessed by a sprawling campus of 8,800 acres and Romanesque sandstone buildings. Football, fraternities, sweaters and penny-loafers for the boys; skirts, blouses, and flat shoes for the girls; there were many more boys than girls; the sun was everywhere. In that era before backpacks, students carried their books cradled in their arms. No one wore caps backwards or sideways. Few rode bikes. Almost everyone was white. The immense campus had not a touch of urban grit. The city of Palo Alto, itself a well-kept community of good homes and leafy parks, was a long walk away down Palm Drive. One might have thought Stanford a paradise, save for the fact that it radiated a peculiar aura of sculpted unreality, a 1950s Hollywood version of "college."

But by the late 1960s, Stanford began to change. In November 1967, students had protested against the presence of on-campus recruiters for the CIA. King's death in April had brought to prominence the voices of the Black Student Union. That same month, students had taken over the Old Union building in an antiwar protest. Thereafter, the building occupied by the Reserve Officers Training Corps was burned down, and on July 4, arson destroyed the office of J. E. Wallace Sterling, Stanford's president. The English department, my new home, hired two women, the first in years, as assistant professors. This was regarded as a bold, even "revolutionary," step by Thomas Moser, who had preceded Watt in the chairmanship (the appointment of anyone "of color" was a few years away). But certainly more revolutionary than that was the announcement by one of the associate professors, H. Bruce Franklin, that he had discovered supreme wisdom in the thinking of Mao Tse-Tung. It was all to be found, as he gleefully told anyone remotely within earshot, in "the little Red Book." Franklin had begun his scholarly career by writing a learned treatise on the

mythical background of *Moby Dick*, and had become passionately interested in science fiction just before coming upon the
astuteness of Chairman Mao. He was soon to become the most
controversial member of the faculty, a *bête noire* to the administration, a Pied Piper to the students, and a lesson to me.

My other colleagues were wholly pleasant and agreeable. They
welcomed us into the life of the department, and we soon found
ourselves at small dinner parties where conversation was cheerful
and easy but, characteristic of Stanford at the time, not given to
the expression of any serious intellectual differences. Perhaps one
of the reasons behind the dominance of the presiding ethic of gentility and generosity was the recent death of a rather contrary
member of the community. Yvor Winters, gifted and eccentric
poet and critic, had been, in his time, a kind of intimidating presence in the department, spreading a form of terror by his zealous
reliance on "rationality" and "morality" in both life and literature. Tales abounded of his badgering this or that colleague into a
corner by demanding a defense—if one could be established at
short notice—of, say, the poet George Crabbe or the novelist
D. H. Lawrence. One way or another Winters inevitably won the
argument that resulted. Perhaps as a result of his behavior, the
department vigilantly maintained a genteel atmosphere. We had
Tuesday lunches together at the faculty club, a facility much like
the "Nineteenth Hole" restaurants and bars at golf clubs. If one
were a member of the club, one could store bottles of liquor and
wine in little wooden cupboards with shiny locks. I began to feel
that Berkeley, only an hour away, existed in another country. The
scholarship my new colleagues had generated over the years was
largely historical and philological; each of them occupied one of
the customary niches provided by chronology or genre. I was slotted as the new "Americanist." Not a hint of "theory" in either
teaching or research was to be found anywhere.

But life in the department was, for me, only peripheral to the
task at hand. I had to learn how to teach freshman English and
how to give lectures to Stanford students. For those beginning
years, those two challenges took up all my attention. As for the
first, I saw that the issue facing first-year students is not "what you

know and what they don't." Freshman English is not about knowledge. It is not about literary matters. Whether at Haverford or at Stanford, it is not about anything but thinking and writing. So I embraced the common notion that no one is born a good writer and that all good writing is the result of practice and hard work. My strategy was to try to have lively class discussions followed by lots of writing. I quickly found out that the more writing assignments I gave out, the better (slightly) my students wrote, but the more I had to read. After some months of this, I concluded that I should reach a compromise point between my eagerness to improve their skills and my willingness to correct what they had written. Another compromise was reached when, acknowledging that the students were not at all interested in what I knew or had written for my dissertation or my scholarly ambitions, I tried to imagine what they *were* interested in. First of all, I came to understand that they, like all able students, had a basic question, never directly put: what is this course and how do I succeed in it? They were beginners like me, and each of us wanted to understand the code of the new place to which we had come. Stanford was just as new to them as it was to me; the only advantage I had over them was twelve years of age and the grade book.

My Haverford days came back to me and I began to imagine that, just as I had started out there—full of hope, anxiety, and awkwardness—they were starting out at Stanford. At Haverford, I wanted to think wonderfully, write wonderfully, and make clear in my essays that I could see with great clarity just how the world worked. These students must, I thought, have the same impulses racing through their minds. And so what first I thought were my twelve years of advantage I should have seen as only twelve years separating one moment of youthfulness from another.

I also knew it would be good to be liked by them. Not only was the opposite unpalatable, but of course my teaching would be better, I told myself, if I were liked. I thus tasted of the illicit wisdom on which much teaching is always based—illicit because it accepts the vices of egotism and self-regard. It encourages one person, the teacher, to make the most of himself in full view of others who remain silent, take notes, or occasionally ask questions. It knows the truth: teaching is an intimate human activity. But while it is intimate, it is not egalitarian. It assumes a hierarchy among the minds that walk into the classroom. One of those minds, just one, is presumed to be superior. With this presumption firmly in place, ideas are introduced and sometimes learning is advanced. But what my Stanford colleague, the poet Donald Davie, once called "the reek of the human" is ever-present within that environment—the teacher's ego must have its way. And so I found myself, with teaching forever in my mind, wanting to become liked and, in due course, being liked by those first Stanford students of mine. I knew I had won at least some affection when two of the more imaginative students tested my patience and dexterity by handing in essays folded and refolded in complex origami patterns; I had to spend some twenty minutes carefully opening what I would then, by way of retaliation, cover with intense red-penciling. I smiled when I returned those essays; those two students smiled back. By such steps, I crossed the first small stream in my teaching career.

Not every relationship with my students was curricular. One of the more ambitious of those students in that first year came to me after class and, with a combination of pride and *savoir-faire*, put six small purple pills in my hand. "For your next trip," he said. I guessed immediately that I was now holding, for the first time, LSD. Recognizing that this was a solemn occasion for the student, one freighted with trust, I thanked him and took the pills home. JoAn and I found a bottle for them and put our illegal stash in the freezer. There the bottle sat, untouched, for six months. We had heard many stories about bad acid trips. But for days thereafter, whenever the student had a chance, he would favor me with a conspiratorial smile. One night we dropped the pills into the garbage.

Yet another student, this one committed to the revolutionary struggle against the war in Vietnam, asked me if I would like to join him and friends around midnight some evening. They had rigged up a powerful catapult made of surgical rubber and had positioned it behind Memorial Auditorium. From that location, they could propel rocks high over the auditorium and down into the windows of the Hoover Institution, a center of conservative, if not downright reactionary, thought. This way, he explained, the war "could be fought at home." Marveling at both their engineering skills and their candor with me, as well as their understanding of military strategy, I thanked my student for the invitation but declined.

If freshman English was one way to learn how to teach, lecturing was another. As I prepared for the spring semester course on black literature, I knew that lecturing was all about expertise, control of information, lucidity, a good and practiced voice, and a commanding presence. Yet I had never spoken in an uninterrupted way for fifty minutes. In fact, fifty minutes seemed to me a very long length of time to talk about anything. Moreover, I would have to repeat such an extraordinary performance dozens of times in the course, always appearing wholly knowledgeable about books that, in fact, I had only recently read. Though dread and fear were, of course, my first reactions in such a situation, my second was to assimilate everything I could on black literature. At the end, I thought, even though I would tremble, I would command the knowledge.

In addition to this private world of anxiety was a lurking suspicion in my mind that the very idea of lecturing was absurd. How had it come to pass that any one person was licensed to loom up above all others and, compelling them into silence, presume that what he had to say was worth their attention? What permitted such arrogance? In fact, how could a self-respecting university permit it? Later I was to read Aldous Huxley on lecturing:

> Lecturing as a method of instruction dates from classical and mediaeval times, before the invention of printing. When books were worth their weight in gold, professors had to lecture. Cheap printing has radically changed the situation which produced the lecturer of antiquity. And yet—preposterous anomaly!—the lecturer survives and even flourishes. In all the universities of Europe his voice still drones and brays just as it droned and brayed in the days of Duns Scotus and Thomas Aquinas. Lecturers are as much an anachronism as bad drains or tallow candles; it is high time they were got rid of.[1]

But when the spring came, I gave those lectures. I had been told that I might expect some 90 students in the course. That seemed a number large enough to be terrifying. But when I entered the hall, 260 people were in their seats. I do not know what kind of apprehension I betrayed that day, but I remember that my immediate tactic was to see if I could enunciate the first sentence of the lecture I had written out. If that succeeded, I could then read the second. I had some twenty-five pages of lecture in my hand and, lo and behold, I was able to move from sentence to sentence, page to page. About halfway through this drama of fear mixed with surprise and attention paid to the clock at the rear of the room, I noted that the entire first row of seats was occupied by members of the Black Student Union at Stanford. They had come to watch. Their leader, Leo Bazile, later to become a member of the Oakland City Council, seemed to be gazing at me as one on shore might look at a surfer about to enter the curl of a gigantic wave. I continued nonetheless to attend to my sentences. And, at the end of the longest fifty minutes I was ever to experience, the time was up. I left the room. So did the leadership of the Black Student Union. They never returned, for they had not registered for the course. Somehow I had passed their test, whatever it was.

I now see, *pace* Huxley, that the lectures served a purpose—a symbolic one—that is always being served in higher education. It was not so important that, by way of my lecturing, the actual poems and novels of writers like Countee Cullen, Claude McKay, Langston Hughes, and Richard Wright, with all of their interior workings and finer delicacies, were brought to the attention of Stanford undergraduates. The crucial fact was that the course itself was taught, and taught for the first time. Those lectures showed that Stanford was marking an historical change.

Another interpretation of the lectures might be that the curriculum of the university was being altered largely in deference to both the presence and the wishes of students. Black students were new at Stanford, and so were their wishes. Clark Kerr was perceptive in saying that "the faculty may, in fact, appoint the faculty, but within this faculty group the students choose the real teachers."[2] He could have added that the students can sometimes

drive the curriculum. This is an essential truth about higher education. Universities themselves rarely revise their curricula.
External realities, when they enter those universities, dictate such
changes. GIs returning from the Second World War made colleges
and universities more serious and less childish places; and no one
now questions the positive intellectual impact made by the presence of Jewish students on higher education once admission quo-
tas against them were lifted. The greater presence of women in the
1960s and after had the same effect—to redefine education itself
and the curriculum.

As that year ended, I understood that it was no easier at
Stanford than at Stillman or Berkeley to make teaching and politics come together in a coherent way. The one constantly
intruded upon, and then began to define, the other. If we read
King Lear in the freshman English course, we soon found ourselves talking not just about Lear's power but about the power
of all kings and leaders, and then, at last, of all presidents,
including Lyndon Johnson. If we read Sophocles' *Antigone*, we
soon were discussing the comparative loyalties one had to "the
state" and to "the self." All around us the war in Vietnam was
in the news. Hundreds of Americans and thousands of
Vietnamese were dying, photographs of napalm doing its hor-
rific work were in the newspapers and on TV, and the nationwide protests were rising in intensity. Those realities entered the
classroom along with the assigned readings.

I sought to teach as well as I could, but I could see all around
me at once: bucolic Stanford, a rise of political insurgency, a defi-
ance of the calm and orderly, and a resentment of authority. Once
again I faced the problem of uniting, if I could, the duty I had to
the classroom and the books I was to teach with the imperatives
of political action. No longer at Berkeley, memories of Berkeley
nonetheless filled my mind. Would I be any more successful on this
campus than I had been there in making sense of situations where
the private and the public met, where intellectual existence and
political passion collided? I did not want, as Yeats would say, to
feed "my heart on fantasies," but I could not ignore the war, the
protests about it, and the ways my students and many of my

colleagues were changing before my eyes as they adjusted to realities for which they were entirely unprepared.

Just as I learned from my students about Stanford's present, I learned from some of my colleagues about Stanford's own recent history as an institution. My curiosity was all a part of being an assistant professor new to the place (but it was also a part of something I only dimly understood at the time: an interest on my part in the academic institution itself, how it worked, how it had succeeded and how it might fail). President Sterling and the provost of the time before my arrival, Frederick Terman, had envisioned a new way for a university to achieve greatness. Sterling was large, affable, charming, and ambitious. He could drink with business leaders, play the piano and sing, and speak enticingly of glorious worlds yet to come for Stanford. Terman was shrewd, sharply focused, and introspective. Wholly immersed in the details of his work, he was reputed to prepare the university's annual budget on Christmas Eve. Together these two men, entirely unlike but working compatibly with each other, explored something that all university leaders were reckoning with at the time: federal and private investment in science, medicine, and engineering. They sensed, rightly, that such new money could transform higher education.

One way to date Stanford's connection with federal funding and national recognition is with the founding of Hewlett-Packard in 1938. Terman persuaded two young engineer/entrepreneurs, William Hewlett and David Packard, both Stanford graduates, to locate their young company in the city of Palo Alto. In the decades that followed their success, Stanford turned out hundreds of other graduates with the knowledge required by the new electronics and aerospace industries. Companies such as General Electric, Lockheed, and Varian established research facilities in what later became known as Silicon Valley (decades later, Google, Yahoo!, Cisco, and Sun Microsystems, all founded at or near Stanford, sustained the entrepreneurial momentum). Government research funds flowed into Stanford and also into other academic and corporate research facilities in the region, especially Berkeley, with its many labs and Nobel Prize winners. Powerful synergies developed between academia, the defense industry, and capital investment. Terman also devoted time and attention to the ways in which medical research could be developed and, with federal help, supported. The thrust of his thinking and imagination attracted more university superstars and financial entrepreneurs to the area. They were happy to find a world of investment funding, experienced managers, and potential customers for what they could do. Stanford had thus become both a creator of, and witness to, an extraordinary display of scientific, technical, and medical productivity. What Stanford did, and did magnificently, was not to look to its past for its importance, but to the future. The Ivy League could root itself in past prestige and the honors of history; Stanford would claim the years to come, and those would be years dominated by science and technology.

Terman also noted, as did others on and off the campus, how sophisticated engineering techniques could be adopted by the defense industry as the nation sought to respond to the perceived threat of the Soviet Union's science in the post-*Sputnik* era. Why not meld the creative energies of the best engineering departments at Stanford with the needs of the nation? Why not ask the federal government to increase dramatically its sponsorship of high-level research on the campus? The defense needs of the United States would be served, as would the aspirations of the university. Stanford did not invent sponsored research or "soft money." During World War Two, President James Bryant Conant of Harvard, and others like Vannevar Bush, who directed wartime scientific research, recognized what it could do: accelerate the powerful connection between government funds and on-campus research. In time, many other universities would follow suit, but Stanford, along with MIT and a few state universities including Berkeley, led the way.

Concurrent with this inspired coupling was Terman's notion of "steeples of excellence," the formula he and Sterling used as a smart and efficient way to build a university: direct money toward a few selected academic departments and charge them to recruit the most eminent professors, urge those new professors to recruit others of their kind in related fields, and then have the invigorated department go after the best graduate students. The expected result would be a sense of intellectual excitement at Stanford. If physics, for example, had become excellent, then biology and chemistry could follow suit. In turn, the recruitment of Arthur Kornberg and Joshua Lederberg would stimulate not only bio-chemistry, but also genetics. If history, with a key appointment such as David Potter, could move toward distinction as a "steeple," then economics and political science could be inspired to do the same. The formula was one of establishing excellence in a few key places and letting the powerful engines of imitation and ambition do their work. Other universities soon followed Stanford's strategy. The idea was simple and brilliant. On the one hand, it is "top-down" management; the president and the provost initiate the idea of the "steeples of excellence." On the other hand, it is a strategy that accepts the most fundamental truth of higher education: it is not the administrators, but the faculty, who dictate the level of intellectual excellence that can be reached. No administration has ever created a great university, but a great faculty, encouraged and supported by an intelligent administration, can.

Sterling's years of leadership sadly came to a close with the burning of his office. The fire, by "persons unknown," destroyed years of his files and memorabilia. A more important loss to Stanford was the sense that the administration could thrive amid genteel tranquility. The arson was followed, in April 1968, by a student sit-in in the Old Student Union protesting the war in Vietnam. That sit-in revealed deep divisions between the administration and the faculty. The administration took a hard line against students, while the faculty, now aroused to action, wanted to be lenient with respect to student activism. I could see the familiar triad of faculty vs. administration vs. students shaping up.

By 1968, when Sterling retired, Stanford had achieved new distinction and new energy. But the connection to federal money also brought with it controversy. If Terman connected academic research with national needs, other people connected Stanford labs with the war in Vietnam. They had a point. In the '60s, some part of the research program at the university not only was sponsored by federal monies but was also "classified" as secret by the government. That meant that it could not be discussed publicly, even on campus. For some people, that kind of secrecy spelled complicity in the war effort. Moreover, the university had spun off a satellite operation, the Stanford Research Institute, in part staffed by Stanford professors, that received federal monies for contract work, much of it also classified. The tension between those involved in classified sponsored research and those opposed to the war partially defined my first years at Stanford.

There was no better sign of that tension than the short and tumultuous presidency of Kenneth S. Pitzer, Sterling's successor. He had been president of Rice University and, before that, a professor of chemistry at Berkeley. At that moment in Stanford's history, the trustees could have picked Richard W. Lyman, the University's vice president and provost since 1967, for the post, but they considered him "too liberal" (this despite the fact that the faculty hardly thought so). They chose badly. Pitzer was white-haired and distinguished in appearance, he was serious, and he spoke in large presidential sonorities. But his tenure in office lasted only 630 days. That brief period was filled with increasing violence and disruption on campus over the prolonged conflict in Vietnam. Students and off-campus youths smashed hundreds of windows all over the campus (my student with the catapult was apparently still busy); protestors held countless demonstrations and marches, many ending at Pitzer's office. The police were called to the campus more than a dozen times. My colleague Bruce Franklin, waving the Little Red Book in his hand, was prominent, enthusiastic, and noisy. In an awful moment characteristic of the times, Pitzer had a bucket of red paint poured over him at a student dinner to which he and his wife had been invited. Everywhere he went, he was perceived as well meaning but confused, sincere but inept. And so, in an understated letter of resignation to the trustees, he wrote, "trends have made it increasingly difficult to obtain the very broad and active support from all those groups who together are responsible for the well-being of the university."

The trustees then wisely, if belatedly, turned to Lyman. Earlier a member of Stanford's History department, he had written a book on Ramsay Macdonald, Great Britain's first Labour prime minister, whom Winston Churchill had once called "the boneless wonder." Lyman proved to be all spine, all bone. His considerable experience with campus activism made him think it irrational and dangerous. He was forceful, articulate, and irritable in opposing it. He spent his presidency, ten years of it, defending the university. Not only did he have to maintain space for civility, but he also had to confront a national financial picture defined by double-digit inflation, a world oil shortage, and a weak stock market. And so with him came the disciplines of cost control and budget cutting. But, as a social liberal, he also brought with him an increase in the numbers and influence of women and members of ethnic minorities as faculty and students. As time went on, I came to consider him a hero of sorts. So did many of his former faculty opponents. He was not always comfortable with others— he did not enjoy idle chat—but he was easy to admire. He was singularly steadfast in keeping the university whole and strong. If he had a "vision," a term later to become popular with university presidents but which he would have thought silly, it was that of "coping." To cope, he would have said, was no easy thing, given campus hostilities, budget woes, and the need to maintain intellectual momentum for the university. In later years, when I became a university president, I looked back on his flinty, no-nonsense, rational, and defensive leadership. It was a model for me. But none of this, war and violence, campus tumult and campus leadership, as important as they all were, trumped then what I had come to do: to be a colleague, a member of the Stanford's department of English, to teach. I was just beginning.

ENDNOTES

1. Aldous Huxley, *Proper Studies* (Garden City, NY: Doubleday, Doran, 1927), pp. 169–70.
2. Kerr, *Uses of the University*, pp. 21–22.

13

Tenure and Its Discontents

Being a member of the English department meant this: as one of two newly hired assistant professors in 1968, I was expected to teach well, contribute to the well-being of my colleagues, and, in time, write something worthy of publication. That trio of expectations— teaching, service, and research—was then, and is today, the established code for progress within the professorial ranks. Its parts, however, were not equally important in the 1960s, nor are they equally important today. When the Day of Judgment comes, when an assistant professor is "up for tenure" and thus for permanent employment at a research university or elite college, research trumps all. Although much rhetorical firepower is employed at every self-respecting university and college to emphasize the crucial significance of teaching, people who devote themselves to teaching and don't publish rarely get tenure. And those who have published something deemed substantial by their peers and by deans and provosts are free to submit a so-so record of teaching and win tenure. As for "service," it runs a distant third. If you have not yet gained tenure, it makes little professional sense to invest time on committees, devote yourself to your students, or work to make the university "a better place." Everyone within the academy knows about this code, and yet the prestige of the academy—any academy—would be embarrassed were it publicly advertised. After all, parents believe their children have gone to college to be taught, and taught well. They have paid for this to happen. Nonetheless, within the academy, research, and nothing else, is gold. Teaching is brass. Service is dross.[1]

Not everyone goes after tenure the same way. Humanists, young "Americanist" professors of English, for example, are expected to write books, as are historians and scholars in foreign languages.

Political scientists and sociologists, on the other hand, are expected to write articles, not books, and the same is true of economists and teachers in business schools. Natural scientists never write books unless or until they have already written many articles and "papers." For a young chemist, spending time on a book is a ticket to failure, but for an older chemist, writing a textbook is acceptable and sometimes can prove lucrative. People in medicine do not write books, but short articles, sometimes a torrent of very short articles (a professional term in medicine is the "SPU," the smallest publishable unit, the instrument by which some medical researchers generate hundreds and hundreds of articles).

Many researchers publish articles arising from their clinical research in labs; that means they have to secure the financial support to maintain those labs. So they seek funding, often year in and year out, from the federal government or other sources such as foundations or private corporations. If they don't find that support, they can't turn to the university for help. Their appointments rest on the understanding that they alone are responsible for their financial survival.

This is hardly the case for humanists—the English professors, the French professors, or the philosophers. They rely entirely on the university for funding. Neither the federal government nor any other sponsoring agency would ever knowingly or willingly pay the salary of a humanist. While lack of such support might seem demoralizing to the humanist, the very same arrangement—with the university providing continuing support—might seem attractive to the natural scientist or the medical researcher. If you must depend on the largesse of external agencies, you will forever worry that your funding could atrophy or even disappear. No support = no lab; no lab = no findings; no findings = no tenure. And thus the peculiar reality of research funding at a university—the humanist forever an institutional dependent, the scientist forever a hunter and gatherer.

Of all these realities I knew only the dimmest outlines in my first Stanford years. In later times, I was to learn much more. But thanks to conversations with my senior colleagues, I became aware in the early '70s that I soon had to publish something—articles first and then at least one book. All I had in hand, however, was what every assistant professor has in hand: a dissertation. For a while I looked at it only occasionally and reluctantly. It seemed a part of a far-away time. But as I watched the time remaining to me as an assistant professor shrink, I began to think of my dissertation as a quarry for articles and the basis of a book. As Samuel Johnson said, "Depend upon it, sir, when a man knows he is to be hanged in a fortnight, it concentrates his mind wonderfully." I concentrated my mind. Slotted into those hours not devoted to learning how to teach or how to be the father of a family (Katie, our daughter, joined us in 1972), I pummeled the dissertation this way and that, adding and subtracting to its pages, eviscerating clotted phrases, and endowing it here and there with signs that it should be taken as written by an "author" and not a student.

Such a book would be my chance to bring together, in one place, two things: the literature that meant most to me and the political sensibility I had come to have. I would make Pound and Eliot come to terms with the political attitudes of someone who had seen the civil rights struggle in the South, student protest at Berkeley, and antiwar demonstrations at Stanford. I saw at the time that I wanted to make a statement about liberalism, about its inability to make sense of the political ideas and affinities of those two writers. If liberals held the two poets in high esteem but couldn't comprehend why they had wound up on the far right of the ideological spectrum, my response would be that liberalism itself was the problem. As a political sensibility, it was inadequate. It couldn't see how certain forms of conservative extremism (devotion to rigid social hierarchies, doctrines of severe orderliness, a belief that democratic priorities should yield to artistic priorities, a conviction that intelligence should come before everything else, and even the snobbish prejudices of anti-Semitism) provided powerful sustenance for these two crucial modern writers. In short, the art of Pound and Eliot sought to bring order out of confusion and bring turmoil to heel; for this reason, they found much to admire in the politics of the boot and the heel. Liberalism had little way to address that disturbing fact. I didn't want to defend Pound and Eliot as extremists or as bigots. But I wanted to point out that the two poets couldn't properly be seen through liberal spectacles.

As I worked, first on the articles and then on the book, I saw that if I couldn't be "political" at Berkeley or on the Stanford campus, I could be political in the pages of what I wrote. At Berkeley, the radical politics of the campus were something I witnessed but did not join. At Stanford, the politics of the day were a frenzy of window breaking, firebombs, and marches against university administrators. I thought the students were wrong to hold those administrators responsible for the war in Vietnam. The students wrongly "brought the war home" by striking out at local targets— any local targets. Berkeley politics had been radical in reputation but only moderate in aims and achievements. Stanford antiwar politics, on the other hand, were radical, misconceived, and dangerous. I had to make my own way. My politics would get mapped out in what I could write, not in what I could do. In civic life, I was a conventional liberal, but I would nonetheless bring liberalism to the bar. Civic life was one thing, intellectual life another. I would shop at the Co-op, drive a sensible car (we had given up the Triumph), worry about civil rights, vote Democratic, and yet all the while have doubts about liberalism. Civic duties are not always intellectual duties.

In time, I submitted a finished book-length manuscript to the Stanford University Press, doing so with some anxiety. On the one hand, the Press was—happy combination—both distinguished and local. Surely, I thought, it would extend some favor to a member of the Stanford faculty. On the other hand, its editor, Jess Bell, had a reputation as a stickler for precision; I heard that he took immense pleasure in rejecting manuscript after manuscript and then letting the authors know exactly—word for word and phrase by phrase—how they failed to measure up.

But with my work resting in his hands, and with a few months' sabbatical leave in our possession, we went to France, there to spend a chilly winter in Provençe. I had never been to Europe, but JoAn had earlier lived in both Lyon and Paris as a Fulbright scholar. After a cheap, bumpy ride aboard Icelandic Air across the Atlantic, the four of us settled into a remote stone farmhouse by the banks of the river Rhône. We huddled before the fireplace, responded to mystified questions from local farmers about why an American family would spend December in a place far from touristic sights, and read. I started a book on James Joyce. The only library I could use was in Avignon, fifteen miles away. I sat day by day in one of its chilly rooms, reading some of my own books shipped across the Atlantic, and filled out request slips for others that would take hours to come to my desk. Stanford was a long way away.

Halfway through our odd sojourn, a telegram arrived from Jess Bell. He accepted the manuscript. I was elated and we all went out for a fancy dinner we could not afford. I told myself that the book, when published, would probably be enough to gain me tenure. I could see Stanford vistas opening up and began contemplating a long career there. But much to my surprise, a few weeks later, while standing in a shed and waiting in a wintry downpour for a bus to take me back home from another day in the Avignon library, an odd thought darkened my mind. I could see a great many years stretching before me at Stanford. As I calculated things, I would have as many as four decades to spend there. I would, in fact, grow old there. Some of my colleagues would for years be my colleagues, would *forever* be my colleagues. Standing in that shed, I found myself arguing against the benefits of tenure. In full perversity, I could not stop thinking that if tenure with all of its security did come to me, it would come too early, with one of the highest hurdles of my professional life surmounted all too soon.

With this thought came another—about professional realities. I had thought, as many young professors in the humanities do, that only the judgment of my departmental colleagues, as they considered the evidence before them, would determine my tenure decision. My future would be the product of their careful consideration, theirs alone. But what about that telegram from Jess Bell? In fact, his judgment would prove the highest card on the table when the decision about me was made. He, not my colleagues, would determine if I had a book to show. His acceptance of that manuscript meant just about everything. External factors turned out, then, to be just as important for me as they were for someone in the sciences seeking funding from the government. As the years passed, I began to understand even more clearly how tenure worked. The emphasis on publication made me appreciate forces—granting agencies, academic presses, popular topics vs. rarefied topics—external to the university. Such realities, I learned, increasingly govern what happens within the academy. Few things are exempt from the marketplace, not even the humanities, not even a study of Pound and Eliot.

This convergence, bringing together the desire of a scholar to have an audience and the desire of a printing press to have more profit than loss, is today an ever-tightening screw. Indeed, as it turns out, few university presses now show any profit at all, and the losses that mount up, book after book, are customarily covered by a subvention from the university. No matter how small the press runs, even in numbers less than 500, the press loses money and then tries to do its part for profits by pricing the books more and more expensively. That in turn diminishes the number of buyers, including university libraries, which are, in fact, the chief purchasers of all such scholarly volumes. But according to Peter Givler, the executive director of the Association of American University Presses, even the libraries each year have less money for book purchases. For decades, the libraries have been spending a greater and greater percentage of their budgets on journals rather than books. In 1986, for example, they spent 44 percent on books and 56 percent on journals; two years later, it was 28 percent to 72 percent. Since then, books have never regained the upper hand. As Givler says, "locked in a vicious spiral, publishers attempt to recover costs from dwindling markets by charging more, as the price of scholarly books balloons past the reach of all but the most determined buyers." But as the years after the '60s were to show, university presses came forward with book titles and book subjects that challenged even the most "determined buyers." The increasing exoticism of scholarly pursuits in those years, particularly in the humanities and some of the social sciences, made it easy to dismiss many scholarly books. As Givler says, they seemed no more than "pompous academic folderol: recondite topics, Orphic titles, pedantic references, obscure footnotes, unspeakable style."[2]

But such wayward thoughts were not on my mind when we returned to California in the early 1970s. Only later in my life, particularly when I had to see things as an administrator, did I understand the incursions of financial reality upon the apparent purity of the humanist's calling. Back at Stanford in the academic year 1974–75, where everything counted for me, the vote on my candidacy for a tenured position in the department was on the calendar. In due course, but only after one senior member of the department said my book was unfair to conservatives and another said it was unfair to liberals, the English department voted tenure for me, the deans approved, the provost approved, the advisory board of the university approved, and, at last, the Stanford trustees approved. I recalled my perverse thoughts on that rainy evening in Provençe, but of course I was happy about the decision. What did tenure mean to me? A great deal. It was a form of permanent employment that I could forfeit only by "substantial and manifest neglect of duty" or "personal conduct substantially impairing" the performance of my "functions within the University community." More than that, Stanford had made an investment in me. Gambling that, over time, I would bring credit to the institution by writing and teaching and, yes, providing "service," it had committed its resources to me as an asset, now and in the future. Tenure was a mutual understanding between Stanford and me. Since we would forever be linked, I had promises to keep.

When the book was published, it received favorable attention, including two long and thoughtful reviews, one in *The New Republic* and another in *The Times Literary Supplement*. I began to feel that I was indeed an "author" and no longer a student. It also seemed that the argument of the book had found traction in the minds of at least those two reviewers, Marjorie Perloff and Bernard Crick. They raised no objections to my argument about the deficiencies of liberalism. They saw, as I had, that neither Pound nor Eliot could simply be written off as extreme conservatives not much worth reading. They were, in fact, among the titans of the literary age. We could not see them solely as aesthetes and ignore their political convictions. We had to see them as what they were: immensely gifted poets some of whose ideas, linked in powerful yet strange ways with the power of their artistic achievement, were repugnant to most of their readers. They made literary modernism puzzling, not least for the reason that they put those appreciative readers in awkward positions. On the one hand, the influence of Pound and Eliot on other writers of their time was unquestionable; on the other, Pound and Eliot had very little sympathy with those times themselves. Readers therefore had to think not only about the poetry Pound and Eliot gave them but also about the cultural ambiance in which to read them.

All this complexity and mystery about literary modernism I tried to teach to my Stanford students—not freshmen, but upper-level English majors—in my first years. Such matters must only have added to the confusion and frenzy they were undergoing. What could the strange ideological fascinations of two poets born in the late nineteenth century mean to them? The war in Southeast Asia was continuing, campus protests were commonplace, and the university must have seemed to those students an odd combination of traditional classroom and huge Hyde Park. For several springs in the '70s, students held "strikes" against the university, the presumed idea behind them being that if students withheld their presence from classes, the White House and the Pentagon would pay attention and peace would come to Vietnam. The absurdity of this logic was not lost on me or on others, but the feeling against the war was strong enough to dislodge logic itself. While I did not honor the strikes and kept on teaching, I allowed my students to stay away. Most of my colleagues behaved the same way; we went on teaching but our classrooms had many empty seats. We all felt awkward and torn: against the war, against the strikes, with and against the students, stirred and depressed by events, simultaneously excited and fatigued. Amid such turmoil, the literary careers of Ezra Pound and T. S. Eliot, as I described them to my dwindling number of students, were doubtless one more fragment of the chaos here, there, and everywhere in their lives. One of them, a girl from Los Angeles, sought respite from the turmoil engulfing her young life and wrote an essay for me with the title: "Moderation Is the Spice of Life." I knew how she felt (but continued to teach Pound and Eliot).

For me, the stay against confusion was to do what Stanford wanted me to do when it granted me tenure: write and teach what

I knew. Protest and anger might surround me, but the university was a safe haven. I began to understand what the traditions of academic insularity, built over the centuries, were all about. They meant that events in the larger world beyond the campus would not, could not, control what went on within the campus. The history of the academy had established a zone that could attenuate, and sometimes even annul, the power of those events. This meant that despite the power of external circumstances, people like me could conduct our research, follow whatever lines of inquiry we had in mind, and advance our professional ambitions irrespective of how the world was behaving.

Students were transient beings and therefore could not take full advantage of that insularity. They might feel themselves drowning in issues too difficult for them to resolve, but within our safe haven we professors did not. In fact, Stanford existed for me and for my colleagues as an engine of enterprise. Other parts of American society might not be working well, but the university seemed to function superbly. Indeed, Stanford had in those years taken off on a trajectory within American academic life that would soon see it rise to preeminence. Working within its protective strength, my colleagues and I could pursue whatever we wanted. Free to do so and encouraged to do so, that is what I did. Thanks to tenure, I had become a part of something giving me both security and incentive. It was now up to me to make the most of it.

ENDNOTES

1. Efforts to promote the importance of teaching in tenure decisions, and thus to mitigate the prestige of research, can have ironic results. A recent study (*Faculty Priorities Reconsidered: Rewarding Multiple Forms of Scholarship*, ed. by KerryAnn O'Meara and R. Eugene Rice, San Francisco: Jossey-Bass, 2005) suggests that calls to give more credit to teaching may simply wind up by becoming demands that faculty members be better in everything, including traditional models of research.
2. Peter Givler, "Scholarly Books, the Coin of the Realm of Knowledge," *Chronicle of Higher Education*, November 12, 1999, p. 46.

14

Tenure Tested

In my first years at Stanford, the value and meaning of tenure were subjected to a profound—indeed, unique—examination. It all had to do, dramatically, with my "revolutionary" colleague Bruce Franklin.[1] As I watched it from the sidelines, the collision in 1971 between the institution and an individual faculty member turned out to be a decisive and historic examination of what security of employment at a university means. The case taught me and many others about the rights a professor has and the rights a university has. It asked me and everyone else watching the affair about how these rights, if in conflict, can be adjudicated. In the end, Franklin lost his job at Stanford, but not before these questions had been thoroughly explored. The conflict was remarkable in part because Franklin himself was extraordinary and in part because Stanford put forward an extraordinary public display of its self-understanding. All of us there at the time—faculty colleagues, students, and the public at large—got to see the expense in time and energy to which an academic community can go, and sometimes must go, to protect the rights of both its teachers and itself.

Although Franklin was a colleague, I never was close to him. But as part of the wooing process that brought us to Stanford in 1968, JoAn and I had dinner with him and his wife before I took up my assistant professorship, and he was eager on that occasion to press into my hands the "other" little red book, "How To Be a Good Communist," by Liu Shao-chi, one of Mao Tse-tung's lieutenants at the time. He readily gave Mao's book to everyone; the Liu Shao-chi book, I gathered, was for special occasions. The book, he said, "will change your life because its author is changing the world."[2] Franklin's wife, even more gleeful than he about the prospects of violent revolution, took us around their house and cheerfully pointed to their various firearms. They bragged about the time "just last week" that they stood in the doorway of the house, rifles in hand, and "faced down" the local Menlo Park police. By the time we started up at Stanford in the fall, I understood that we had dined with a celebrity of sorts. I could not wait to tell my Berkeley professors. This was not "the Farm" as they had condescendingly spoken of it.

Franklin was in the news, on television, and discussed as a phenomenon never before known on the campus: a "Maoist." Forever in motion, he presented himself as a messenger of the future. He had zeal; he had energy; and he was untouched by the kinds of irony, particularly self-irony, endemic to faculty life. He *knew* where the world was headed, while the rest of us were uncertain. This gave him a purity of understanding most academics had long ago written off as impossible. But he was no dark and brooding revolutionary. Although he had read here and there in the history of communism, nothing of Lenin's implacable anger, or Trotsky's steely intellectualism, or Stalin's brutal menace touched his persona. His was the face of happy American utopianism. He let us know that as soon as the rest of us got around to understanding the Truth, we would be as enthusiastic about overturning our country as he was.

The chronology: in February 1971, President Richard Lyman suspended Franklin, a tenured professor, from his duties, and in September he brought a number of charges against him. The most serious of these was that, earlier in the year, Franklin had led an occupation of the university's computer center, then urged the crowd outside to disregard a police order to disperse, and later "incited students and others to engage in disruptive conduct which threatened injury to individuals and property. Acts of violence followed." Rather than accept whatever sanction Stanford might impose on him, Franklin eagerly asked to have his case heard before the Advisory Board, an elected group of seven distinguished faculty members whose normal duty was to oversee the processes leading to faculty appointments, particularly those involved in the granting of tenure. He saw it as a public relations gift—an even larger audience for his zeal. The board members held public hearings on the Franklin case in 1971 from September 28 until November 5, five hours a day, six days a week. Those hearings were broadcast over the Stanford radio station and telecast to rooms beyond the large hearing room. I went many times to see what he would say, how he would be answered, and how the process worked. Testimony and argument, which ran to about one million words, were preserved in a transcript of more than five thousand pages. Legal counsel helped both Franklin and Stanford, but he conducted his own defense. One outside helper, Harvard law professor Alan Dershowitz, quit when he saw Franklin had mounted a large photo of Joseph Stalin above the defense table. One hundred and ten witnesses were called. When the drama at last came to an end on January 5, 1972, the board, by a vote of five to two, recommended his dismissal from the university. That meant, of course, that his tenure would be stripped from him, the security it provided deemed less strong than Stanford's need to protect itself. Franklin quickly denounced the finding and publicly stated that he hoped for more violence on the campus, saying, "whatever happens is not enough."[3] Lyman and the board of trustees accepted the recommendation, and Franklin was expelled from the university on January 24, 1972. With the help of the ACLU, he then took the matter to the civil courts, where it dragged on for eight years. In the end, the courts affirmed Stanford's decision.

As I watched the process, I believed that what Stanford did was fair. From everything I knew about both the strength and the fragility of academic life, I thought Franklin had to be removed from the university community. His tenure was rightfully forfeited. That is because he represented an extremely rare, but nonetheless dangerous, hostility to the very idea of such an academic community. His considerable intelligence, matched by his considerable passion, found its fuel in a radical ideological interpretation of everything in the world. He looked with blithe contempt on any explanations that differed from his own, routinely writing them off as "bourgeois." At the core of his sensibility was the belief that the prevailing academic standards of truth-telling need never guide or detain him and that his calls to violence against the university were entirely justifiable, in fact, obligatory. He believed that "revolutionary truth" was superior to the form of "truth" pursued in places such as Stanford.

Once, after he had publicly denounced our mutual colleague Ian Watt as a "paid agent of the CIA," I asked him how he could say such a thing, knowing as he did that his charge was preposterous. He replied: "Yeah, sure, but you forget that I am a guerilla warrior; guerilla warriors pick up any tools they find." Nor did he have any scruples about employing his students, enrolled in classes such as "Melville and Marx," as pawns in his efforts at never-ending campus disruption. Those students were assured of both good grades in classes (he saw grading as a form of invidious distinction and just another bourgeois poison) and lively marches at his behest. While a few faculty colleagues, looking on from afar, supported in general his activities, none joined him in the melees he led. His ranks were made up of starstruck undergraduate students, a few embittered graduate students, and a troop of off-campus followers (some of them armed) called "Venceremos." His entourage was that of the young, the exploited, and the exploitable. While the threat of violence against the university was forever in the air when he spoke, rallied, and marched, he was watchful not to commit violence, proclaiming, "the Movement needed [my] presence as a faculty member."[4] In effect, he employed his tenured position as a protective shield while he acted to weaken the source of that protection.

The phenomenon of Bruce Franklin at Stanford was not without its moments of comic absurdity. I came to think of him as a combination of volatile self-proclaimed revolutionary and wide-eyed adolescent innocent. Once, after a departmental colleague had sheepishly confessed to him that he had spent the entire summer surfboarding and swimming off the Northern California coast, Franklin eagerly responded by saying: "That's great! When the Revolution comes, we'll need frogmen!" His wife, matching his every folly with some of her own, declared, with childish naïveté, that the 1969 oil spill off the coast at Santa Barbara, "has split the ruling class and half of them are now with us!" Both the Franklins apparently believed, like fundamentalist Christians waiting for the Apocalypse, that the revolution, no theoretical abstraction, could occur at any moment, and that like-minded people should get ready by committing cathartic acts immediately.

The question for the Advisory Board was whether an institution pledged to free and open discourse could afford someone whose entire being was pledged to the idea of violent overthrow of that institution. As the board put it:

> We believe the university's prohibition of incitement, given the criteria of intent, risk, and imminence . . . is fully justified when speech threatens two central university interests: (1) protection of members of the university community and university facilities against risks of serious injury or damage; (2) protection against coercive intrusion on the intellectual transactions which the university seeks to foster.

In sum, Stanford defended the fundamental terms by which it existed. It said that its basic instruments of intellectual exchange must not themselves be damaged. It judged Franklin (correctly I feel) an enemy of those instruments.

Such a situation is unlikely to be repeated. It drew together a seductive individual, a troubled time for the nation, an institution repeatedly put on the defensive, and students and others willing to act in dangerous ways. The case also revealed something dismaying about some of my colleagues in the English department and elsewhere. The Advisory Board, made up entirely of faculty members of considerable distinction, worked diligently and reasoned well in concluding (5–2) that Franklin had to be removed from Stanford. Their labors safeguarded the core values of academic life. But a few other faculty members said that Franklin was unfairly persecuted and that the board was no more than a "puppet" of the administration (Maoist terminology was all the rage those days). These differences in judgment taught me something about the ways in which some faculty members will choose always to be at odds with the administration, any administration. I had seen the breakdown of trust between the faculty and the administration at Berkeley in the '60s. While I thought it weakened the institution, I also believed it an appropriate reaction, given the circumstances on that campus. And I knew it would be naive to think that the intellectual spirit of a university would, or should, perfectly mesh with the administrative apparatus. But the unwillingness of some of my colleagues to come to terms with what Franklin meant, and meant to do, dazed me.

As I studied the Franklin case, day in and day out, I knew it could tell me a great deal about the university where I worked, about the academic profession in general, and about how political claims of an extreme sort would be met by moral claims on behalf of institutional protection. The facts, as I saw them, were these: Franklin had often incited students to damage the institution that paid and protected him. He had announced that his own colleagues were either fools or knaves (in his words, "ignorant, self-deceived parasites"[5]). He had urged students to disrupt the classrooms of members of the Advisory Board.

I also came to see that the campus threat he posed was a companion to the things he published. He soon edited a book—*The Essential Stalin*—that championed the ideas of the Soviet leader (whom he affectionately called "comrade Stalin" and described as "the key figure of our era") and argued that the millions of deaths Stalin caused were no more than the price one would expect to pay for a successful Russia;[6] he believed that Mao Tse-tung's "Cultural Revolution" in China, despite the murderous ruin and horror it had brought to that country, was a singular triumph of political strategy. Franklin's few faculty defenders were silent about these toxic notions. Instead they found Stanford at fault.

Most members of the English department were wholly reluctant to take a clear position about Franklin. Despite what he had written about them, Franklin was, to some of them, a friend; to others, he was an embarrassment; and yet to others, he was a burden to be borne out of professional courtesy. All of us knew that the student protests, in which he was intimately involved, had changed our daily lives. And we knew also that Franklin was involved in the disruptions and anxiety we then faced. On one occasion, the business of a department meeting was rendered inaudible by the noise of a police helicopter hovering above our building and looking for a knot of angry marchers. On another occasion, anxious about the safety of colleagues and students, Ian Watt recruited members into round-the-clock protective vigils at our buildings. While some scoffed that this wartime emergency measure was unwarranted, they were astonished to find a cache of Molotov cocktails, ready to use, stored in the attic of the department. Watt's "Blitz mentality" no longer seemed so strange. In private, Watt had little use for Franklin, thinking him representative of one of the maladies of the modern personality. About such people he was to write that they are "romantic, anti-historical; . . . they all show a belief in rapid and absolute solutions of military, political and social problems; they are all, in the last analysis, [representative of] ego-centered institutional patterns disguised as anti-institutionalism."[7] But Franklin was a member of the department of which Watt was the chairman. He had to be treated carefully.

When Watt heard in February 1971 that Franklin was facing imminent dismissal, he called together all of his colleagues—some thirty of us—for a Sunday afternoon meeting at his home in Los Altos Hills. For the occasion, he had composed what he thought was an evenhanded appraisal of what the department should say and what it should not. Alas, it said very little. It began: "We personally regret that we must now face the possibility of losing a colleague and a gifted scholar and teacher." To this phrasing, Watt's fellow Cantabrigian, the distinguished poet and critic Donald Davie, took exception. "Ian," he quaintly pleaded in making his only suggestion of the afternoon, "might we not say *severally* instead of *personally*?" After hours of such punctilious editorial nit-picking, the document was released to the world in the form in which Ian had constructed it ("personally" remained). Given its lack of substance, it gained no attention.

I learned from this meeting and from the Franklin case in its entirety that in a time of political stress and conflict, professors only rarely act courageously. I include myself. I did no more, and no better, than they. It is always hard to speak against a colleague. Even in the face of danger, an easier way—conciliation, compromise, and elaborate evasiveness—can usually be found. This is a sad truth about the academy. In later years, particularly when I found myself the president of a university, the frailty of the academic sensibility in such awkward and dangerous situations took on immense, and negative, implications for me. But the picture is never entirely bleak. Faculty ranks are not entirely made up of colleagues who shrink from responsibility. Stanford's Advisory Board did its duties well, providing Franklin with elaborate due process before it decided that his presence could no longer be tolerated on the campus. And later, when I was the president of Wesleyan University, a "saving remnant" of faculty colleagues did come forward when, at a profoundly critical moment, the life of that school was at stake. I learned that such places are strong enough, just strong enough, to sustain the unique mission they have. This is not wonderfully consoling, but it helps.

I learned from the Franklin experience, and then was to learn at Wesleyan, that institutional loyalty is a struggle for many professors. They often feel more responsibility to the professional guild—historians, biologists, philosophers, cardiac surgeons, East Asian experts—than to the university where they find themselves employed. This is a standard pattern at school after school. In addition, many of the best scholars are nomadic in their careers, moving from one place to another, perpetually seeking *the* station of ultimate distinction and honor (as well as the highest possible salary). These academic superstars do not woo their employers with protestations of loyalty; the wooing comes entirely from the would-be employer. At the other end of the professional spectrum, that of teachers employed on one-year contracts and never landing a position leading to tenure, the college and university asks of them no loyalty and they would never imagine rendering it. Given the fact that the number of such "parafaculty" is growing every year, institutional loyalty as a whole is increasingly in jeopardy.[8] Employing both the nomadic stars and the nomadic yearly workers, institutions learn to expect, as I learned to expect, loyalty to be a sometime thing.

If, with my Stanford tenure, I had become a part of something giving me both security and incentive, I had to keep in mind that I had entered a profession in which many other people would never earn tenure and the safety it offered while yet others, possessing tenure, would be so eminent that, for them, tenure would be irrelevant. And as the years passed, I was to understand, at Wesleyan and then at Emory, just how delicate and vulnerable professorial attachment to the institution can be.

ENDNOTES

1. A concise history of the case is Herbert L. Packer, "Academic Freedom and the Franklin Case," *Commentary*, April 1972, pp. 78–84. See also Donald Kennedy, *Academic Duty* (Cambridge, MA and London: Harvard University Press, 1997), pp. 132–34.

2. Historical irony: in October of 1968, Mao expelled Liu Shao-chi from the party. With his departure, the Cultural Revolution ended. Mao had removed a potential rival in the party and saw no need for the Cultural Revolution to continue.

3. See *A Chronology of Stanford University and its Founders: 1824–2000* (Stanford, CA: Stanford Historical Society, 2001), p. 107.

4. See Packer, "Academic Freedom and the Franklin Case," p. 78.

5. See Franklin's "Teaching of Literature in the Highest Academies of the Empire," in *The Politics of Literature: Dissenting Essays on the Teaching of English*, ed. by Louis Kampf and Paul Lauter (New York: Pantheon Books, 1972), p. 102.

6. The introduction to the book *The Essential Stalin* (New York: Doubleday, Anchor Books, 1972) is characterized by statements wholly detached from empirical evidence that today are embarrassing in their political naïveté (for example: "according to all accounts, the great majority of the Soviet people still revere the memory of Stalin"). In a mere 37 pages, Franklin triumphantly defends the annihilation of the kulaks, the Moscow show-trials, and the Soviet-German non-aggression pact of 1939.

7. Ian Watt, "The Humanities on the River Kwai," as reprinted in *The Literal Imagination: Selected Essays*," ed. by Bruce Thompson (Palo Alto, CA: The Society for the Promotion of Science and Scholarship, and Stanford, CA: The Stanford Humanities Center, 2002), p. 250.

8. Data from the American Association of University Professors show that part-timers constituted some 42 percent of instructors nationwide in 1998,

compared with 22 percent in 1970. The proportion of full-time professors working on contracts grew from 19 percent in 1975 to 28 percent in 1995, while the proportion of those on the tenure track fell from 29 percent to 20 percent in the same time period. The number of full-time but non-tenure-track professors almost doubled between 1975 and 1995, while the number of full-time professors on the tenure track dropped by 12 percent. See Robin Wilson, "Contracts Replace the Tenure Track for a Growing Number of Professors," *Chronicle of Higher Education*, June 12, 1998. In 2002, the National Center for Education Statistics said: "that there has been an increase in the number and percentage of part-time faculty over the last 20 years is undeniable." See "Part-time Instructional Faculty and Staff: Who They Are, What They Do, and What They Think," http://nces.ed.gov/pubs2002/2002163.pdf.

15

Teaching and Its Discontents

In the first years of teaching, I thought about the words of a student, Eric Cross, who returned punts for the school's football team. When asked why he could run so quickly after receiving kicks from Stanford's opponents, he said: "Fear. I run out of fear. I don't want to get caught. They're fast and so I run faster."

In lecturing on black literature for three years, and later when I was given "American Literature, 1917 to the Present" to teach, fear was my fuel. I wanted to get things exactly right and make no mistakes. That meant controlling, for fifty minutes, three times a week, the classroom. It was the arena of my pedagogical testing, my modest ordeal by fire. The thought of the students waiting for me to deliver the material focused all my attention. I imagined them to be tough, critical, even severe. With them in mind, I wrote out my lectures, page by page. Everything got included. I wrote out the "spontaneous" asides; I wrote out the jokes. I thought about the teachers —Sargent, Davenport, Satterthwaite, Flanagan, and Rader—who had taught me, recalling their way of talking, their strategies, the way they organized the hours they had in front of classes. I asked myself how they would teach a certain book and, in my imagination, could see myself teaching just as I had been taught. I filled lined yellow pads with everything I needed. Starting with these pads at eight in the morning, I worked on them through lunch and then, at 1:15 I was ready. For three years this was my routine.

In the fourth year, I looked up from my work and stopped. I knew I couldn't go on, year after year, that way. I reduced the yellow pages to 3-by-5 cards, lots of them, moving through them as I spoke to the class, adding here and there, interjecting remarks when I felt I could, reading less and speaking more. The asides and the jokes, not included on the cards, now were to come as they

came. After a few more years of lecturing, even the cards themselves became less important, for their contents had been
imprinted on the equivalent of cards in my head and I learned to
speak from them. And in this way, I became a lecturer—not an
excellent one but not a bad one. With a small sense of victory, I
said to myself that fear no longer was my fuel. At last I had gained
the confidence I needed to speak to undergraduate students.

But with this acquisition of skill came a peculiar, if wholly private, anxiety about the value of what I was telling those students.
In "American Literature, 1917 to the Present," my syllabus was
Eliot's *The Waste Land*, a few selections from Pound's poetry,
some short stories by Hemingway, Wharton's *The Age of
Innocence*, Fitzgerald's *The Great Gatsby*, Dos Passos's *The Big
Money*, Faulkner's *Light in August*, Wright's *Native Son*, poems
by Robert Lowell, Elizabeth Bishop, and Allen Ginsberg, and,
usually, some essays by Norman Mailer. I provided biographical
information and placed the works in an elementary historical context. I reviewed the basic plot structures and inner complexities of
the novels and how the poems worked as poems. I told the students about the connections, if they existed, between the writers.
And I highlighted those moments in the works, sometimes reading
from them, that I thought deserved special praise.

But was this real work for an adult?

While I knew that my Stanford colleagues in, say, chemistry,
were imparting solid information about the structure, composition, and properties of the things of the world and that the knowledge they were providing was not otherwise easy to come by
outside such lecture halls, my lectures were, in fact, saying no
more than what a reasonably attentive and responsive reader
could get out of those books unaccompanied by my help. I paused
to think: was there anything to understand about *The Great
Gatsby* that needed my guiding hand? Was my assistance required
by the curious and ambitious reader in getting to the mysteries of
Allen Ginsberg's *Howl*? I began to think that instead of being a
teacher I was more like a museum docent, politely pointing this
way and that, ever friendly and engaging, ever the gentle hand by
the elbow. But how essential was I?

These worries about my lecture classes led on to others just as distressing: what indeed is the function of the teacher in the humanities? Is there, in fact, a real discipline for the humanist to teach, an orderly body of knowledge not otherwise available to the intelligent and inquiring mind? How do the humanities compare to the sciences with respect to the coherence of the material imparted, the firmness of the data, and the configuration of the parts in relation to the whole? Perhaps this worry was part of being a humanist at Stanford, an institution with enormous strengths in the sciences and engineering, an institution that was then developing "Silicon Valley" and supplying it with innovators, ideas, and skills. But my worries were no less real for all that. How could the teaching of something like novels, short stories, and poems constitute a "discipline"? I knew I would always have a lot to talk about: authors and dates and "movements" and the existence of literary traditions, what Gore Vidal once called "book chat."

I did talk about these things, with feeling and some knowledge. I could have talked about them forever. But I was bothered by the fuzziness of everything I brought up, by the profound differences that changes in literary taste could make, or by the dislocation that strong critics could effect as, every once in a while, they reassembled the "traditions" and made of them even newer and better "traditions." What did we really know for sure about the books we taught? What besides the simple fact that a certain person at a certain time wrote a book and thereafter the book was variously judged, understood, and misunderstood? Was this enough; was this something really to be *taught*? What was once sufficient, at Haverford, as a discipline now seemed to me, as a young teacher, all too fragile and arbitrary. Did English and American literature really constitute a stable body of knowledge that could, like chemistry, be the same thing to all who encountered it? If it were, as it seemed to me, everywhere open to question, entirely susceptible to modifications over time and open to innumerable personal interpretations, then what was I teaching?

These uncertainties joined with another. To what were my students paying attention? I took this a step further: when I was a student, to what was *I* paying attention? An embarrassing fact: I now remembered my teachers better than the material they taught me. Could it, I worried, be personality, rather than knowledge, that is at the heart of teaching in the humanities, my teaching and the teaching of those who had taught me and whom I admired? Of course it is better to be liked as a teacher than to be disliked. But what are the costs of being liked? What if (painful considera-tion) I had not really been teaching "American Literature, 1917 to the Present," but had instead been teaching "William M. Chace and the Books He Prefers"? Like him, like his books. What if my teaching, what if teaching in the humanities in general, is not so much the command of a body of knowledge as it is the self-presentation of the teacher as he or she happily consorts with the chosen material?

Despite such concerns, which seemed at times no more than idle sophomoric musings helpful to no one, I continued to teach the American literature course. I knew, however, that I wanted to teach something else, something in which the knowledge I could give would exceed in importance the turns of personality I could bring to the occasion. I wanted a subject that the ordinary reader would not read easily, or read at all, without help. And I sought something wonderful, something astonishing as a work of art and yet something true to life and astute about the travail of being human. I chose James Joyce's *Ulysses*. Joyce, after all, had been on my mind since that sophomore year at Haverford when I wrote my ungradable paper on *A Portrait of the Artist as a Young Man*.

Ulysses is rightly regarded as the most important novel in English in the twentieth century. It combines extraordinary tech-nical ingenuity, moral force, and human wisdom. Joyce's treat-ment of its "plot" (on a given day, an unimportant man leaves his house, meets a variety of people in his city, helps a young man in trouble, and returns at end of day to that same house—which, during his absence, has been the scene of his wife's infidelity) is a powerful reminder that much of human life, while apparently "ordinary," is saturated with meaning if only we pay close atten-tion to it. Yet while everywhere praised, *Ulysses* is a book largely unread. I thought that if I were able to teach it, even doing so as a simple docent in its presence, I would help my students explore something that, on their own, they might never read or read only in part and then discard in confusion or despair. So, for three months, I read the book, then read all I could find about it. I marked it with a density of marginal notations that made it my own; my scribblings became Talmudic. I assembled an entirely new set of 3-by-5 cards about Joyce and *Ulysses* and committed them to memory. And then, in 1973, I taught the book for the first time. I believed that at last I had something genuinely useful to teach. Several decades later, I have not stopped teaching it, and my reasons for doing so have not much changed.

In those days at Stanford, while teaching *Ulysses* as well as the American literature course and other courses, I came to the melancholy observation, not unmarked by admiration for them and for their many abilities, that my students did not have much knowledge of the historical and literary culture preceding them and surrounding them. They were among the most talented young men and women to emerge from some of the best secondary schools in the country. Having gained admission to Stanford, one of the most selective schools in the country, their abilities and promise had been certified. But what they did not know, or rather what I could never assume they knew, was considerable in its range. Here are some examples in no particular order: anything about the French Revolution, the First or Second World Wars, Joseph McCarthy, the Renaissance, the causes of the American Civil War, Irish immigration into the United States, the Lindbergh kidnapping, John Milton and his poetry, the painter Goya, Marshal Tito, Jonas Salk, the San Francisco Gold Rush, Mozart, the case of Emmett Till, the Dreyfus Affair, Charles Darwin. You name it—I could not count on them to know it. This meant in practice that they collectively had no stable fund of knowledge on which I could base my teaching. A kinder way of putting this: much of what I knew, they did not know, and much of what they knew, I did not know. But, after all, I was teaching them, and only informally were they teaching me. What they had were supple and energetic minds—in many cases, much stronger and more fertile than my own—largely empty of a common core of references, templates of knowledge, and historical markers on which I could proceed in class. I could not say, for instance, "We are all familiar with Machiavelli's lessons about the use of power." Some but not all had heard of Machiavelli; some fewer still had read *The Prince*. And therefore it fell to me, should the occasion arise, to review basic information about Machiavelli and his influential book.

This problem was, of course, not visited on me alone. All of my colleagues knew that, as intelligent and enterprising as our students were, they were largely unread. Nor was this problem unique to Stanford, nor unique to that time at Stanford. The best universities with the best students have been struggling for decades with the fact that, after rigorous admission tests, high SAT scores, and Advanced Placement courses in secondary schools, students arrive on campuses all over the country with remarkable deficiencies in their intellectual preparation. (I was no different than they when I arrived that first day at Haverford.) And so those schools have, over time, established courses or curricula meant to remedy such deficiencies. To that end, Columbia long ago invented its "Contemporary Civilization" course; Harvard devised its "Red Book"; the University of Chicago thought up a "Great Books" course; and Stanford, for most of the twentieth century, required courses that, under various headings and with various rationales, were meant to bring beginning students into an awareness of what was of central importance for them to know.

Stanford began in the 1920s with a course titled "Problems of Citizenship," its purpose being to introduce the student to civic responsibilities in the United States. But by the mid-1930s, that required course, along with its implicit notion that the United States had much to fear from the threat of "strange doctrines" from afar, was shelved. In its place, "The History of Western Civilization" was introduced, becoming a staple of the curriculum until the watershed years of the late 1960s, when it in turn was dropped as a result of a major (and radically libertarian) study that concluded that every "faculty member should be free to pursue his intellectual interests wherever they lead him. The student, other things being equal, should be similarly free."[1] The only thing left standing after this revolutionary change was the vague recommendation that the beginning student take a one-semester course in historical studies. But by the early 1980s, Stanford reversed direction once more and created a new required course, "Western Culture," complete with a required reading list whose purpose was to remedy the very problem of inadequate knowledge that earlier courses, at Stanford and elsewhere, had been created to remedy. The reading list had these works:

Hebrew Bible, *Genesis*
Homer, major selections from *Iliad* or *Odyssey* or both
At least one Greek tragedy
Plato, *Republic*, major portions of Books I–VII
New Testament, selections including a gospel
Augustine, *Confessions*, I–IX
Dante, *Inferno*
More, *Utopia*
Machiavelli, *The Prince*
Luther, *Christian Liberty*
Galileo, *The Starry Messenger* and *The Assayer*
Voltaire, *Candide*
Marx and Engels, *The Communist Manifesto*
Darwin, selections
Freud, *Outline of Psychoanalysis* and *Civilization and Its Discontents*

This new course had a feature appropriately designed to address the complicating factor that the faculty members who would be teaching it had, all of them, held rather different ideas about "Western Culture" and what was important in it and how it should be taught. Therefore a number of "tracks" ("Western Thought and Literature," "Ideas in Western Culture," "Western Culture and Technology," "Great Works in Western Culture," "Europe: From the Middle Ages to the Present," and so on) were established, each suiting the intellectual preferences and preparation of the instructors. Each one of them provided the student with a way of satisfying the same basic requirement; each student had to enroll in one of the tracks. Some tracks were strong on historical fact; others were strong on textual readings; yet another saw Western Culture as the history of technological innovation. Some of the tracks had lots of students and lectures; others were small and seminar-based. But all shared the common reading list, even if it proved difficult for those devoted to the technological approach to make much of, say, selections from the *New Testament* and for those with literary sensibilities to deal effectively with Darwin.

Wanting to teach courses that were both substantive and helpful to undergraduates, and doubting that the traditional courses in English and American literature could satisfy those basic standards, I asked to teach in one of the "Western Culture" tracks. I soon found myself responsible for one of the sections of "Western Thought and Literature." It would be, for my students and me, Voltaire, Marx and Engels, Darwin and Freud, along with a few selected others. As the change in name from "Western Civilization" to "Western Culture" suggests, those who had seen to the revival of this required freshman course responded to pressures to strip from its title the implied honorific sense of the "civilized" and to substitute the neutral anthropological sense of "culture." We would not necessarily ascribe glory to what had happened in the West, only note that it had occurred and had given us the cultural framework, the "soup" in which we lived. Many of my colleagues believed this to be an adroit strategic shift, anticipating the arrival—on campus among some students and faculty, and elsewhere in the nation and world—of sharply critical reservations about Western civilization and its so-called achievements.

But the move was not adroit enough. As the course continued through the 1980s, criticisms continued to rise up about the readings, the authors, the approaches and, in fact, about the very idea of requiring a course that was so skewed in favor of male writers, male writers no longer alive (and thus allegedly irrelevant to the modern condition), and male writers who all were members of a privileged elite (the white race). Hence "DWM"—dead white males—the pejorative abbreviation flung about on the Stanford campus and elsewhere in the nation as the critics of the course and others like it vented their outrage that anything so "parochial" and "bigoted" should be inflicted on college students. The

Stanford students themselves did not, most of them, voice this criticism (indeed, many of them said they very much liked the course when they filled out questionnaires about it), nor did every faculty member, but enough did to force "Western Culture" to a crisis on campus—one that attracted the attention of the Academic Senate, the national press, and political opinion from every quarter, including two harshly conservative voices from Washington: Lynne Cheney, then the head of the National Endowment for the Humanities, and William Bennett, then the Secretary of Education. The character of the negative attitude toward the course is captured by these remarks by Bill King, the president of Stanford's Black Student Union at the time:

> I know Professors . . . are simply preserving that tradition which they consider correct and which guided their life in a positive way. But by focusing these ideas on all of us they are crushing the psyche of those others to whom Locke, Hume, and Plato are not speaking, and they are denying the freshmen and women a chance to broaden their perspective to accept both Hume and Imhotep, Machiavelli and Al Malgili, Rousseau and Mary Wollstonecraft. . . . The Western culture program as it is presently structured around a core list and an outdated philosophy of the West being Greece, Europe, and Euro-America is wrong, and worse, it hurts people mentally and emotionally in ways that are not even recognized.[2]

Some African-American and Hispanic faculty and students and some women added censorious remarks of their own: the course was not only "racist," but also "sexist" and "provincial." They charged that it omitted too many things and gave excessive attention to only a small part of history and the world. As someone teaching the course, I found their criticism rhetorically and politically interesting, even powerful, but beside the point. No course could be all-inclusive, and this one had never pretended to be. My approach, and that of many others teaching it, was not to celebrate the authors, but to tell about what they had written because I believed that my students were, by and large, ignorant of both the authors and the books. For that reason, the reading list was wholly acceptable to me. I did not think it either racist or sexist.

In fact, many of its books were sharply critical of Western culture: Rousseau saw it as a prison, Marx and Engels thought it rotting from within, and Freud thought it a veneer of make-believe shielding from view a cauldron of repressed psychological turmoil. Many of the books, far from championing "the West," were written in opposition to it. But most importantly, I believed that those books had been part of the "ABCs" of educated people for a long time. And we at Stanford, teacher and student, were living in the West, not elsewhere. The books the course taught had served for a long time as the furniture of the minds of people like us, women as well as men, black and white, Hispanic and Asian-American. To ignore these books or to substitute others for them would be, I thought, a mistake. Of course I wanted the students to read many more things than those given to them in "Western Culture," but chances were that they would not be the same things for every student. The course had the simple virtue of a list shared by all, each of the works eminently worth knowing if for no better reason than that they had supplied part of the vocabulary of knowledge and reference for so many people in the West for so long.

But reasoning as straightforward, perhaps even as simpleminded, as that was not to prevail. In the late 1980s, after two years of deliberation played out in full public view, the faculty once again created a new course, this one titled only with a neutral acronym, "CIV," instead of "Cultures, Ideas, Values," with the hope that the students would not feel an unwanted celebration of Western values and ideas was being imposed on them. Most of the "tracks" remained in place, but no single reading list was required. Rather, the instructors collectively chose books, authors, and issues each year, for that year. The one preserved remnant was that in all of the tracks, students had to read one epic, part of the Bible, a classical Greek philosopher, an early Christian thinker, one author from the Enlightenment, a Renaissance dramatist, Marx, and Freud. All the other assigned reading from the list of the fifteen books was jettisoned.

By naming the course "CIV," by thinning its list, and by keeping the names of required authors to a bare minimum, the course survived for several more years until it underwent, with renewed campus commotion, yet another change. For more than a decade, then, "Western Culture" as a course endured a great deal. The West itself didn't suffer, but everything about it was rendered suspect on the campus. Believing that some such course was better than no course at all, I regretted the cycle of changes and wanted the course to continue. But by the mid-'80s, the course called "Western Culture" resembled a toxic dumpsite. Many people on campus approached it warily, fearing that if they said anything positive about what students had been asked to read they could be subjected to withering attack. Nor could the instructors in the course any longer agree on what was important to teach about the West. We reached bottom at one meeting when those of us teaching the course discussed the reading list for the next year. What, we asked ourselves, was absolutely essential for every first-year Stanford student to read? We took a vote and I was dumbfounded and dismayed to learn that Shakespeare did not make the "top ten." His inadequacies? Insufficiently philosophical, historically inaccurate, culturally insular, and dim about science. Poor Shakespeare. That he was a great playwright—the creator of a world of characters; a poetic genius; a master of tragedy, comedy, and historical drama; and the single greatest contributor to how the English language can be used for expressive purposes—didn't count for very much at all.

The history, then, at Stanford of a course originally designed to provide students with an elementary understanding of some of the basic texts in Western cultural history—a course once thought of with their basic interests in mind—had become instead a course plagued by two problems that, by the mid-1980s, almost destroyed it. The first problem was that the texts themselves were seen, by some students and even some members of the faculty, as insulting to those students because what was being taught was deemed insular in coverage and narrowly pro-Western. The second problem arose from the faculty: they simply could not agree about what specifically was important to teach. These two problems gave me an understanding of academic life at the time: students have real political power on campus, particularly over what they are to be taught, and faculty colleagues could not be counted on to provide unified support for basic educational purposes. I learned that not only are students "customers" or "clients"; they can also become key participants in negotiations about the curriculum. And faculty members, I also learned, are likely to be less devoted to the common aims of education than to the imperatives of their own respective disciplines.

Although what happened to the course in Western culture proved discouraging to me, it also drove me to understand better and more completely the character of an institution like Stanford. What made it work? What made it stumble? Where was power found, and how did it make itself felt? How was an older system of authority changing under the impact of student concerns, and what constituted "the university" if the faculty was focused less on the institution than on itself? Asking those questions was to ask administrative questions. And trying to answer them would, in time, lead me away from teaching and research. I did not understand it fully at the time, but I was on the way to a new career.

ENDNOTES

1. A thoughtful and elegant study of the shaping of the curriculum at a number of major American universities is provided by W. B. Carnochan, *The Battleground of the Curriculum: Liberal Education and American Experience* (Stanford, CA: Stanford University Press, 1993).
2. As quoted in Herbert Lindenberger, *The History in Literature: On Value, Genre, Institutions* (New York: Columbia University Press, 1990), p. 151.

16

The English Department in Disarray

But I was no administrator yet. I still had much to learn about my own department and my own teaching. I became attentive to how the incorporation of non-mainstream cultures into the curriculum was changing not only the required freshman course but also Stanford's English department. The "Western Culture" requirement, newly established, brought in its wake another requirement, that students also take a course in a non-Western topic. The old geographical restraints were being loosened and new topics revealed. This change sat well with some of my departmental colleagues, for they had discovered enthusiasms about literary areas earlier thought to be outside the "canon": gay and lesbian, Caribbean, Yiddish, post-colonial, Latino, and "oral" literature. Over the years they also became interested in topics only loosely associated with English and American literature: computer technology, cognitive science, Sigmund Freud, the art and music of the Holocaust, transatlantic culture and society, feminist rhetorics, literature and hypermedia, cultural geography, and postmodernity. The reasons for the changes were many; so, I thought, might be their costs. Although I worried about these shifts in interest, and what they would do to the traditional study of English and American literature, I kept Joyce in mind. He accepted no constraints on what the written word, any written word, could do. The "non-mainstream" was his mainstream. His last work, the uniquely and monstrously difficult fictional achievement *Finnegans Wake*, is a monument to the ways the English language must take its place, but only its place, in the constellation of myriad languages and verbal inventions. By the time he wrote the *Wake*, English had become for him a hindrance to his expressive ambitions. He would have understood, I thought, how a

department of English could see the traditional "canon" as
another kind of hindrance.

But I nonetheless worried, for what I noticed happening in
Stanford's department, and in other departments across the country, seemed to be one of the most dramatic changes in recent
American academic history. In part these changes happened
because student populations were changing. If slightly less than
two-thirds of students in 1965 were men and more than nine in
ten were white, thirty years later four in ten students were men
and slightly less than three-quarters were non-Hispanic whites.
Louis Menand has remarked:

> The appearance of these new populations in colleges and universi-
> ties obviously affected the subject matter of scholarship and teach-
> ing. An academic culture that had, for the most part, never
> imagined that "women's history" or "Asian-American literature"
> might constitute a discrete field of inquiry, or serve to name a
> course, was suddenly confronted with the challenge of explaining
> why it hadn't.[1]

As teaching black literature had taught me, demographic
changes bring with them curricular changes. One way to understand those changes is to look at their costs and benefits. Among
the benefits: professors and students have more to teach and learn,
and that is a positive change. Let's call this expansion—of new
things to be known—"Joycean." Among the costs: the erosion of
any clear sense of the disciplinary core of the average English
department or Comparative Literature department. For some
observers, this is very bad news; for others, the notion of a "disciplinary core" is part of the problem. In the eyes of these observers,
even to have a "disciplinary core" is an unwelcome constraint, one
rightly to be jettisoned from the academy.

But how did these extraordinary changes take place? The explanation customarily offered is that curricular expansion opened the
doors to hitherto unheard voices, idioms, and forms of expression.
What was once denied became welcome; a history of exclusion
was rectified. The mission of higher education, after all, is to
absorb and integrate knowledge, not to shun it. Thus the

humanities have brought into the house of learning the works of women, African-Americans, Latinos, Asian-Americans, gays and lesbians, as well as many others almost wholly unknown or unwelcome in curricula before the changes came about.

But again the costs: the "new" knowledge, while always welcome, thrusts some "old" knowledge into obscurity. That was my worry. The logic of "zero-sum" addition and subtraction meant that every new work brought into the curriculum supplanted an earlier favorite. Semesters are only so long and only so much can be included on any reading list. So Kate Chopin might get to replace Theodore Dreiser in American literature courses; Maya Angelou might take the place of William Carlos Williams in modern poetry. The result? What once looked like a stately parade now looks like a free-for-all. The old-fashioned effort to define the curriculum as a stable "tradition," with one writer succeeding another in an unbroken line of influence and assimilation—all congenial to the semester system and all part of my days long ago at Haverford—has given way to the presence of many writers, all shouldering into the arena of knowledge, many of them having entered as "representative" of one kind of ethnic or racial or gender classification, their collective presence making the semester more diffuse and harder to handle.

Another result of the curricular changes, as I saw them at Stanford and elsewhere, was that the twentieth century assumed a primacy of place while other, earlier periods were slighted. That is because of the nature of the earlier reading lists. They included few writers coming from racial and ethnic groups. How was this to be remedied? Although certain women writers in previous centuries (one thinks of Jane Austen, George Eliot, or Emily Dickinson) wrote so well—indeed wrote with supreme mastery—that no one could question their inclusion in earlier English department course offerings, their numbers were small. Only the twentieth century produced many women writers of distinction. The same is true of writers who were black—few in earlier periods and many in our own time. The result is that, in many classrooms, the real action in the humanities is only recent action, the action of the last hundred or so years.

In addition, then, to the fact that an earlier and once apparently plausible notion of historical tradition and continuity has been destabilized, the weight of the curriculum in many English departments across the nation has fallen on the modern period. These two changes—disrupted continuity and an emphasis on the very recent past—have weakened the notion that the study of English and American literature is a "discipline." To many observers, inside and outside the academy, it looks less like a coherent field of study and more like the result of political and social compromises arising from political quarrels which themselves have little to do with English and American literature. One result of such changes in "English" as a major field of concentration is that almost all "comprehensive examinations," such as the one I took at Haverford in 1961, have been abandoned across the nation. What department could now ask its majors, no two of them having studied the same thing in classes that have been taught by professors who themselves are unlikely to agree about what the field has become, to take such a test?

If this is the new curriculum, what of the scholarship linked to that curriculum? Here another kind of cruel logic, similar to "zero-sum," has arisen. Along with publishers and committees reviewing tenure files, humanists have come to fear that many scholarly areas have been over-farmed and over-harvested. As Menand put it, "it may be that what has happened to the profession is not the consequence of social or philosophical changes, but simply the consequence of a tank now empty."[2] Given that kind of depletion of resources, only the most ingenious young humanist could now dare think that he or she could come up with an entirely new reading of, say, John Keats's "Ode on a Grecian Urn" or the character of Falstaff. Good things, many good things, have been said and even resaid by the most eminent critics on these matters.[3] With the possibility of something genuinely original diminishing, young scholars in the humanities have thought to themselves: what can I write that will attract a publisher, convince a committee that I deserve tenure, and promote my career?

They have found their answers by going outside the traditional and apparently arid constraints of the field. For example, while they might not write about *Macbeth*, they might write about Orson Welles's movie based on *Macbeth*; if someone else has already done that, then they might write not about the movie, but about the sociological attributes of the audience that once watched it or even about the nature of the advertisements about it in newspapers at the time. They can put the work itself aside and inject life into ancillary topics. They can become sociologists of literature or commentators about popular culture or film and TV critics. But in so doing, they wind up being part of the energy distending the boundary of the field.

Given the power of intellectual creativity and the kind of mental inspiration that can be found when academic promotion is at hand, the results of these transformations have not been all bad. Good and intelligent things can always be written by good and intelligent people. But the cost of such ingenuity has been a growing difficulty in saying what the field of "English literature" is and what it is not. When an area of knowledge starts to lose its disciplinary profile and becomes, even for understandable reasons, shapeless, and when it seems perpetually at the mercy of ideological clashes, people are likely to take notice. If "English" becomes everything, then it might turn out to be—in disciplinary terms— nothing in particular. And one sign of becoming nothing in particular is that some English departments now look like thriving cities—literature and film, queer studies, post-colonial seminars— surrounded by deserted villages—the eighteenth century, early American literature, and pre-Shakespearean drama.[4] This, I began to think, was at the heart of what had gone wrong: "English" seemed to have lost its way and, in becoming so much while at the same time becoming so little, had become, in the public eye, disheveled and incoherent. The distinguished scholar Tzvetan Todorov reminded his readers what tradition has always meant and what its loss can cost:

> The goal of a humanist, liberal education is to form minds that are simultaneously tolerant and critical. The method employed to attain this goal is the mastery of a specific tradition: no path leads to the universal except through the particular.[5]

By the time Todorov was writing, the "particular" had granulated into myriad particulars. Every young scholar was at home with his or her specialty, and the reaction of most departments to this spectacle was to practice the policy of *laissez-faire* accommodation: accept my particular and I will accept yours, but let us not interfere with each other.

I knew at the time that the public, always attentive to the laughable shenanigans of professors as reported in the popular press (witness the gleeful anticipation in many newspapers of the annual meeting of the Modern Language Association, with its apparently ridiculous paper topics such as Eve Kosofsky Sedgwick's "Jane Austen and the Masturbating Girl"), had concluded that the humanities were a dead end. But what of the students themselves? The numbers here are genuinely dismaying: from 1966 to 1993, even though the number of nationwide bachelor's degrees more than doubled, those in the humanities dropped from just over 20 percent in the late 1960s to a low of about 10 percent in the mid-1980s, increasing only to 12 percent in the early 1990s.[6] The economic decline of the time was in part to blame for this deterioration of interest in the humanities, always a victim because always a "luxury." With a decline in U. S. economic growth and productivity from 1970 to the mid-1990s, with nearly 50 million American workers terminated in mid-career or forced to retire early between 1981 and 1996, and with continued "outsourcing" of jobs to other nations,[7] many students did not believe they could afford to study topics not directly leading to secure jobs. Thus it was not only those beyond the campus gates who had grown leery of what the humanities, particularly English departments, were up to. Those on campus, the students who could have voted with their feet to support literary studies, decided to travel elsewhere.

Critics of the humanities, of whom there were many at the time, were busy citing critical theory as the culprit in this drama. This, I think, is wrong. Strong critical approaches have existed in the study and understanding of literature forever. Samuel Johnson exerted a profound influence in his own time and thereafter; so did Matthew Arnold in his time, T. S. Eliot in his, Cleanth Brooks and Robert Penn Warren in theirs, Northrop Frye in his. There has never been a moment in the interpretation of literature when the critical voice was not present, sometimes commandingly so. The revolution in our time, however, has been that some critical theorists have violated what once seemed inviolable—the stricture that said the literature came first and the criticism came after. I was witnessing a revolution in my department and elsewhere in the 1980s that was upending the basic presupposition that the literature is primary and the criticism secondary.

And so in classrooms the students who remained to study "English" might indeed know a great deal about critical theory but not much about literature. While familiar with Jacques Derrida or Mikhail Bakhtin or "reader-response" theory or neo-Marxist strategies or Orientalist critiques or notions of "foregrounding," they may not have read, actually read to the very end, many poems or novels, these things being mere grist for the critical mill.

As I said to myself at Stanford when Joycean in spirit, all knowledge is good. To know critical theory is a genuine intellectual achievement; and many intelligent students have learned from many intelligent teachers how to feel at home with demanding modes of critical discourse. But I came to believe that those students had equipped themselves with an occult mastery. If their study was not primarily literature itself, but was focused on the theory hovering around literature, they and their teachers would leave the public, and perhaps even themselves, puzzled about what departments of literature do and what is meant by "humanistic studies." Of course, they could refuse to worry about the public and say that intellectuals who worry over such matters really are not intellectuals at all. As for puzzling themselves, they might well call that "jouissance," the seductive play of mind, the pleasure of well-wrought obfuscation.

To me, however, the plight of the humanities was disturbingly real. I thought I could see its origins and causes: the incorporation of new curricular materials inflating the field and giving it a modern and contemporary focus; the poverty of new and worthy things to say about traditional materials; and the supremacy of critical theory over the texts themselves. But what a spectacle remained! An academic activity that was hard to define or explain, one that had lost both institutional support and prestige in many universities and colleges, and that had suffered an almost complete erosion of understanding among the public at large.

As I continued my teaching at the time, I noticed another painful fact about the troubled enterprise of the humanities. No discipline had done more to enlarge its curriculum to embrace that which had previously been excluded: in particular, racial and ethnic minorities. The course I inaugurated at Stanford in 1969 on American black literature and that other teachers began at other schools in the 1960s and '70s had become a staple in colleges and universities across the country by the 1980s. Yet minority students were not choosing in the 1980s and 1990s to major in English or comparative literature, the very places that seemed to be inviting their presence. As Lynn Hunt speculated, "it is possible that minority students have been especially alert to the potential decline in status of the humanities."[8] If so, they have responded as if in harmony with all other students and with the public at large.

The question for the department where I made my intellectual home—English at Stanford—and for all other departments in the humanities was how they could recover the stature, among students, among colleagues in other fields, and, yes, among administrators, they once enjoyed. Perhaps they could purchase that stature, but I feared that it would be at a cost no one would be willing to pay: a more constrained and exacting curriculum; a rededication to teaching the central texts while admitting that profound new scholarly findings about them might only rarely be made; and a concentration, in the classroom, not on theoretical but on traditionally literary pursuits. Such costs might be high indeed, but perhaps not as high as the cost of witnessing what the study of "English literature" was becoming: an increasingly shapeless, rarified, and irrelevant endeavor.

That concern and my continuing reservations about my own contributions as a teacher made for a powerful ambivalence in my thinking. Haverford and Berkeley had given me a sturdy foundation on which to study, to learn, and to teach. The literature I once read was real, very much seemed to have meaning, and could illuminate life, even life in its most delicate and complex patterns. Although nothing was simple about the relationship of the words on the page to the patterns of human life as they played themselves out all around us, that relationship was eminently deserving of our study and understanding. It could enrich our moral codes, deepen our sense of ethical and spiritual duties to one another, and enhance our awareness of what was uniquely human in all we did.

But that foundation had begun to creak beneath the pressure of ways of reading that questioned the very connection between the words on the page and anything else; it also was weakened by arguments that questioned the meaning of so "bourgeois" and intellectually provincial an idea as a "moral code" or a "tradition." The "hermeneutics of suspicion," a fashionable way of undermining everything in sight, were potent and omnivorous; little could stand in the way of approaches that questioned the structure and meaning of all known entities and constructs. Nor was I in a position—either by training or by intellectual power—to refute these approaches with absolute conviction. So, in a spirit of what I acknowledge now as reactionary discontent, I wrote a book in the early 1980s whose implicit message was that American literary culture had once witnessed a moment when books did carry moral meaning and did offer reflections of life amid even its most intricate configurations. That moment was best represented, I argued, by the critic and Columbia University professor Lionel Trilling (1905–1975), my book being a biography of his intellectual development. It was also, truth to tell, a cemetery marker. The kind of criticism he practiced, essay by essay and book after book, was dead. What I wrote, as homage, accepted that fact but sought nonetheless to claim the importance of his extraordinary career.

Trilling, who found his métier in the reflective essay, customarily began his writing by explicating a literary work (usually fiction, not poetry) and then moved to a meditation on the situation of its contemporary American readers. For some forty years, he sought to represent the class of those readers in a variety of little magazines such as *Partisan Review*. In so doing, he interpreted the culture surrounding him as much as he interpreted the literature.

He was armed by two considerable bodies of knowledge: Marxism and Freudianism. He deferred to the former while having great doubts about its explanatory power; he saw the latter as a way to appreciate the essential tragic condition of being human. His devotion to Freud, while unstinting throughout his career, was not based on the technical nomenclature and dynamics of psychoanalysis; it focused instead on the prophetic and somber qualities of Freud's thinking. Trilling found the "real" Freud in such works as *Civilization and Its Discontents* and in such comments, alien to Marxism, as "there are difficulties attaching to the nature of civilization which will not yield to any attempt at reform." This Freud stood for Trilling as a way to tell his readers that their social and political optimism was fatuous and that much of modern literature was abrasively hostile to anything but a soberly realistic appraisal of the human condition.

As his career came to an end, Trilling turned his saturnine intelligence to what he called the "adversary culture," contending that American intellectuals and their readers had wrongly become hostile and negative toward the culture that had nourished them. He argued that readers had wrongly internalized the violence, menace and bleakness of much of modern literature—in writers such as Dostoevsky, Lawrence, and Kafka—with the unfair result that the structures and artifacts of traditional society were under constant and casual attack. Art could no longer "shock" because, he argued, the very idea of "shocking" had become absorbed and thus trivialized in everything we do. As the "anti-social" became "socialized," what once had served as moral "verities" lost their power.[9]

I had a good idea of what Trilling would have made of the new vogue of critical analysis and theory found in virtually every English department in the land. Although he had much to say about the ways in which the "adversary culture" could go about misreading books, he had no doubt that books could, in fact, be read, understood, and widely discussed with agreement about their meaning. To arrive at such agreement was, he believed, an end both desirable and achievable. "Misreading" was a regrettable fact but not inevitable, not a constituent of the text itself. But by the time I wrote the book, Trilling was dead, dead as a man and dead as an inspiration to young scholars and critics. I was memorializing a lost tradition of reading, doing so for reasons local to my own situation. I would have to find a new way, a better way, of being a teacher and member of the academic community. Writing on Trilling had served as a memorial to a moment in American cultural history that once was alive—at Haverford and Berkeley—but now, I thought, was lost. Nonetheless, I had to find how to fit into the academy, a place changing beneath my feet. The question was the same one I had been asking for years: how to bring together the world of ideas (or what I knew of it) with the desire to make a difference (if only small) in the world itself. If I could not find an answer to that question as a professor, where could I find it?

ENDNOTES

1. Louis Menand, "The End of the Golden Age," *New York Review of Books*, October 18, 2001.
2. Menand, "The Demise of Disciplinary Authority," in *What's Happened to the Humanities*, ed. by Alvin Kernan (Princeton: Princeton University Press, 1997), p. 215.
3. As Andrew Delbanco has written, "while old works will always attract new interpretations from new readers, and the canon will continue to expand with the discovery of overlooked writers—a process that has accelerated enormously over the last twenty-five years with the entrance into the profession of women and minorities—the growth of English departments at anything like its former pace cannot be justified on the grounds that literary 'research' continues to produce invaluable new knowledge." "The Decline and Fall of Literature," *New York Review of Books*, November 4, 1999 http://www.nybooks.com/articles/318).
4. With the teaching often carried on in an atmosphere described by the literary critic Frederick Crews as made up of "epistemic relativism, pop-cultural leveling, radical proselytizing, and the tunnel vision of 'subject positions.' " *New York Review of Books*, December 1, 2005.

5. Todorov, "Crimes Against Humanities," *New Republic*, July 3, 1989, p. 30.

6. See Lynn Hunt, "Democratization and Decline? The Consequence of Demographic Change in the Humanities," in *What's Happened to the Humanities*, ed. by Alvin Kernan (Princeton: Princeton University Press, 1997), p. 22.

7. See David Pearce Snyder and Gregg Edwards, "Roller Coaster 2000: Forces Reshaping Daily Life and Work in America: 1990–2010," http://exploringleadershipcolloq.gsfc.nasa.gov/1998-99/snyder2.pdf.

8. Hunt, "Democratization and Decline?," p. 20.

9. See Trilling, "On the Teaching of Modern Literature," in *Beyond Culture: Essays on Literature and Learning* (New York: Harcourt Brace Jovanovich, 1978).

17

Why Join the Administration?

Very few professors think they will become administrators. And few do. Seen from afar, a career in administration looks dull or suggests that one's career as a scholar has dried up. It is true that deans, provosts, and presidents make more money than professors and enjoy some perquisites unavailable to faculty members. But since the work is reputed as at once tedious and labor-intensive, the perks don't seem entirely enticing. If you are to spend long hours with paper, better the paper in books and research reports than in committee minutes and budgets. And to separate oneself from the special guild of which one has long been a loyal member—that, say, of biologists, or of historians, or of mathematicians—and to associate with a collection of people from other guilds in an administrative office is to join a society of strangers. Moreover, the real work of the academy, as everyone knows, is not done in administrative offices but in the disciplines; administrators are only there by necessity: to be stewards of the organization that supports the authentic intellectual labor.

And yet. Professors, some of them, do become administrators and some of them for reasons not entirely embarrassing. The best of them are drafted into the work. They have run a search committee particularly well, or they have been reasonable and fair while chairing their department. Or they have successfully served on a committee to resolve a complicated issue in university governance. They are then urged to serve, but only for a limited time, as "junior" deans, or they are recruited to take over a failing academic department in need of an outside manager. In each of these instances, should they again be successful, the recruitment process leads to yet another, and more advanced, administrative role. As this process develops, the professor can at any time stop and return "home" to his or her department. But some continue as administrators.

Almost everyone who starts this process experiences anguish about leaving aside, even if temporarily, the work in the field in which they were trained. The tension between the work of the day as an administrator, a dean, for instance—claims on the budget, space problems, laboratory expenses for a natural scientist, handling committees, tenure grievances, departments recently weakened by the departure or death of a distinguished colleague—and the "real" work that one once knew can be intensely painful. No truly good administrator ever departs from his or her discipline without some regret. But they do depart.

The best universities and colleges do not seek out administrative leaders who have been formally trained as administrators. Most faculty members might themselves not want to be administrators, but they want administrators to have done genuine academic work, and the more significant the work the better. Hence deans and provosts and presidents at distinguished universities are those who have earlier been, say, very good scientists or humanists or economists or teachers in the law school. A form of "projection" operates: a professor must somehow see part of himself or herself in the person of the administrator, even if that administrator has, for mysterious reasons, left the home discipline.

Bad reasons also exist for wanting to become an administrator: crass careerism; a childish fascination with the perquisites; or the belief, without much foundation, that the administrator possesses "power" and can unilaterally effect great institutional changes. In most cases, the careerist is sooner or later found out and cast aside; the perks turn out to be baubles; and the unilateral power proves to be a chimera. But this does not mean that the wrong people do not sometimes find roles in administrations. They do and the institution inevitably suffers. By and large, however, a complicated sorting process does its slow work: few people want to be administrators, but if they think they do, they are first given apprentice roles where they flourish or flounder; if they are happy and successful, they then move on to more substantial roles. If success follows success, and if their own satisfaction with the office is sustained, they become, at last, journeyman administrators. Thus the creation of deans and provosts and presidents.

At Stanford, the deans, provosts, and presidents I saw had begun as historians or mathematicians or legal scholars and had then become—for reasons peculiar to each—administrators. They did not seem careerists interested in "power." Perhaps they had figured out that their supposed "power" would be drawn from obliging others, that it was, in effect, borrowed power, and that it could always be taken back by others in the university who, in a spirit of trust, had lent it to them. No academic administrator gets his way for very long without the willing consent of those with whom he works. And these Stanford deans and provosts all seemed to have been quite good in the disciplines from which they had come. I got to watch them from my vantage point in the English department. Richard Lyman, Stanford's president my first ten years there, had been a fine scholar of British history (even though he often announced that he no longer possessed expertise in the field); Donald Kennedy, who succeeded Lyman and served for the next decade, was a distinguished biologist and an eloquent spokesman for all the sciences and for academic life in all its dimensions. I saw how they handled things: a tenure case or a budgetary problem or a matter affecting humanists. And from these experiences I formed a tentative idea of what prompted them to do what they did.

I conjectured an interest on their part, a curiosity, a fascination, with the institution itself. What made it work? What held it together? What principles could be enforced to make it work even more efficiently? Why were some operational ideas superior to others? How could assorted colleagues be assembled to complete a given task? Who was helpful and who was not? The strategies of the two men were different, even though the basic interest in the institution was the same: to look after and advance its well-being. For an entire decade, Lyman—tough, clear and resilient—defended Stanford when it was in trouble; Kennedy—a more ebullient and gregarious man—went on the offensive during the next ten years to enlarge the university's capacities and bring it to the greater attention of the world. They both succeeded, but in different ways—one to protect and stabilize, the other to celebrate and augment.

Added to these attributes was their apparent acceptance of the unusual thing a college or university is. They each knew it is an institution not held together by any of the forces governing other important institutions in our society—year-end profits, more viewers, larger audiences, greater sales, more subscribers, or the ability to swallow up the competition. Instead, both saw that universities and colleges have as their uniting purpose the creation and the preservation of knowledge. This purpose is given energy by another: a relentless search for that elusive entity, the "truth." Everything else depends on this pursuit. The implicit understanding of this goal carries the institution forward. The administrators I watched—Lyman, Kennedy, and others—did not continually give voice to that understanding (save on festival days like Commencement) but it suffused everything they did.

No more than any other professor did I think of becoming an administrator. But I had been on search committees in my department. I had tried to help graduate students find their first jobs. I had served in the Academic Senate and one year in the 1980s had chaired it. Nothing unusual. But in 1979 the Dean of the School of Humanities and Sciences, Halsey Royden, asked if I would serve on "A & P," the Appointments and Promotions committee, a group he would periodically gather to review the files of candidates for tenured positions at Stanford. It was made up of six persons, each of them with a good reputation for scholarship and institutional service. I accepted his invitation and was happy I did so. The satisfactions were many, all of them new to me. I learned that if a given case proved complicated for the committee, our discussions would be lengthy, turning into an occasion when each of us would articulate our basic principles about academic excellence, institutional responsibility and risk-taking, and where we thought the department or academic unit should be going. I got to know a great deal about how different colleagues saw the university, given the various kinds of intelligence and disciplinary training—scientific, humanistic, and social scientific—we brought to bear on problems. How was "excellence" to be judged? What was a genuinely new achievement in a field and what was false gold? Who was an intellectual innovator and who a camp follower? What disciplines were lively and which worn out? Who was revamping a field and who was an "exhausted volcano"? It all depended on how we thought. (A mathematician once told me about solutions to problems that were not just "correct," but "elegant"; this notion, new to me, was a welcome antidote to my belief, as a humanist, that all good thinking was "complex" thinking.) We would discuss a candidate who had produced enormous quantities of "good" scholarship and then another candidate who had produced little scholarship but all of which was unequivocally "brilliant." Which one was better? We discussed departments that rarely forwarded to us a case, believing that their internal standards were rightly high and that few of their young scholars were worthy of tenure. And we looked at other departments that forwarded all their cases to us, prompting one member of the committee to say: "We are being told that all their geese are swans." What I learned was invaluable, and it was all about "quality control," the rules and standards by which a university regulates itself and demonstrates, over time, if it knows what genuine excellence is and if it is willing to be tough enough to demand it.

Serving on this committee ventilated my mind. It gave me a way out of my anxieties about teaching and about the direction of the English department. It opened up ways of looking at Stanford and higher education in general. The low-grade claustrophobia that had come to characterize my sense of myself as a scholar and teacher faded a bit. In being uprooted, I saw contours of the place I had never known existed. I began to understand how the university—a much more complicated place than I had imagined—worked. Although it seemed at times to behave awkwardly, even in a bumbling fashion and with confusions and redundancies characteristic of all bureaucracies, I knew it was getting stronger, more eminent, and surer of itself. Stanford was on the rise; the surge was all around me. And I noted that the once rather "faceless administrators" I was getting to know were, in fact, people who took Stanford's growth seriously and had invested an extraordinary amount of time in its development. Most surprisingly, each of them worked without the friction of ambivalence, or so it seemed. For me, to whom the ironic aside and the dismissive challenge had become psychological and rhetorical staples, this was a new world, one in which competence, clarity, and demonstrable results were the currency of the day. Moreover, some of the administrators I met seemed to have found what I had been seeking since my graduate days at Berkeley: a way of uniting intellectual capability with political aspiration. They could exercise their minds and could also make a difference to the world in which they had found themselves. Of course they did so within the circumscribed domain of the university and sought no influence beyond those limits. This was not politics writ large, but it was a form of leverage—benign because the university itself was benign—that seemed honorable and useful. From this new vantage point, I felt myself drifting away from the comforts of my earlier Stanford life. I liked what I found.

This turned out to be only one of many steps I took toward administrative duties and away from scholarly ones. After I'd served three years on the A & P Committee, from 1979 to 1982, the new dean of the School, Norman Wessells, a quiet and circumspect biologist, asked me to become one of his three associate deans. The other two were James Rosse, later to become Stanford's provost, and a good friend, David Kennedy, a superb historian with whom I had for several years co-taught a course called "Reflections on the American Condition," and who years later was to win a Pulitzer Prize for his book on the United States during FDR's presidency. I was responsible for a scattering of departments, some in the humanities, some in the natural sciences, and some in the social sciences. I was immediately plunged into budgetary allocations, salary reviews, search committees, meetings with chairs of departments, and—the enduring fixture of all administrative labor—refereeing squabbles among faculty colleagues.

As I learned more about the pressures and personalities and constraints collectively making up the life of a research university, I addressed my new reality with a kind of double-mindedness. At any moment, I could step back and find footing within that framework of ironic detachment that had been my long-term companion as an English professor. I could cavalierly dismiss the issues coming my way as no more than transient and therefore, given the "long run," inconsequential. But I also could find satisfaction by bearing down on those very issues, getting to understand them fully, and then pressing toward their resolution. I discovered the happiness of solving certain problems and leaving them behind me, a sensation rarely granted to a professor in the humanities who learns that most of his major problems are only temporarily settled. I liked helping to negotiate the appointment of a senior professor and remembered, on the other hand, how difficult it had been to determine how successful a poet Ezra Pound had been. The second problem is more important than the first, but is forever hedged with doubt and ambiguity. In preferring at times the first kind of problem, I felt no guilt in my new mental pleasures.

But life as an associate dean was not, I learned, all pleasure. Before too long, I became the kind of "faceless administrator" whose actions make deans such unsympathetic characters to the faculty. A tenure case coming from the History department in 1982 was forwarded, as was routine, to the A & P Committee. The mixed vote of "Ayes" and "Nays" from the department was disclosed; letters from external referees were read and discussed; and considerable mention was made of the fact that the candidate was a feminist scholar. The discussion around the table was lengthy and detailed. We in the office—the dean and his two associate deans, David Kennedy having recused himself owing to the principle of conflict of interest—listened and observed but offered no opinion about the merits of the case. At the end, the committee's vote was decisively negative, 6–0. We then met in the dean's office and the three of us (Kennedy again absent) decided that we could not, and should not, forward the case to the provost with our endorsement. The A & P discussion had been substantive and, we thought, fair. Some of the best faculty in the School had thought, talked, and decided. The candidate's case was not strong enough to elicit a positive vote. We agreed that we should not move it ahead without A & P endorsement.

As the "cognizant" dean for the department, I called its chair, Peter Stansky, to tell him about the decision, adding that I thought it was correct. His only response to me was a weary sigh and then:

"Bill, I see a *terrible* shit storm coming your way." He was right. The case involving Estelle Freedman was to preoccupy me, the dean, then the provost, and much of the rest of the Stanford academic community for the next several months. Faculty and students wrote letters pro and con about Freedman; over the months in that academic year, her proponents mounted protests in her favor; some circulated allegations of unfairness and sexism around the campus. Scholars from other institutions wrote in; threats of lawsuits emerged; the national press picked up the story. For many people, the case was much more than a matter of the fate of an individual scholar. For them, it was about women in American society and gender discrimination in general. And for some people, the issue turned on the fact that Freedman was a lesbian, their letters charging that those involved with the case—including me—had made their decisions on homophobic grounds.

The pressures became so great that the dean asked the A & P Committee to reassemble late in the spring of 1983 to look at the case again. Its membership had changed slightly in the interim and was no longer wholly male in its composition. A & P took another vote—again it was emphatically negative, 5–0, with one abstention. I again let the chair know, and the predicted fecal tempest increased in intensity. Much to my personal surprise, and yet not at all surprising to me as someone who had begun to understand the problems of administration, I was in the direct line of that storm. After all, I had been the messenger, the one who had given the department—and the world—the bad news on two occasions. I had thereby become the face of insensitivity and the representative of institutional prejudice against women.

At such times, the complicated apparatus of university decision-making gets reduced to a person, a name. Even though most people knew that a committee of otherwise distinguished (and until that moment, unimpeachable) colleagues had analyzed the merits of the case on two occasions and that the dean (up until that moment, also unimpeachable) had reflected on the matter and on the department with his colleagues and had accepted the advice of the committee, Freedman's proponents had sought a simple explanation. Their answer: I was the problem. Better a drama featuring a villain than a drama featuring a committee. And, for years, my reputation as a "misogynist" pursued me.

In the end, after more internal and external appeals and more general university consternation, the provost, Albert Hastorf, decided late in the academic year that he would remove the case from our office and would, on his own authority, move it toward tenure. Provosts can do this, for they are the officers ultimately accountable for the institution's academic integrity. I accepted this fact of life, as did the dean. Our writ went only so far; the provost's went further. We had done what we had thought right; now it had come to him to do the same.

And thus the case concluded: Professor Freedman gained tenure. In the end, the A & P Committee performed honorably, the provost saw something we did not see, and the department of history gained a tenured colleague. For my part, I learned a lesson about how any action I might take could be interpreted to suit the psychological and dramatic needs of the community surrounding me. In the eyes of some, I became something less than a person and more an administrative stooge and, at that, a wholly reprehensible one. I began then to understand that the defense of what I was as a person would henceforth fall more directly upon me. Up until that time, I had thought I would get a break on that point: I could entrust my merit as a person to others. I could no longer be sure of such support. I began to understand much more about the isolation of administrators.

Cases such as the one in the History department are unusual and telling. When tenure matters become celebrated causes, they are usually freighted with meaning and implications beyond the specific merits of the given candidate. In this case, questions of feminist historiography, of the place of women in the academy, and the situation of lesbians in our society were at stake. A great many people had intensely strong feelings about these larger questions and attached themselves to the case in vigorous ways. When something that extraordinary happens, the institution is left in the acutely uncomfortable position of deciding whether it should judge an individual scholar, evaluate a divisive topic, or do both. The crucial issues of "merit" and of "quality control" become interlaced with issues of social justice, perceived historical wrongs, and the championship of ideas deemed progressive or "right for the university." At the center of this drama stand the administrative officers. As a dean, I came to recognize this fact as a formidable challenge. What aspect of the university should I represent: intellectual excellence as defined and regulated by established peer review, or "doing right" on behalf of the institution in accordance with those who saw it as an engine of social change and virtue? I knew where I stood. I agreed with the A & P Committee's judgment on the Freedman case. I also could see why the provost had decided otherwise. The university had been on the side of doing right by women, but I worried that the department of History might become intellectually weaker as a result of this decision.

Nothing about this case was easy. The weight of the discomfort fell on everyone. I learned that to weigh the best interests of the institution while at the same time factoring in the criterion of academic excellence can be a form of exquisite mental and ethical torture. One could argue, for instance, that the first—an institution's needs and obligations—has little to do with the second—individual merit. But, I wondered, are the two, in fact, dissimilar? If so, how much? Could one not argue that insisting on individual excellence is ultimately a means of guaranteeing institutional excellence? In the end, a university is only as good as its faculty. Yet insisting on institutional excellence might be a good way to reinforce individual scholarly excellence. After all, no faculty stands on its own; it needs the full support of the institution to survive. Hence the institution should be able to assert a supererogatory power to influence events in its favor. In some cases this power might push toward academic excellence. In others it might mean that the institution declare itself, for the good of everyone, in favor of affirmative action.

The Freedman case and the discussion surrounding it taught me that while I had once known much about the complexities of difficult cases of literary merit and achievement (for example, exactly how good were some of Shakespeare's history plays?), these new matters, local and now intimate to me, of academic merit and institutional power, were exceptionally compelling. They called upon everyone to exercise the best judgment they had. Both young faculty careers and the integrity of the university were at stake. As I saw colleagues use their best wisdom amid intricate processes, I sensed that what I was witnessing—the drama of administrative management—would provide the sustenance of my career for a long time to come. Step by step, I was learning to become an administrator.

18

Exchanging Reflection for Action

As I learned about working in a dean's office, I would sketch rough drafts of the world, organized and disorganized, that I observed. The chief feature of that world was that the faculty populated it. Budgets were important; space in which teaching and research could be conducted was important; and the many rules, some of them the legacy of academic life for centuries, were also important. But nothing was more significant than the presence of hundreds of professors. A taxonomy of a university faculty reveals that each and every professor is a specialist, not a generalist. Over time, the specialties define the professors. The greater the mastery of the specialty, the more esteemed the professor has become. Hence each professor occupies a separate well-appointed chamber of which he or she is the solitary master. Each has developed hypertrophy of a particular intellectual muscle. Deans oversee a vast gallery of men and women who have sharpened the intellectual distinctions between themselves and all others who might at first, by the unknowing, be confused with them. These differences are what make their reputations. And reputation is at the heart of the standing, and thus the compensation, the office, the teaching duties, and the other perquisites of every faculty member.

Much is rightly made, at every university, of the virtues of "cross-disciplinary" activity and the need to have greater and greater faculty cooperation in many projects, but professors know how to guard what they have made and cultivated. They are not likely to surrender it to cross-disciplinary enthusiasms. Although everyone likes to celebrate the liberal feeling of a campus, the way it opens outward to learning and new ideas, deans learn that faculty members are profoundly conservative about what they know and what they possess. The liberal faculty is never liberal about what it considers most important—its own work.

As a dean, I also learned about other basic realities shaping the lives of faculty members. Every dean or provost must be steadily attentive to them. While it is a mistake to confuse one professor with another, it would be even more ludicrous to imagine that "the faculty" is made up of fungible assets—that the physicist can be refashioned to become the sociologist, or that the philosopher can take up the duties of the historian. A university is not a repertory theater with each of the actors schooled and willing to play a variety of roles. As Alison Lurie says in her novel, *The War between the Tates*, "Teachers, especially university professors, often have an elective affinity with their subjects. Whether through original tropism, conscious effort or merely long association, language instructors born in Missouri and Brooklyn look and act remarkably like Frenchmen and Italians, professors of economics resemble bankers, and musicologists are indistinguishable from musicians." You become what your discipline instructs you to be. Nor does retraining go on in the academic workplace; only further refinement does.

This entrenchment of mind is reinforced by tenure, that unusual privilege possessed by a good percentage of the faculty at America's better academic institutions. Established almost a century ago to protect professors who could be fired if they expressed ideas offensive to a university's proprietors or administration, tenure today rarely serves that purpose (as witness the wholly exceptional Franklin case). Instead, it bestows permanent security of employment on a distinct class of professional workers, few of whom today would be inclined to write or say anything politically or socially offensive. Despite the fact that tenure has largely outlived its original purpose, however, it is not likely to be abandoned. In universities, merely to be obsolete is not reason enough to be set aside. Tenure is, moreover, one of those perquisites of academic life that serves to compensate a group of highly trained men and woman for their relatively low salaries. Such a class of people—whose training has taken many years and whose expertise can be considerable—do not earn what similarly qualified lawyers, accountants, and physicians earn. But they have what those professions do not have: lifetime security of employment. Tenure is now enjoyed as an employee benefit, not a protection, by most of the professors who have it. And about two-thirds of those teaching full time in colleges and universities have that benefit or can imagine acquiring it.[1]

But for deans or provosts, the protective entitlement of tenure means that professors are immune to most of the means of suasion or constraint that govern employment in most other professional realms. Moreover, as those deans and provosts know, tenure is no guarantee of institutional loyalty. A tenured professor is not bound to the institution in any way. While he or she can choose to be very responsive to it, devoting much time to its well-being, indifference to it or even downright hostility are also options. Academic administrators get to know that the only true dedication—across faculty ranks—is not to the institution but to the career and the discipline. One is first an art historian or chemist, and it is to the body of fellow professionals—other art historians or other chemists—that one first looks for acknowledgment, status, and honor.

All of which, as I learned those first few years as a dean in the 1980s, makes the management of faculty a subtle and difficult art. In fact, much of a dean's work is not managing faculty members but satisfying them. The better the institution and the better the faculty, the less a dean's work is to spur people on or to improve their productivity. Rather, the main job is keeping the best of them from migrating to other institutions. With institutional loyalty registering a low pulse rate at even the best schools, what does a dean do to retain the presence of a "star"? As a Stanford dean, I first saw stardom when it came to the tenure decision for a young and exceptionally enterprising biologist. In reviewing his file in 1983, I noted that he had never, in fact, taught a Stanford course, not one. He had given lectures in other people's courses, had given seminars at other universities, and had directed graduate students in his lab. But an actual class under his own name? No such thing was on the record. I was left with an odd profile to share with my colleagues and the members of the A & P Committee who asked about his research, teaching, and service. But such a remarkable absence did not really matter. The trump card on the table, proudly submitted by the department, was that three other institutions, all of them with prestige equal to that of Stanford, were actively seeking the young professor, and all of them were offering him tenure and other perquisites. What did it matter that no record of teaching existed? Our response therefore had to turn not on what he would offer us, but what we could offer him. At such a moment, as we thought of various blandishments, it became clear to me that a dean is foolish to think that he directs people or events but wise to keep in mind that he responds to them.

Successful deans are skilled, then, at understanding the resources they have and allocating them in ways that gratify the best faculty members while keeping the others at least not unsatisfied, all the while maintaining that everyone is being treated in an egalitarian fashion. However, any close inspection of the budgeting of a large school, such as one embracing the social sciences, the natural sciences, and the humanities, reveals that while all colleagues are equal, some are more equal than others. While everyone accepts the fact that universities should pay senior professors more than their junior colleagues, it is hard to explain why schools pay economists more than language professors or why chemists more than art historians. A standard explanation (one that cries out to be demystified) is that "economists can compete for jobs in the outside corporate market" and "chemists can nail down big salaries with pharmaceutical companies." But many economists neither would nor could work for the corporate world, just as many chemists would refuse to work for BigPharm. Nonetheless, it is a tradition that some disciplinary callings customarily live uptown and others live in the low-rent districts. Thus faculty life is like American society in general: a society made up of many classes, richer and poorer, suffused by the reassuring ideal of equality.

Other lessons came to me that first year in the dean's office. Many professors, I learned, can become quite skilled at determining just what part of their day will be spent in teaching vs. research, with their preferences customarily coming down in favor of research. But a dean must keep in mind something not always on the minds of the faculty, namely that the university has presented itself to the public as an institution devoted to teaching and has charged parents large annual tuition payments for that very teaching. One duty of a dean was long ago noted by Henry M. Wriston, an experienced university president, namely, "to make the college what the president has long asserted it already is." Thus, while observing the faculty who are behaving in ways invisible to those parents, a dean, working with the several departments and their own leadership, has to preserve the honor of the institution, and, in this instance, to make sure that the students are, in fact, being well taught. This a dean must do while recognizing that teaching "loads" vary widely and that many natural scientists will do most of their teaching in labs with a few graduate students or postdoctoral assistants, not in classrooms, while those in English will mostly see students in lecture halls and seminar rooms at definite hours. My days were spent in nudging, suggesting, and even challenging a large and wholly heterogeneous body of professionals to do certain things like teaching—on behalf of the larger mission of the university—while knowing that my power to command that behavior could be exposed at any time as the frail reed it was.

A dean's work can consume, as mine did, many hours and yet can generate the feeling that one has accomplished little. Henry Rosovsky, the revered former dean of the Harvard faculty, noted that "my activities would consist of seeing many people, shuffling papers, writing letters, and chairing innumerable committees. Frequently these activities did not result in measurable progress or benefit, but I always returned home at night convinced that my time had been used productively."[2] I know how he felt, and was also able to convince myself that I had spent my time effectively. This kind of confidence, based on very little, is like all forms of faith and must be understood as such. It can be fortified, and often is, by the belief that another person in the same place would have been less competent and hence the outcome worse. I employed that argument when talking to myself and assumed other deans and administrators made use of it too. Like all people employed in odd ways, I learned early on as a dean that whistling in the dark was part of the job.

The most painful lesson coming to me when in the dean's office was that while my circle of acquaintances had greatly expanded, my number of friends had not. Even my slender power seemed to act as a disincentive to friendship. Once people believed I could "do something" for them or fail to do so, easy amicability withered. In later years, when I became a president, this lesson about friendship became even more poignant to me. Yes, I would get to know many more people—and from many more walks of life—than had I remained in the English department. But acquaintances do not become friends as long as power, or the perception of power, is hovering in the background.

Over my office desk, I kept a quotation from Abbot Lawrence Lowell, the president of Harvard from 1909 to 1933. It said: "An administrator should never feel hurried, or have the sense of working under pressure, for such things interfere gravely with the serenity of judgment that he should always retain." But down below on my desk was my daily calendar, a careful record, broken down into fifteen-minute segments, of meetings, obligations, and appointments for each of the days of the week, weekends included. I liked to imagine what President Lowell, looking down from his serenity, would think of the way I spent my time. Perhaps he would be aghast but then would understand, as I did, that a certain kind of person, having once known the scholar's pace—long meditative considerations of books, quiet dialogues with students, and leisurely conversations with colleagues—could reorder his life so that his attention span resembled that of a five-year-old: spasmodic and inconsecutive. Meeting followed meeting; appointments came by the dozen; I suffered no existential anxiety about "what to do" because my calendar told me precisely what to do.

But I would have told Lowell that I took pleasure in this new tempo, it being a kind of response to the first years of my life at Stanford, defined as that early period had been by long gestations, delayed gratifications, and all the other typical features of the scholar's inward ways. I would have told him that I was learning to exchange "reflection" for "action" and to replace the customs of intellectual self-initiation with the realities of external demand. I reacted to the challenges of others—the faculty, my administrative colleagues, and budgetary pressures—rather than to challenges I could impose on myself. And I was, as I now and again reminded myself, uniting what seemed, in my graduate school days and in my days in the English department, disparate: thought with action, mental pursuits with "political" pursuits (even though my politics were institutionally confined).

Perhaps Richard Russo is right in his novel *Straight Man* when he says, "a liberal arts dean in a good mood is a potentially dangerous thing. It suggests a world different from the one we know." Looking back on my days in the dean's office, I think I was in a good mood most of the time. While that did not make me dangerous, I can understand why a fair-minded observer might have thought me strange. But what may have been strangeness to others was compelling to me. Even after acknowledging the various limitations within which I worked—chief among them, the autonomy of the faculty and the constraints of the budget—the fact remained that I was continually at the center of decisions and processes that propelled a massive organization. And here was the great consolation: the goal of that organization—the creation and the conservation of knowledge—was of unquestionable social good. In addition, the oddity of the organization appealed to me: its ancient roots, its peculiar customs, and even its tolerance of inefficiency and redundancy, but most importantly, the way it was unlike anything else by virtue of its obsession with getting down to the truth of all matters, be they philosophical, biological, linguistic, chemical, or artistic. It pursued that obsession in ways much more intricate than I could have imagined had I not entered the dean's office. Russo's words stuck with me: I had entered a world different from the one I had once known. And while cynicism was always an option for me—and while a cynical tone perhaps marks these paragraphs—I was too interested in the immense structure of higher education of which I was a part to let cynicism take over. Deans, I decided, are built that way: they believe that the importance of the work overrides all the arguments against it.

In the fall of 1985, after I had spent four years as a dean, I was named vice provost by Stanford's provost, James Rosse. Rosse, who had been my colleague in the dean's office, now asked me to help him with academic planning and development. The consequences of taking that job were twofold: I came to learn a great deal about how a university raises money, and I recognized that I would never return to the English department. I continued teaching (the number of students interested in reading *Ulysses* seemed inexhaustible), but I was losing my identity as a professor and assuming another role at the university. I was swept up in Stanford's campaign to raise an amount of money—one billion dollars—that no university had tried to raise before. Under the direction of Rosse and the vice president for development, the campaign became a highly sophisticated machine to locate and rate potential donors around the world, to stimulate academic departments and schools to propose specific goals for their own enhancement, to hire an army of fundraisers, and, with Donald Kennedy's charismatic leadership, to persuade thousands of people that there was no better place for their philanthropic dollars than with Stanford University.

Campaigns, as Rosse saw them, were best defined as "wartime." Everything on the campus got mobilized and the institution picked up its pace, used new language to describe itself, and paid less attention to what it had been than to what it could be. Of course, for the Stanford I knew, this was nothing novel. That kind of ambition had been part of the institution for decades, for Stanford had undergone an acceleration of reputation and power that few universities could match. It had been one kind of place in the '50s—good, pleasant, and relaxed Californian—and had become quite another in the '80s—hot, competitive, and international. The campaign was created to take advantage of that growth and visibility and to amass the kind of financial resources to move it further ahead. To make that excitement possible and to give it substance was largely Rosse's job. Not every good academic idea could find a donor; and donors sometimes wanted to give money for programs the university did not need. He had to make sure that he could match the announced needs of the individual academic units of the university with the interests of donors.

Month by month, meeting by meeting, Rosse showed me how to pair philanthropic capacity with academic aspiration. He was a deft teacher. An economist by training and an expert on the complicated issues of newspaper ownership and monopolies, he came from Omaha and showed his Midwestern background at every turn: wholly ungiven to any form of ostentation or self-important remark, he was fair, terse, and unerringly objective. He knew what he was doing and did it expertly, with no wasted motion. Problems were like nuts to be cracked. Choose the correct angle, apply the right force, and then move on to the next problem. I admired the competence he brought to every problem and once told him so. But, in a characteristic response, he said: "Thanks. If I can keep my rate of error down to thirty percent, I feel good." (That kind of modesty gave me considerable solace in later years.) In time, all that money and more was raised, with the university completing its "Centennial Campaign" in February 1992, with a total of $1.27 billion. The success of that campaign, five years in duration, stimulated other universities to mount campaigns even more ambitious than Stanford's. Something momentous had thereby happened in higher education, and by the late 1980s, I had seen what historical momentum, ambition, and diplomatic expertise with donors could do for one university. I took the lessons I learned with me later to other institutions.

Perhaps it was Stanford's success, perhaps it had to do with the way search firms work, perhaps it was the workings of the academic grapevine, but early in the academic year 1986–87 I began to receive letters from other universities and colleges asking if I would be interested in being a candidate—dean, provost, president—for a position: the University of Pennsylvania, Indiana University, Southern Methodist, Reed College. This was a heady experience and stimulated my imagination and ambition. What would it be like to have a much more important administrative job at a good school? All the key positions were already occupied at Stanford. If I were to test myself as a mature administrator, it would have to be somewhere else. I took all the possibilities seriously, sent the schools my curriculum vitae, and flew to interviews. By now, I recognized that if the right position came, I would leave Stanford. But no such position materialized. That seemed to be all right; I would remain patient with what I had. I had a wonderful job at Stanford; our family was happy; I had some minor success as a teacher and scholar; the weather was perfect; and Stanford was in the ascendant. On the other hand, I knew I wanted yet more administrative experience and challenge. Out of such odd yearnings are careers in midlife made. By the winter of 1986, I knew I was ready to go.

ENDNOTES

1. "About 45 percent of all full-time faculty at Title IV degree-granting institutions were tenured in fall 2003 . . . an additional 20 percent were nontenured but in tenure-track positions." See *Staff in Postsecondary Institutions, Fall 2003, and Salaries of Full-Time Instructional Faculty, 2003–2004*, report from the National Center for Education Statistics (http://nces.ed.gov/pubs2005/2005155.pdf).
2. Rosovsky, *The University: An Owner's Manual* (New York: W.W. Norton, 1990), pp. 213–14.

19

Diversity University

In fall of 1987, Haverford College, my alma mater, announced a search for a new president. Twenty-six years had passed since I graduated from the College. I was still using the intellectual capital it had given me. Haverford had formed my understanding of intellectual and ethical standards. My most intense memories of not knowing and then knowing came from that campus. I had made big mistakes there and I corrected them there. When I wrote, I could feel my Haverford teachers still standing over me, watching and editing. No institution in my life had left a stronger imprint on me. And so, without hesitation but with a sense of elation that such an opportunity had come about, I put in my name as a candidate for the presidency. I wanted to go back.

The elaborate dance of "the presidential search process" then began. This highly structured and labor-intensive ritual typically involves a committee, sworn to absolute confidentiality, made up of school trustees, faculty members, representatives of the staff, a few students, and a search firm. This committee's role is to winnow the list of candidates to a small number of people who are then inspected by others on the campus. What it does not usually recognize is the role it plays for the candidates. While the committee rightly thinks its function is to scrutinize candidates and then, one by one, eliminate them, the candidates all the while are rightly scrutinizing the committee members to see what it can learn from them about the school. Each party studies the other. The committee can lose interest in a candidate; but the candidate can always make the first move and go home. Both the wooing and the drawing back go on continually, with each party to the courtship presenting itself in the most attractive fashion possible while keeping open the option to withdraw.

But no matter the time spent in the process (at least half a year), neither gets to know much about the other. That is why mistakes are sometimes made. The interviews are too short and can play to attributes (such as the talent to generate sound-bite responses to complicated inquiries) that are irrelevant to how a person would perform in the job. Immediate impressions trump substantive inquiry. Letters of reference are usually superficial, composed of laudatory but vague adjectives. Informal background checks, if permitted, tend to be hit or miss with respect to the kinds of information gathered. And the committee, by virtue of its size and composition, often guides itself into the safe waters of compromise, minimizing risk and maximizing the public benefits of a unanimous selection. In sum, the committee is governed, for good and for ill, by the venerable conventions of all committees. But no better way of selecting presidents has been found.

In time, I learned that I had been selected as a finalist for the Haverford position, and JoAn and I were invited to the campus for a frosty fall visit of three days. Scores of people in various settings, morning, noon, and night, carefully looked us over. I worried that some Haverfordians would bring up the theft of the silverware, my poor grades in the sophomore year, and the woeful immaturity I had demonstrated when first a Haverford student. Then, amid great embarrassment, my candidacy would end. To my great surprise, nothing like that happened. Instead, the entire silverware episode and everything surrounding it was happily told and retold as an illustrative tale about "how it was then." While I felt a considerable weight lifted from my consciousness, I wondered whether the College had lost some of the ethical Quaker edge.

Although I ended up as one of two finalists in the search, I was not selected as Haverford's president. Tom Kessinger, whom I had known when we were both students there, was. I was acutely disappointed and, for a while, felt that the very best job I could ever have would not be mine. I could see, however, why Tom was chosen. A University of Chicago Ph.D., he was well respected in the community of experts on international affairs; during the late 1970s and into the 1980s he worked with the Ford Foundation in India and Southeast Asia, publishing a book about North India; he also was a Quaker. All of these attributes spoke to important values of Haverford. And I knew he revered, as I did, the College and all it stood for. Good for Haverford, I thought, but too bad for me.

But that same fall, another presidency opened up: Wesleyan University in Connecticut. It seemed to be just like Haverford: small, Eastern, serious, liberal in spirit, with a history rooted in early-nineteenth-century religious enthusiasm (Methodist rather than Quaker). I talked to people at Stanford about it and read as much as I could about the school's reputation, its faculty, and its present standing. Everything looked excellent. I sent in my name. In due course, and in obedience to the same ritual of meetings, interviews, and a campus visit, I became a finalist for the job. The search committee was led by the chairman of Wesleyan's trustees, Steven Pfeiffer, a young man who, after his four successful years at Wesleyan as a student-athlete, his Rhodes scholarship to Oxford, and his graduation from Yale Law School, had fitted himself out with the grave sobriety of a man many years his senior (this, I took it, was obligatory for him in his role as a Washington corporate lawyer). Conducting me through the search process, he gave me to understand that his job was delicate and immensely complicated, and that he had to contend with a variety of competing interests, factions, power bases, and difficult personalities. He told me in hushed confidential conversations that Wesleyan was a mosaic of liberal, moderate, and conservative blocs, that the faculty members on the search committee were not entirely in agreement with the trustee members, and that the student representatives had particular interests of their own. He intimated that the person ultimately to be selected for the presidency would have to be every bit as astute and sensitive as he himself was. He also told me that whoever became Wesleyan's next president would "have very big shoes to fill," for the retiring president, Colin Campbell, had served superlatively amid enormous stresses and challenges for almost two decades. I took all of this in, thinking at the time that Pfeiffer seemed to be overdramatizing what was, after all, a normal event in the life of every university or college, the succession from one presidency to another. Little did I know.

After the next-to-last meeting, in New York City, with the search committee—during a three-hour question-and-answer event that felt like my Ph.D. oral exam at Berkeley—I asked if I could visit the campus, never having seen it. How could the committee say No? So, on a Saturday in Middletown, Connecticut, I spent the day peering into a few classrooms, walking on the grounds, and trying to imagine what being Wesleyan's president would be like. I noticed oddities here and there: pennies colored red flung on the grass, artificial spider webs fastened to campus trees, and posters everywhere denouncing racism, sexism, and monopoly capitalism. The webs, a passing student told me, stood for the nefarious conspiracy between the trustees of the institution and South African apartheid; the pennies, he said, stood for the blood money that such a conspiracy had generated. I thought: Berkeley. I felt at home in such an atmosphere, given what I had known of radical politics elsewhere, while I was startled by the contrast between the lovely old Connecticut brownstone buildings and the fervency of the political expressiveness. But I felt I could handle all of this. Again, little did I know.

In midsummer, I was summoned from California to meet one last time, and on this occasion with all the trustees, not the search committee. The day was muggy and the venue was a down-at-the-heels motel near LaGuardia Airport. But inside the motel, an elaborate and delicate drama was to be enacted. The ritual of question and answer, challenge and response, was again invoked. The inquiries were by now familiar to me—what academic values did I prize most highly, how important was teaching to me, what was the future of a liberal arts college that carried on research, how did I make decisions—and so, inevitably, were my responses. As the afternoon wore on, I sensed that although I was being interrogated, I was, at the same time, being courted. The trustees wanted me to like them and the instrument of their wooing would be their excellent questions. So while they made me stand and deliver, they seemed to want me to admire the intelligence of their inquiries, and I was glad to do so. Now and again a trustee complimented me on the way I had put things, and I did not lose the opportunity to smile admiringly at the phrasing of some of their questions. Thus we played our respective roles as the time went on, each party knowing what to say, how to react, in short, how to behave in order to bring the search to a gratifying and appropriate end. After some two hours, Pfeiffer, who had adopted the role of interlocutor and diplomat, took me outside and told me again that his job leading the search was more complicated and difficult than I could imagine and that Wesleyan was "different." Not knowing what to make of this rather cryptic remark, I blurted out that, given all of its complexities, perhaps he should take on the job himself. But he was quick to remind me that his job in Washington was, in fact, much more difficult than that of the Wesleyan presidency. So I wished him well in the search, thanked all the trustees, and got on a plane back to California.

That same evening, back at home and at dinner with friends, I received a call from Pfeiffer offering me the job. The terms of his offer were generous but carried, unmistakably, the tone that one of the pleasures I would have would be working with him. With company present, I was able to tell JoAn the news only in a whispered aside. The next day, I called Pfeiffer back and accepted the offer. That would mean that we would be leaving Stanford and I would be taking up the presidency of Wesleyan in the fall of 1988. I could not have been happier. This, I was utterly sure, would be a wonderful chapter in our lives.

But what did I know about being a president? What knowledge, what skills, could I bring to Wesleyan? Although I had spoken with calm confidence to the search committee and the trustees when asked the formulaic questions about my approach to problems and my understanding of academic life in all its aspects, my inner self told me that the difference in "talking president" and "being president" was immense. The first day on the job would close that gap swiftly and decisively. After that, everything would change and I would begin a new and different role. In anticipating that day, I knew I would need a picture of myself as president. I would have to have a way to understand the most demanding job I would ever have. The word "role" kept coming back to me. Presidents aren't just people. They also represent something; they symbolize, for everyone in the university community, a way of being. But what would be my role, my way of being?

After some long walks through the streets of Palo Alto, the answer came to me: I would be a "teacher." After all, that is what I had been for most of my professional life. At Wesleyan, then, I would seek to explain things, clarify things, and encourage people to see things as they had not seen them before. My "class" would be the Wesleyan community in its entirety. Because I knew that excellent teaching lay at the heart of all the institution was, I would not seek to transform the place, but try to make it the best possible version of its teaching self. In building upon its traditions, I would find ways to explain and illuminate them—to the faculty, to the students, and to all others. In reaching out to the alumni, I would remind them of what they had once learned. I would teach courses myself and, in thus joining with my faculty colleagues, would work to exalt teaching as a wonderful profession. With such a role fixed in mind, and having readied myself as best I could for Wesleyan and all it would be for us, JoAn and I drove across the country in the late summer of 1988.

That fall, as we were settling in, moving our meager belongings into the handsome presidential home located in the middle of the campus, *Vogue* magazine published an article about Wesleyan, titled "Twenty Something," which laid out, in excited terms, the kaleidoscopic nature of the place: "the *hot* college of the moment . . . politically liberal and academically rigorous . . . passionately compassionate . . . activist . . . raging social life." One word dominated the article: Wesleyan was "diverse."[1] It was, *Vogue* said, politically diverse, racially diverse, pedagogically diverse, and diverse with respect to all sexual matters. And indeed, for the six years I was to serve as president, "diversity" dominated the campus. It was used as a term of praise, or an explanation, or an apology, or a defense, of everything and anything that happened. As I came to understand the school, even the conservative faculty members on campus, who themselves may have wished that the prevailing culture were not quite so diverse, had gotten used to describing themselves as one part of the diversity. As I began my presidency, I knew I would have to understand the term better, would have to find out how it had come to pervade the campus. Recent history gave me part of the answer.

Until the mid-1960s, Wesleyan had been a solidly good, somewhat patrician liberal arts school with a wholly attenuated
Methodist heritage. It could compare itself, with only a little
reaching, to Amherst and Williams. Not quite as selective nor
quite as prestigious as they, it nonetheless was proud to be one of
the "Little Three" of superb New England liberal arts colleges. Its
student body, coming from both private and public secondary
schools in New England and the Eastern seaboard, was almost
entirely white, mostly Protestant, and middle class. As part of an
early manifestation of a liberal attitude, it had been the only one
of the "Little Three" to admit Jews in any appreciable numbers in
the 1930s and 1940s. Coeducational in the nineteenth century, it
had reverted to being an all-male institution in 1910 (as the story
went, the male students resented the fact that the women did well,
the women were made to leave, and, as a result, Connecticut
College—for women—was founded in 1911). It did not admit
women again until 1970. Wesleyan was preppy, proper, and proud
of its identity.

But two forces changed all of that: money and the 1960s. As a
result of being forced in 1965 by the Internal Revenue Service to
divest itself of American Education Publications (an entity publishing *My Weekly Reader*, the popular news magazine for school-
children) as "unrelated business income," Wesleyan wound up
owning stock from the buyer. That buyer was a new company—
Xerox—and, in short order, those stock holdings became enormously valuable and Wesleyan became rich. Its endowment became
one of the largest, for a liberal arts institution, in the nation.
Wesleyan then went about changing itself from a school with only
modest means and modest ambition to a school with very large
ambitions. It changed the structure of its academic departments,
converting them into multidisciplinary "colleges," such as the
College of Letters and the College of Social Studies. It strengthened
its graduate programs and its Center for Advanced Studies, and
invited to the campus such celebrated personages as Hannah
Arendt, Daniel Patrick Moynihan, Carl Schorske, C. P. Snow, and
Luigi Barzini. It set up a university press. In 1967, it appointed as
president Edwin D. Etherington, the youthful and dashing former

president of the American Stock Exchange. It had money, it had aspiration, and it believed it had nowhere to go but up.

After the assassination of Martin Luther King, Jr., and in the spirit of the activist '60s, it also decided that it should use some of its wealth to respond to the problems of racism in America. In 1965, only 14 black students attended Wesleyan. But in 1970, as a consequence of a new admission policy instituted that year, 12 percent of the entire student body and 20 percent of the first-year class was black. At the same time, Harvard and Yale had black enrollments of no more than 5 percent. Black students were recruited to Wesleyan from inner city projects, from poor rural areas, and from the suburbs. The strategy was "instant assimilation." The idea was that every black student would have a white roommate and, in time, or so the thinking went, racial differences would dissolve and racial understanding would flourish in the larger fabric of the place.

The actual results quickly turned out to be nothing like that. It did not take long for the school's noble dreams to fall victim to distrust and suspicion. The black students did not mix well with the white students and thought many of the professors were condescending if not worse. Cries went up from those newly recruited students that Wesleyan was not a good place at all, but "racist," and the administrative leaders and faculty were no more than "white liberal swine"; some felt they were patronized tokens. At the same time, many of the faculty members grew to have serious doubts about the entire experiment, many were bewildered, and some became resentful of the presence of students they believed unprepared for Wesleyan's academic challenges. Some white students feared that their black roommates were little more than hoodlums. The result was a situation so heated and tense that it generated national publicity. In early 1970 the *New York Times* published an article, "The Two Nations at Wesleyan University,"[2] portraying the institution as having undertaken a social experiment that had gotten badly out of hand. The *Times* suggested that Wesleyan was a place where liberalism was ravaging itself, and, as it reported, "No one on the Connecticut campus has any illusions left." But the administration, undaunted, forwarded its agenda even in the face of threatened violence, the takeover of buildings, and several instances of arson. As a spokesperson said to the *New York Times*, "We have passed the point of no return."

Because Wesleyan pressed on, and as the civil rights movement became connected with the antiwar movement, the school found itself deeply enmeshed in all the political and social problems of the time. To each of them, it responded with liberal hope and liberal activism, supported, where possible, by money from its newly handsome endowment. If the concern was the situation of women, Wesleyan would champion coeducation; if the concern was the presence of too few financially disadvantaged students, Wesleyan would put more of its resources into financial aid; and if the younger generation wanted to relax the rules about marijuana and other "recreational drugs," Wesleyan would look the other way.

This, then, was a new Wesleyan, one that attracted more and more activist students and, in some areas, a more liberal faculty. But as these extraordinary changes were going on, there was also another Wesleyan, an older Wesleyan, an institution characterized by a football team, fraternities, a reputation as "the singing school of New England," ivied buildings, secret societies, and, above all, its alumni. The older institution had a hard time speaking to the younger one. The trustees of the institution, the men and women who appointed me, were almost entirely from that older place. All schools, of course, change over time, with a generational difference between "today's" students and those who, once students, periodically return to the campus, sometimes as trustees. At Wesleyan, however, this difference had become, as almost everything else on the campus had become, exceedingly sharp and filled with tension. Thus the red-colored pennies and the symbolic spider webs. And thus also an event that again thrust the school into national headlines: the arrest, in May 1988, of 110 students who had been protesting for fifteen days against apartheid and who at last decided to block access to the administration building. Protests against apartheid were common at many good universities and colleges; the arrest of four percent of the student body was not.

By the fall of 1988, the Wesleyan administration was putting forward "diversity" to explain, and then to justify, everything. Just as Steve Pfeiffer had said, the place was different. Since the late 1960s, it had never backed away from an issue involving race, or gender, or poverty, or war. In fact, it savored those issues. In time, prospective students took note of this identity, as did high school counselors. Wesleyan's identity as a liberal institution became its "brand," the way it got to be distinguished from other places. If Wesleyan was your kind of place, then you were Wesleyan's kind of person. The press, always ready to fasten on the unusual and dramatic in American higher education, found Wesleyan a lively subject. The momentum affecting admissions and enrollment increasingly characterized the institution. This put the students of Wesleyan, year in and year out, in an unusually powerful position. The "brand" increasingly defined them and what they did, and this gave the school its profile in the eyes of parents, counselors, and authors of college guidebooks. The faculty, along with the administration, found itself uneasily adjusting to the position Wesleyan had achieved, and by 1988, this adjustment had created underlying strains and awkwardness. Not everyone agreed that Wesleyan was what the students and *Vogue* said it was: an intensely "liberal" or "progressive" or even "radical" place. Most of the trustees, as I was to find out time and again, were not happy with what had happened to "their" school. The conservative faculty members, those not caught up in ideological fervor but wanting to focus on their respective disciplines, were not at ease. I learned that many of my administrative colleagues, wanting to imagine that they were employed at a typical college, did not enjoy hearing about campus oddities. In short, if institutions can have crises of identity, Wesleyan had endured a prolonged one by the time the Chaces, fresh in from California, came to the campus in the fall of 1988.

ENDNOTES

1. Lisa Wolfe, "Twenty Something," *Vogue*, September 1988, pp. 682–85, 754.
2. Richard J. Margolis, "The Two Nations at Wesleyan University," *New York Times*, Jan. 18, 1970, pp. 9, 49, 54, 60.

20

Marching to a Different Drummer

Much has been written about being a university president—by those who, at one extreme, glorify what presidents can do and by those who, at another extreme, doubt the entire enterprise. A real job with much to do, or an impossible job with only ritualistic functions? Some see the office as a glorious station and others regard it as a kingship empty of power. In anticipating what I thought I could do at Wesleyan, I found comfort in the words of William Rainey Harper, long ago the president of the University of Chicago: "The life of a university officer is in many ways the most ideal that exists. The minister meets everywhere sorrow and sickness and death. The lawyer struggles against dishonesty, dissipation and fraud. The physician is almost wholly occupied with want and pain and suffering. With the college professor and the college president it is essentially different. They have to deal with all that is uplifting in life, with the constructive and not the destructive forces of life. The satisfaction which this brings no man can describe." On the other hand, I worried about what A. Bartlett Giamatti, once the president of Yale, came to feel: "Being president of a university is no way for an adult to make a living. Which is why so few adults actually attempt to do it. It is to hold a mid-nineteenth-century ecclesiastical position on top of a late-twentieth-century corporation."

Harper's lofty tone inspired me; Giamatti's dismissive analysis worried me. But no words from any former president could detain me as the new president of Wesleyan. I believed I was responsible for the welfare of the school. True, others—the faculty and the trustees—also had power and influence. But the presidential search would not have taken so long, nor would it have consumed so much thought and energy on the part of so many people, had my office been irrelevant. I knew as I began that universities consist of circles of power and inertia that work to constrain presidential power. I took that as a given. One of the dramas of higher education, enacted again and again, is the contrast between the publicly celebrated functions of the president and the residual power of the faculty. The president, occupying what he and others might believe is a bully pulpit possessing the power to promote change and new institutional direction, must consider how long the faculty has been in place, how deep-seated its interests are, and how strong its stamina to outlast the latest presidential initiative.

But new presidents do not spend time dwelling on the possibility of their impotence. Their terms are new. The omens are bright. The greetings are many and almost all are friendly. The campus looks like a garden of possibility. What could be more inviting than a community with brilliant faculty, lively students, eager administrative colleagues, and the energy that change always evokes? That's the way I began at Wesleyan in the fall of 1988.

That first year I met many people—faculty colleagues, other administrators, and scores of students, alumni, and parents. I concentrated all my attention on knowing the place—its history, buildings, traditions, and aspirations. Although I had proposed to myself that I would come to Wesleyan as "teacher," I spent those early months as "student." I brought together my six most important administrative colleagues into a council and I listened to them as they explained the place to me. Buttonholing people on the campus or taking them to coffee, I asked them to tell me what they thought I should know. The year passed quickly and pleasantly. Everyone was happy to remind me that I was in my "honeymoon" period, yet they were also likely to repeat Steven Pfeiffer's refrain, that Wesleyan "was different." While seeking always to define that important difference, we took in the pleasures of the New England landscape, met scores of people at receptions, and were month after month paraded before alumni groups in Connecticut and elsewhere on the Eastern seaboard. Being president seemed quite enjoyable, but I watched and listened. The prospect of Wesleyan being too "different" haunted me.

After several months of such study, my mind focused on three questions about Wesleyan. The first concerned what it called itself: "Wesleyan University." Since its founding in the nineteenth century, that had been its name. But in what proper sense was it a "university" and not, in fact, a "college"? I had come from Berkeley and Stanford and knew for certain they were universities. Their research activities were prodigious, and between a third and a half of their students were at the graduate level. The official gatekeeper for such nomenclature, the Carnegie Classification of Institutions of Higher Education, says that "doctoral" or "research" universities must offer a wide range of baccalaureate programs, and commit themselves to graduate education through the doctorate. They must award fifty or more doctoral degrees per year across at least fifteen disciplines. On the other hand, "colleges" emphasize baccalaureate, not graduate, programs. They award at least half of their baccalaureate degrees in liberal arts fields. While Wesleyan did offer a small number of graduate degrees in a few fields, fewer than 200 of its 2,850 students were not, in fact, *under*graduates. So Wesleyan, I thought, should be considered a "college" and not a "university." While I certainly did not want to change the name of the place, I thought I should resolve this confusion.

The second question for me was how I could best address an imbalance on the fiscal ledger. Although Wesleyan seemed sound with respect to money, I soon discovered that it was operating an $80 million annual budget with a $3.5 million deficit (this fact had not surfaced during the search process). In addition, it faced a $35 million budget of deferred building maintenance. Even a former English professor could recognize that this was not how things should be. The institution could no longer carry such a deficit, nor could it allow its buildings to continue in such disrepair.

The third question was how I could ask the campus community a delicate question: if the school had seen the many benefits of diversity, could we now tally up its costs? Wesleyan had achieved a reputation—much of that a product of the concentration, for twenty years, on diversity in all of its aspects. What now were the virtues of that concentration? What were the liabilities? Should we make a mid-course correction? If so, what?

These were all formal questions for me as president to answer. But another question, a private one, was just as important. It had to do with how JoAn and I now were to live—as we had never lived before. JoAn was an independent and resourceful woman with a Berkeley Ph.D. and her own intellectual ambitions. But now she was "official" and married to someone whose official identity was going to define everything he did. We lived in a grand and imposing place—a large and handsome nineteenth-century pile of brick, stucco, and capacious rooms. In that house, men and women came and went, preparing some of our meals, cleaning the rooms, and tending the gardens. At times, people we did not know moved about the place—planners, repairmen, delivery people, and even security personnel. Being residents of such a dwelling put us on display, even at times to ourselves. Across the rooms where receptions were held that first year, we caught ourselves looking at each other with mixed humor and embarrassment as she was introduced as the "First Lady." She thought it oddly amusing that people would call me "Mr. President."

When visitors came to the house for functions, they would sometimes inquire if the furniture was ours. Of course the answer was "No," but the question made us reflect on the fact that, only months before, we had lived in a small house most of whose modest furnishings descended from our days as graduate students. Our only real possessions at Wesleyan were books, photographs, musical records, and memories. Our surroundings, which others might take as appropriate to our station, we took as accidents of fortune. And therefore, as long as we were at Wesleyan, we were never able to take them seriously. But they were there, all around us: chairs and tables, chandeliers, linen and crockery, cooks and servers, flowers and mahogany, the appointments and accoutrements of presidential life in a dwelling on the National Register of Historic Places.

That first year ended quietly. I had learned much about the school, and about New England, and so had JoAn. She began a book on adoption and how the needs of adopted children and the rights of their biological parents could best be balanced. She quickly learned the roles of the "First Lady." We saw the seasons in Connecticut: a lovely autumn with colors, a cold winter, and a spring, all too short. Northern California seemed a long way away, and it was, even though I brought it close to me in dreams of sunny days, cool nights, and air untouched by humidity. Commencement, with the sense of happy completion for everyone, came and went. I began to feel that, whatever the complexities of the job and all the surprises it might spring on me, I could hold up my end. I turned my attention to the next academic year, 1989–90.

During that year, the words of one of Wesleyan's trustees, Gerald Baliles, echoed in my mind. He told me that when he served as the governor of Virginia he learned that the single most important feature of administrative life was the "unexpected, the things you can't control, the accidents." He was right. It is a good way of thinking about our second year. It was one of disaster, pain, and, at the end, death.

It began with the presidential inauguration. This was to be a grand event. After all, the school had not put on such an inauguration for almost two decades. The date was selected—September 23—and invitations were sent out. I was told that "special music" had been created for the occasion. My extended family was present and accorded special seating. We invited friends, former teachers, people from Haverford and Berkeley and Stanford. Tom Flanagan and Ralph Rader, my two best Berkeley teachers, came. Donald Kennedy and Nan Keohane, respectively Stanford and Wellesley presidents, were to speak, as was Dana Gioia, a former Stanford student, now a poet of renown (and later to become chair of the National Endowment for the Arts). Another scheduled speaker was my Stanford colleague Arnold Rampersad, the eminent scholar of African-American studies. A lovely long green field was set aside for the formalities, and the audience of faculty, representatives from other institutions, and the administration was to face a stage richly overflowing with flowers. Elegant flags and gonfalons were designed and set on high. A procession was majestically to lead the platform party from the center of the campus, around Wesleyan's stately buildings, and then into the field while the new music set the tone for the proceedings.

In fact, what happened was Hurricane Hugo. The moment the procession got underway, what had once been a beautiful autumn day became a scene of sodden chaos. Hugo, a category five hurricane, was the single most destructive storm to strike the United

States for more than 100 years. In the twentieth century, no tropical cyclone along the United States east coast (north of Florida) ever recorded a lower pressure, stronger winds (160 mph), or higher tidal surges at landfall. When it discovered our little procession that Saturday, it hit with brutal force. The temperature dropped some twenty degrees in twenty minutes. The day darkened as if by biblical command; the sidewalks and lawns ran with water; gowns and caps were drenched; and everyone, cold and soggy, desperately sought haven. The long green field became pools of water and islands of grass; the flags drooped heavily; the chairs, all thousand of them, sat vacant beneath the rawness of the storm.

After an hour or so waiting in a basement room, and thanks to the extraordinary efforts of the buildings and grounds crew, we were all ushered into a dry and safe place—the old gym, fondly known as "The Cage." The crew moved the chairs and wiped them dry; they set up a stage and found a lectern and microphone. The platform party was brought together and again we took our places for the processional. Then, as we entered, I learned what kind of "special music" had been designed for the occasion.

A composition arising from the avant-garde ingenuity of one of the music professors, it was named "Clackers and Swoopers" and consisted of several students slapping two pieces of wood together at a regular beat while other students laboriously cranked the handles of antique sirens. As we solemnly approached the stage accompanied by this sound, I could see that some members of the audience were under the impression that a fire warning had been given. But then they looked at their programs and learned, to their astonishment, that the noise was part of the ceremony.

After others gave introductions, acknowledgments, and expressions of hope for the future, I went to the microphone to present my inaugural address. During that address I made my thoughts known about the name "Wesleyan University" and what it might erroneously imply about the level of research at the institution:

If being ever-expansive, enriched by professional schools, and driven by larger research imperatives of the state or of the whole nation, is being a university, we are not a university. If being far-flung and receiving large amounts of funding is being a university, we are not a university. The term can only bewilder us, can only blur our vision.

I thought I was pointing out an obvious truth—about where and what we were. But from the faculty came a voice: "This is war!" Of course I imagined objections from faculty members proud of their research activities, but I could not have imagined anyone interpreting my words as the equivalent of Pearl Harbor. I had issued no preemptive strike against research. I had sought only to remind everyone that teaching must come first at such a place: "unlike a university, which can be freely responsive to the inner imperatives of a discipline, no matter where they might lead, we must recognize that our research must forever circle back to our teaching. This is a hard truth, but truth it is." For weeks and months thereafter, word circled back among the faculty that I was "an enemy of research" and must be resisted at every turn.

As I continued to deliver my address, I turned to the question of Wesleyan's "diversity." Believing that the school's "diversity" had, in fact, made a fetish of difference and had only called attention to what was dissimilar about people rather than what united them, I asked the audience "to learn more about the building of a community, more about the establishment of a sense of commonwealth." I called on the spirit of Alexander Hamilton to help me, reminding my listeners that when he wrote one of the Federalist Papers, he saw how the young American nation could fly asunder if it did not pay attention to binding forces and unifying principles. As I quoted him,

> "it happens, that in every political association which is formed upon the principle of uniting in a common interest . . . , there will be found a kind of eccentric tendency . . . by the operation of which there will be a perpetual effort . . . to fly off from the common centre."

At this point, six African-American students strode to a position beneath the microphone, lowered their heads, and raised their hands, handcuffed together, in a show of silent militancy. I proceeded with my remarks, but after a few minutes of their demonstration, one of them handed me up a note. While continuing to read my own words, I sought to get some idea of what theirs were about. To what must have been the bewilderment of the audience, I continued with this double reading, my words aloud, their words silently to myself. The six students were demanding many things, all of them unanswerable at the time: that the university upgrade the African American Studies program to a department, increase the number of minority faculty, completely divest from South Africa, complete a comprehensive study of race relations on campus, and provide sensitivity training on issues of race for public safety officers. They then departed. The audience sat stunned.

I ended my remarks by drawing the audience's attention to Wesleyan's curriculum. I wanted to see if we could make more sense of the school's teaching efforts, and thus reduce the budgetary deficit. I said the institution

> embraces a cornucopia of interests, desires, hopes and impulses. With almost one thousand courses offered each year, and with more than 1500 individual tutorials and lessons, that curriculum is a celebration of our intellectual enthusiasm. It is also a glorious way of distracting ourselves from the duty we have, particularly to freshmen, of disclosing what our *credo* as scholars and teachers really is.

I thought I knew what I was doing; what I did not know at the time was how ridiculous my project would seem to many in the faculty audience. Each of those thousand courses and those 1,500 tutorials was proudly owned by someone, and while it might be admirable for us, in a *general* sense, to bring clarity and order to the curriculum, it was unlikely, in an *individual* sense, that we could make any changes at all. Collective will was one thing; proprietary control was another.

Having sounded these notes and announced my hopes to the audience, wet and perplexed, I was happy to bring this odd and memorable inauguration to an end. If ever an event was an omen of things to come, I had been given that omen. Baliles was right: the "unexpected, the things you can't control"—like torrential rains and agitprop student theater—would shape my presidency of Wesleyan. I had my aspirations, but circumstances beyond my control had their power. On the other hand, the faculty resistance to change would prove, as I would learn, more predictable and steady. On it I could always count.

If that was the beginning of the year, its end was no less jolting. In November, the student newspaper ran a story headlined, "Campus Tensions Running at an All-Time High," and quoted the student affairs dean as saying, "I can't remember a time in my association with Wesleyan when [human relations] were this bad with the possible exception of the late '60s." He went on to say that while there were some expressions of frustration on campus, he didn't anticipate any "major explosions." How unprophetic he was. On January 2, some 60 African-American students seized the admissions office and presented the administration with a list of concerns, requests, and "nonnegotiable" demands. Threatening to destroy the files of applying students, they said their takeover was a "peaceful protest, perhaps for the last time." They were right about that. It was the last peaceful protest, and a cascade of events followed: in early April, three separate acts of vandalism clouded the gala preview celebration of the new $22 million athletic center; shots were fired at night at the administration building; bulletins coming from organizations identifying themselves as D.A.G.G.E.R. (Direct Action Group to Generate Education Reforms) or S.T.R.I.K.E. (Students Rebuilding Institutions for Knowledge and Education) threatened further violent assaults if the curriculum did not soon include more courses on Africa, African-Americans, Latinos, and women.

On April 7, Wesleyan's head of public safety awakened me at 4:30 in the morning. "Bill, your office has been firebombed." I left the house, walked the few steps to the office, and saw both the early spring snow falling and the yellow-orange emergency lights of the fire department. Giant exhaust fans were sucking smoke out of the building and knots of firefighters and police officers surrounded it. When I was able at last to enter my office, I saw a chamber darkened by smoke, grime, and a greasy film covering every surface. Several Molotov cocktails thrown through a window had exploded across my desk and then caught the carpet on fire. No one had been hurt, but a firefighter told me that a custodian working in the building would have been instantly incinerated had the kind of backdraft common to such fires started up. The physical damage would take weeks and more than $60,000 to repair. More costly was the psychic injury to Wesleyan. It would take months to heal, and for many years the firebombing left a legacy of negative images of the school in the media. In those days, the serene language of William Rainey Harper came wafting back to me: the college president has "to deal with all that is uplifting in life, with the constructive and not the destructive forces of life. The satisfaction which this brings no man can describe." Happy William Rainey Harper.

The campus reaction to the event was paralysis. For weeks, no faculty member said anything to me about my burned office. No student spoke, though many of them had a good idea who had thrown the bombs. The trustees were disturbed but not surprised; they had endured years of protest against the school's policies, particularly its investment policies in South Africa. For them, student resistance to the administration had become perfectly ordinary, even familiar, perhaps part of the unusual charm of the place. The chairman of the board, now aware of a "complexity" at Wesleyan not even he could have imagined, adroitly distanced himself from me. What I, as the newcomer, was witnessing was a campus that had grown wholly accustomed to conflict and adversarial relations. A firebombing, at once spectacular and disruptive, could be seen as "diversity" in practice.

Yet there was no way, despite my best common sense, not to blame myself for what had happened. Given that my office—in a sense, my person—was the direct target of the bombers, I asked myself: what had I done to cause the firebombing? Was not the silence greeting me—the utter absence of any commiseration—a way that Wesleyan had of letting me know that something I had done had caused the calamity? With JoAn, I reviewed everything that had happened since we arrived. We backtracked over the days we had been on campus to locate the error of my ways. At the end, despite my willingness to accept responsibility, we could not find that error. Before the event, I had taken to lunch both of the students who were widely perceived—by the entire community—to have been the bombers. I had spent time with them and with scores of other students, many of whom seemed angry, at loose ends, and ripe with grievances. I had sympathized with them over the barbarisms of apartheid. Some knew that I had taught in the South and had been jailed there for civil rights activities. At the end, however, JoAn and I concluded that I was what I was: an administrator, a figure of authority, and thus, *ipso facto*, part of the malicious power structure. That was not going to change, and so I turned to the work I had been hired to do: be the president.

Even that duty was complicated for a few days. The head of public safety persuaded me to wear a bulletproof vest when I walked to and from my office. The distance was only some three hundred yards, but he was certain that the territory was dangerous. I wore the vest until the weight of its absurdity seemed heavier than the Kevlar itself.

Then, to make campus matters worse, in early May African-American students discovered that the basement walls of a residence hall they occupied had been defaced, overnight, by obscene racial epithets. Some referred, mysteriously, to "nigger bombs" and others were grotesque invitations to rape black women. The resident students were frantic with fear; the TV cameras arrived; and Wesleyan was once again in the news. Campus scuttlebutt pointed to the same two students behind the bombing as having stage-managed, with extraordinary cynicism, this event. One of them was African-American and had absorbed, as I well knew from talking to him, all he could read of the violent rhetoric and racial antagonism of Malcolm X. His strategy seemed to be one of imagining the worst that racists could do and then performing the acts himself. He must have contented himself by thinking that, after all, a racist *could* do such things.

At this point, when Wesleyan seemed hopelessly sapped by events and devoid of the psychological strength needed to recover, and when the faculty seemed incapable of assuming any responsibility for the institution, four professors at last came forward and publicly announced that neither I nor any other administrator could save Wesleyan. Only the faculty could do that, they said, and they asked colleagues to join them in protecting campus well-being. I rejoiced. In time, other colleagues answered affirmatively;

we joined forces; the students rallied with a large and festive "Unity Day," and just in time we brought the year to a peaceful end. Archbishop Desmond Tutu spoke at Commencement, and he brought his own healing power to us as he said: "Because of its greatness, Wesleyan has been the scene recently of reflection, perhaps in an intense form, on the kind of tension that exists in American society. It is a great privilege to be part of an institution that refuses to be an ivory tower."

No, not an ivory tower at all. There was even more to come. After the semester ended in late June, and as a terrible coda to a year disfigured by violence, one of the two suspected students was murdered in a park in nearby Hartford. His short life had been defined by profound instability of mind and confusion about his identity. Although entering Wesleyan as a conservative who upbraided me for not establishing a mandatory curriculum focused on the "enduring books" of Western culture, he quickly moved from the political right to the political left. By his sophomore year, infatuated with the notion of revolutionary violence, he proclaimed himself an African-American (although he was from a family of Lebanese-Americans), and at the end of his second year he purchased three high-powered automatic weapons and a cache of ammunition. Luring two other young people into his world of fantasy and guns, he told them he had a plan to spark a revolutionary uprising in the United States. He would give them several thousand dollars to buy illegal drugs; they were then to resell the drugs at a profit to addicts; the money would be used to arm American blacks. He added that he would give each of them a pistol for protection against the drug dealers, warning them both that if they lost the money, he would kill them. Wholly inept, they immediately lost the money, returned in full panic in order to see him, and, thinking to defend themselves against his threat, shot him in the back of the head.

No other school experienced what Wesleyan endured in 1989–90. Some things are unique, and the events of that year tell us little about American higher education in general. But what the year helped me to understand is that a president's reach does not extend to all those larger forces beyond the campus where many of his school's problems have their genesis. Baliles had been right: it is good to be prepared for exactly that for which no preparation is enough. Students are young, some are volatile, terrible things can happen. In part what occurred that year at Wesleyan had to do with only a handful of students who came to that campus bringing with them the violent pathologies of their lives. But in part it also had to do with the spirit of the place that received them.

In addition to the antiestablishment and rebellious attitudes it absorbed from the 1960s, Wesleyan also absorbed, and then magnified, a set of lessons stemming from its historical roots in New England. From Ralph Waldo Emerson's essay "Self-Reliance," it had heard these lines:

> Whoso would be a man must be a nonconformist. . . . Nothing is at last sacred but the integrity of your own mind. Absolve you to yourself, and you shall have the suffrage of the world. . . . No law can be sacred to me but that of my nature. Good and bad are but names very readily transferable to that or this; the only right is what is after my constitution; the only wrong what is against it. . . . What I must do is all that concerns me, not what the people think.

And from Henry David Thoreau's *Civil Disobedience* it had heard this:

> Let every man make known what kind of government would command his respect, and that will be one step toward obtaining it. . . . The only obligation which I have a right to assume is to do at any time what I think right.

Independence, the singular mind, the self in its absolute rightness, and the separation of the individual from society: these were first New England lessons, which became the lessons of the '60s, and they are American lessons. For Wesleyan, however, they became the paramount lessons. By the time we arrived on campus, the institution had no need to worry about its skill in marching to a different drummer. But its mastery of that one skill had left it impaired to learn another: how to build a community, how to establish a working commonwealth. And thus, when students in violent rebellion met an institution whose sense of commonwealth had withered, their eccentric tendencies could not be constrained by any common center.

The end was pitiful for the student who died, painful for all who saw the school in deep jeopardy, and injurious to Wesleyan's reputation. Those four faculty members who recognized their responsibility to the institution had to reassemble the pieces of the commonwealth that alone guaranteed their professional security. They labored on behalf of all their colleagues. I helped them in every way I could, for they needed my attention and my resources. But I also needed them, knowing as I did that while one year had ended, another was soon to begin. We would all be back. When we returned, we had to work together. What we knew is what every teacher and administrator knows: nothing is more regular in higher education, even when tested to the utmost, than the rhythm of the semesters. During the summer, we all had to get ready for the next year. It would come quickly enough.

21

The Puzzle of Leadership

The academic year 1990–91 was my third year at Wesleyan. I thought at the time that I would stay there for many years. I had only begun to work on some of the major issues of the place: its budgetary shortfall, its far-flung curriculum, and, above all, the painful question of its identity. There was a great deal to do. Over the years Wesleyan had lost key faculty, and these individuals, I knew, had provided much of the intellectual lifeblood of the place. We had to replace them with scholars who would replenish and then increase the school's educational capital. Everything I knew about colleges and universities had told me that you build institutional strength on the quality of the faculty; nothing can substitute for it. And I wanted to fulfill the pledge I had made to the campus that at least four of the nineteen vacant professorial positions would be filled by people of color, and ten of the nineteen by women. This was not going to be easy to do.

I was pleased when the fall semester opened in a subdued way, even though several students wrote to say they would be taking the fall semester off, giving as their reason that they could not face the prospect of returning to so troubled a campus. The place already felt different to me, and I thought those students would have returned to a calmer institution; the terrible storm had passed. But memories stayed on. Wesleyan's morale had been shaken badly by the events of 1990. In the public eye it was a place where a key building had been firebombed and a student had been murdered. And the local newspapers followed closely the trial of the other student involved in the firebombing (he pleaded not guilty, saying he had been at home with his mother when the attack took place, and although an accomplice testified otherwise, the jury found him not guilty).

As the year began, I proceeded to do what, on occasion, presidents must do. Concluding that Wesleyan did not have the administrative strength it needed to resolve the issues it faced, I asked for and accepted the resignations of several officers who had served the school for a long time. The chief academic officer had worked for Wesleyan in a meritorious way for years, exercising considerable diplomatic skill in countless situations with his faculty colleagues, both good and troublesome. He gracefully returned to the faculty and resumed his career as superb teacher and scholar. The dean of students, who, years before, had been one of the first black students at Wesleyan, had risen to administrative prominence, contending again and again with difficult students, impossible students, and some very good students. But exasperated and fatigued by his job, his for seventeen years, he left Wesleyan to take a position with the Ford Foundation. The third officer, who for years supervised in a distant and supercilious way both fundraising and public relations, seemed wedded to the style of my predecessor and considered me an unfortunate and unwelcome interloper. After several failed attempts to get him to accept the fact that I really was the president, I told him that I would begin a search for his successor. He left the university in anger and resentment.

New college and university presidents find that the changes they want to make in the administrative structure are not accomplished easily or quickly. That was my experience; it is the experience of every president. The administrative colleagues I had inherited had been at the institution for a long time. Each of them had allies, networks of memory and friendship, and a sense of rootedness. For me to make personnel changes was to challenge the weight of institutional history. While some observers might believe that a university president can behave like a CEO, striking with impunity down through the layers of personnel to achieve an instant result, everything the president does is subjected to the closest and most protracted possible reading. Universities, not being corporations, are profligate with time. Hence nothing on a campus is viewed only once; every change, as well as every possibility of change, is scrutinized again and again. Moreover, the "hermeneutics of suspicion," as literary scholars term it, is visited upon all new things. And it does no good to consider the job I had to be equivalent to that of a CEO. The business CEO is responsible only to a board of directors and to shareholders; the university or college president is responsible to a greater array of parties, each of them attached to its own system of values and its own proprietary relationship to the institution. Chief among these parties are the trustees and the faculty. Each of them has a hold on the president's tenure, and a faculty that has lost confidence in a president possesses as much authority as the trustees who officially appoint presidents and accept their resignations.

The personnel changes I made were more or less accepted by the campus and Wesleyan seemed ready to work with new people. But I did not appoint them all by myself. Everything important on a university campus is done collectively. For example, a search committee, made up almost entirely of faculty members, and chaired by a senior member of the faculty, was established to find the new chief academic officer. Because authority is oddly dispersed on the Wesleyan campus, as it is on every campus, this new officer would formally report to me, but the faculty group would have a great deal to say about his or her selection. The principle of "dual control" would be in force, a principle that recognizes two facts: (1) presidents are the receptacles in which power is nominally placed, but much of that power is informally in the hands of others; and (2) faculty members are not so much the employees of the institution as they are its intellectual engine and its most important asset. They are "capital" rather than "labor." The faculty rightly demands primary control over educational processes, and considers trustee or presidential involvement in those processes as unacceptable. All of which makes "control" of the institution an ambiguous matter. Sometimes it's hard to know who is in charge of a college or university, and while the fiction of "presidential leadership" is often employed to mask this reality, the president—every president—learns after a while how much of his or her authority is, in fact, in the hands of others.

After a strenuous search, Wesleyan appointed Joanne Creighton as the new chief academic officer in the fall of 1990. She had been successful as the dean of the College of Arts and Sciences at the University of North Carolina, Greensboro, where she also was a professor of English. She brought toughness of mind and an admirably imperturbable manner to Wesleyan. "Another day, another problem solved" seemed to be her motto. She looked at the academic budget, winced once or twice, and got to work. She did not make the mistake, easy for someone new to the job, of first looking for items to cut; instead, she framed the process as one establishing what had to be saved. After that, in time, but with certainty: the cuts.

Beginning with a sense of priorities, she looked at her work as objective exercises in academic planning. This formalized her labors and depersonalized the process. For several painful months during the 1990–91 academic year, the faculty reared back and pleaded self-rule, but she briskly informed the chairs of departments that, after all, she held certain important cards, they being the collection of faculty positions reverting to her office upon the death or retirement of colleagues. She would reallocate them on the basis of her judgment of which departments were making good sense of what they were doing, what they were teaching, and where they were going. She was aware of the narcissistic tendencies of the faculty and their preference to cast blame rather than take responsibility for the institution, but she reminded them that Wesleyan would likely be their professional home for the rest of their lives. They had better care for it.

At times the faculty accused her of playing favorites, and this was true in an admirable sense: she gave preference to academic departments that were well organized and productive. And week by week, month by month, she employed her every resource to chip away at the culture of entrenched fiefdoms. In the spring of 1991, we together created a new committee, the Institutional Priorities Advisory Committee, made up entirely of faculty members. We asked its appointed members to use every fact available about the institution to establish what Wesleyan, at its best, could be. We would listen to their advice and then we, not they, would make the most of it. I wanted, and she wanted, the faculty to take what they already had—namely, a sense of rights and privileges—and to add to it a sense of responsibility and obligation. By the end of that academic year, I had willingly given up my position as chair of the academic council, announcing that a member of the faculty should take on the job—as occurs at most schools. Either it was an academic body or it was not. Although several faculty members first saw this as a ploy so ingenious that its malign administrative intent could not be discerned by even the closest inspection, everybody finally accepted it as only right and proper.

We were less successful in our efforts to make institutional sense of the process by which Wesleyan awarded tenure. We inherited a highly inefficient mechanism that presumed perfidy at every turn: within the department recommending a candidate, within the elected advisory committee that would spend hours mulling over the department's action, within the office of the provost bringing the case forward to the full complement of tenured faculty members, and also within the president who would take the case forward (if I deemed it meritorious) to the trustees for final approval. Although the faculty claimed to be interested in "quality control," the system confused the labor-intensive with the rigorous, adding to the mix the special ingredient of suspiciousness.

While Joanne and I only partially succeeded in making the system more rational and less wasteful of faculty time, we reconciled ourselves to the fact that the faculty should indeed figure prominently in that most crucial moment: the tenure decision, the means by which they would look after their own posterity. We could supervise the fairness of the system and mop up after the occasional derelictions of faculty duty, but we had no right to extract from the faculty the dignity of their own self-determination.

In time, and with the customary indulgence of other search committees, I found able successors to the remaining vacated positions. Although I was concerned about the institution's budgetary deficit, the chief financial officer, Bob Taylor, was a man of thoroughgoing integrity and competence. He had struggled for years with the institution's predisposition to live beyond its means. He had learned, as I was to learn, that no chief financial officer can alone balance the budget if the institution continually exerts a pressure to do things for which it does not have the money. I found at Wesleyan a collective desire—rooted in faculty hopes and dreams and endorsed by administrative sympathies and trustee lenience—to be a certain kind of institution, indeed a wonderful institution, but one that could not support itself. The chief financial officer could minimize here and there, look for savings, and exert discipline where possible. But Joanne Creighton and I had to exercise authority and judgment about how most of the money was found and used.

As the three of us—Joanne, Bob, and I—worked on these problems, I began to see that the three major issues at Wesleyan—its identity, its financial condition, and its curriculum—really were just one problem: could the institution shape its curriculum to reduce costs and also project to itself and to the interested public an attractive and compelling self-portrait? As I faced that issue, I asked others to face it too.

In addition to this imposing task, I also dealt at regular intervals with the single most exotic component of a college or university: the trustees. Those times came when the full complement of 33 men and women (mostly the former) descended upon Middletown from New York, Boston, Washington, Houston, Philadelphia, San Francisco, and other cities to accomplish their regularly scheduled work. They undertook their tasks through five or six standing committees but always left themselves plenty of time to see again the campus at which most of them had once been students, have drinks and dinner, and chat about Wesleyan as they believed it to be or as they wanted it to be. Their visits were occasions for the administration to present carefully designed "show and tell" exercises, to give the best possible interpretation to any situations under review, and to demonstrate that the school was in good hands. They were also occasions for the trustees to comport themselves in a way that would reinforce their belief that they were exerting general control over the institution.

After I participated in these ceremonies several times, I reflected on the historical reasons for the existence of trustees and considered the kind of asset—or deficit—they were to the institution. Richard Hofstadter and Walter Metzger observe in their magisterial *Development of Academic Freedom in the United States* that only this country and Canada have boards of private citizens governing

their private universities and colleges. European universities are
characteristically under their own control but have evolved under
the additional impact of both state and church. On the other
hand, schools like Wesleyan (and Harvard, Princeton, Haverford,
Emory, and countless others), founded by nonconformist Protestant
churches, are quite different from the medieval universities that,
thanks to church sponsorship, were held at a distance from civic
authorities. As Hofstadter and Metzger observe, "both the church
principle of ecclesiastical independence and the guild principle of
corporate self-government provided [European] universities and
society at large with dominant models of autonomy."[1] Such
autonomy was not a part of the formula that created America's
private universities and, in being deprived of it, schools like
Wesleyan found that the lay government establishing them wound
up exerting considerable control over them. One early consequence was the reduction of the faculty's freedom to determine its
own affairs. As Hofstadter and Metzger point out, lay government, with trustees holding fiduciary control of the institution and
thus, at least legally, retaining the power to hire and fire faculty
and administrators, has

> hampered the development of organization, initiative, and self-
> confidence among American college professors, and it has con-
> tributed, along with many other forces in American life, to lowering
> their status in the community. Other professional groups have far
> greater power to determine the standards and conduct of their own
> professions.[2]

And thus the strange spectacle of the Wesleyan trustees, a spectacle common to all such American trustees. While regarding their
sporadic duties with utmost seriousness and working without any
monetary compensation, these well-meaning men and women
brought to their duties no special knowledge of education, of
either teaching or research, the twin functions of the school. They
brought instead affection and loyalty. Knowing the school had
changed them in positive ways, they offered it their time, their
respect, and, in some cases, their philanthropic support. Officially,
they were "in charge." That is what "fiduciary responsibility"

meant. But none of them, in fact, knew the school well, nor could they, given the limited time they could spend on campus. The faculty, which did possess an intimate knowledge of the institution, nonetheless felt inferior to trustee power and prestige as it was periodically visited upon the campus. This peculiar situation, in which the local education experts on the Wesleyan campus—the faculty—were by tradition made to feel inferior to the distant entities setting policy for them, was at the root of their anemia, an anemia of morale. But what was true at Wesleyan is true also of other schools. Physicians have the AMA; lawyers have the ABA. But professors at American colleges and universities have no self-governing body, no association that sets standards, makes rules, delivers sanctions, and extends honors.[3]

The faculty and I recognized that the trustees saw in the school what it once had been in the past—sometimes in the imaginary past—not what it currently was. Their link was to a place that only partially continued to exist. We, on the other hand, were on the campus as it was and there we made our respective ways. There is an endearing pathos to this situation, but I soon concluded that trustee sentimentality, as poignant as it might be, is a poor guide for stewardship.

I had to keep in mind that the duty of trustees is, in fact, to "contribute." I learned, however, that trustee contributions are a mixed blessing. At their best, they bring, as the euphonious clichés go, "time, talent, and tribute" or "work, wisdom, and wealth." But only rarely did any Wesleyan trustee, even one with "talent" or "wisdom," possess the kind of sophisticated knowledge about the academic workings of the institution to be any more than a kindly observer of it. And we in the administration behaved as if indeed we were being observed. Hence the careful design of our staged presentations to the trustees, the formal introduction of one or another precisely selected star faculty member or student to speak to them, the scrubbed and polished views of the budget. We did not seek to deceive, but to convey what we could to a body of people who knew far less about the institution than we did and whose connection to it was, in sum, charitable but quite imperfect.

During those meetings, often taken up by topics with which some trustees felt affinity, such as investment management or the maintenance of the physical plant, I would wish that I could take them to witness the genius and magic of the place. It did not exist where, in light of their business or legal experience, trustees felt most comfortable—the management of money and the repair of buildings—but in the classroom, that extraordinary arena where young minds could be challenged and enlightened through the touch of a teacher. Wesleyan had such teachers, many of them, and such teaching constituted the core of the school's value. But, to the trustees, the classroom seemed inaccessible, a foreign territory made up of odd young people and slightly eccentric older men and women. For me, the tragicomedy of the trustee visits was that these decent men and women were unequipped to comprehend the essence of the institution they were pledged to guide and support.

Some, but hardly all, were financially generous. One in particular, the CEO of a large national company, had long since seen the school change from the place he knew as a student. He had become a Republican businessman in Texas, but something arising from his largeness of spirit and his ability to recall with genuine love the quality of his youth prompted him to support, in a wide variety of ways, and usually anonymously, his alma mater. Student radicals, incensed by one thing or another the trustees had done (usually concerning their investment policies), customarily called him terrible names whenever he visited the campus. He would smile gently at them and, after a while, call me to say that another handsome check was in the mail. Another wealthy trustee, wise and generous about young people, set up a splendid fund along the lines of the Rhodes Trust to support fully some eighty students from ten different countries in Asia who, carefully selected, would enrich the student body and would, in time, return to their native countries with a strong American education. Such trustees exemplified what a combination of "wealth" and "wisdom" could do. But in their generosity, and in their benign understanding that the school they now supported had moved leagues away from the school they had known as students, these two trustees were exceptions. Others, including those few who seemed prompted only by parsimony and intrusiveness, behaved differently.

Perhaps the oddest trustee behavior arose from those who felt that the school should have a specific and unique "mission" and that I, as president, should sound a rallying cry to let the world know what Wesleyan, as opposed to all other liberal arts colleges, stood for. Shortly after the firebombing in 1990, one trustee, looking at me with eagerness and hope, asked what my "vision" of Wesleyan was. He wanted to relay this precious idea to others in his alumni class. At the time, all I wanted was to end the year peacefully, with no other buildings burned, and students taking their final exams in peace. I thought back to Richard Lyman's defense of Stanford in a time of violence and fear. Lyman had a "vision" then of Stanford: it should survive. That seemed to me a paramount aim for Wesleyan at the time. To the trustee, I responded that I had tried to make my "vision" of the institution as clear as possible in my inaugural address. I then added, by way of digest of that address, that I saw Wesleyan as a place where the highest standards of teaching and learning, reinforced by research, would be upheld, a place that would have the means to take good young minds and make them more responsive, capacious, and informed. He looked at me, deeply disappointed. To him, my words must have seemed little puffs of presidential air. I was sorry that he had nothing to take back to his classmates, but Wesleyan's survival was my main mission at the time.

On another occasion, during the 1991–92 school year, a trustee volunteered the idea that, to achieve fiscal equilibrium at home and uniqueness among all our "competitors," we should consider simply dropping a wide range of curricular offerings. He suggested the social sciences—economics, political science, sociology, and history. When I responded that without those things we could not call ourselves a liberal arts institution, he asked that I think about moving away from "timeworn tradition" to establish a genuinely special "brand." This I knew was "thinking outside the box," but, as a result, we would destroy the box.

Unworkable ideas like this, born of business practices, now and again occur to trustees, and I learned not to be surprised by them.

Trustees speak of what they know and where they have been. This
man was an aggressive and successful investment broker. He
moved money and thought I could just as easily move the curriculum. Although he was extraordinary in the boldness of his
misunderstanding, he was no more than typical in other ways.
Trustees tend to fit the following general categories: they are male,
in their fifties, white, and financially successful. They are mainly
in law, business, and medicine. Few are musicians, artists, or writers. Almost none are teachers. One of the most striking facts
about them is that they are almost wholly unfamiliar with the
basic literature about higher education. By and large, according to
several studies of their habits, they do not read *The Chronicle of
Higher Education* and they do not know studies such as the popular book by Henry Rosovsky, *The University: An Owner's
Manual* (whose title might seem tempting to them). One study of
their reading habits concludes: "the trustees' lack of familiarity
with the literature serves to underscore the peripheral nature of
the trusteeship for most of the board members."[4] Yet most
trustees are not peripheral in the affection they have for "their"
institution. The contrast, then, between the emotional weight they
bring to their roles and their shallow knowledge of higher education in general creates a considerable challenge to all presidents
and their administrative colleagues. At Wesleyan, we faced that
challenge three or four times a year.

In a gesture of solicitude, a trustee would now and again tell me
that he thought the presidency "must be the toughest job in the
world." Usually this meant that in his business or profession, the
lines of command authority were clearer, and thus he could exercise power more directly than I could. I would respond with
thanks, adding that the scholarly literature on the presidency supported his thinking. Many people who have looked at the job have
concluded that it is, if not impossible, at least very difficult. Clark
Kerr delivered the classic summation of the duties of a university
president:

> The university president in the United States is expected to be a
> friend to the students, a colleague of the faculty, a good fellow with

the alumni, a sound administrator with the trustees, a good speaker with the public, an astute bargainer with the foundations and the federal agencies, a politician with the state legislature, a friend of industry, labor and agriculture, a persuasive diplomat with donors, a champion of education generally, a supporter of the professions (particularly law and medicine), a spokesman to the press, a scholar in his own right, a public servant at the state and national levels, a devotee of opera and football generally, a decent human being, a good husband and father, an active member of the church. Above all, he must enjoy traveling in airplanes, eating his meals in public, and attending public ceremonies.[5]

With the exception of those duties the president of a public institution alone would have, Kerr's droll description fit what I found myself doing. I knew that people thought my job very difficult, but perhaps blinded by excessive self-regard or limited in imaginative intelligence, I thought it a good one, not an impossible one, and I enjoyed almost all of its aspects. In performing all those duties Kerr described, I was glad to be active, happy to be involved in many committees, and eager to learn more about how the place worked, what made different people tick (or not tick), and what held such a curious thing as a liberal arts college together. I slept well, exercised a lot, went to work every day with a smile, and thought myself a lucky fellow to be at Wesleyan.

When gloomy days descended, as they now and again did, I consoled myself with little mental games. Thinking about the profusion of advice I continually received from every quarter of the campus, I would say to myself: "Being president must be the easiest job in the world; after all, everybody seems to know how to do it." Or I would think about how the "leadership" of a campus is so amusingly different from leadership elsewhere. I would recall that George Shultz once said that the biggest difference between his life as a corporate leader and his career as dean of a business school was that, in business, he had to make sure that his orders were precise and exact, given that they would likely be followed, whereas no such danger existed in academia. In sum, the very peculiarities of the job were its most appealing feature.

Much of the literature on presidential leadership concludes that the job is impossible, but it is worth noting the obvious: at any given time, about 3,500 men and women do the job. The situation is much like that of the airplane: there is no obvious reason why so large and heavy a piece of metal can fly through the sky, yet it does. Despite the impossibility of their work, thousands of presidents go to the office every day, successfully complete some tasks, and return home.

Robert Birnbaum, one of those scholars who claim that the job is unworkable, argues that the problem of presidential leadership is that the criteria for success and failure are elusive:

> there is no accepted criterion presidents can employ to judge the benefits of one course of action over another, and little assurance that they could implement their preferences even if they could specify them. Presidential authority is limited, complete understanding of the scope and complexity of the enterprise exceeds human cognitive capability, and unforeseen changes in demographic, political, and economic conditions often overwhelm campus plans.[6]

But the "impossibility" of such places can serve as a healthy reminder of what they are not. A university or college is not a business, does not make a profit, cannot declare quarterly earnings, "wins" nothing, hopes to flourish forever, will never be bought out, cannot relocate, is both in and out of the world, studies everything including itself, considers itself a meritocracy while continually worshipping the idea of community, and has as its greatest asset an odd assemblage of self-directed intellectual entrepreneurs who work on the most complicated aspects of their respective disciplines. What a university does is expensive, time-consuming, inefficient, wayward, hard to understand, and yet prestigious. It also helps young people and, more and more each year, looks after them in all sorts of ways. It is exclusive in admissions and appointments, but generous in sharing the fruits of its labor. It stands on ancient ceremonies yet accelerates the workings of democracy. All in all, I thought, a good place to be, even if my job was "impossible."

As we worked in the academic years 1993–94 to establish financial equilibrium for the institution, one of the greatest costs we had to absorb each year was connected to Wesleyan's "need-blind" admissions program. Like many other distinguished private colleges and universities, we subscribed to the notion, admirable in all moral respects, that we would admit students first and then establish financial aid for them if they qualified for such aid. We would not, that is, skew the admissions program according to the financial capabilities of the students or their families. But such a policy is expensive. More than expensive, it is also dangerous. A senior member of the faculty, an economist, thought it a "running spigot" policy, for we had no precise way to control how much financial aid money we would need in a given forthcoming year. If we were lucky, it would be not much larger than the amount we had spent the previous year. But if we were unlucky and it got much larger, it could inhibit our support for other programs—curricular or physical—that Wesleyan needed.

There was one safety valve in the program: the single most important factor in admissions to the school was self-selection. Even though we spread out our arms in all we said about Wesleyan, thus to encourage the widest possible range of applications, only a tiny percentage of the hundreds of thousands of secondary school students in the United States would even imagine applying to the school. Nor did we recruit everywhere; we tended to fish where we knew good students swam, and we enjoyed returning to high schools from which good students had come before. Thus we limited the number of applicants and, over the years, got to know a lot about who they most likely would be and what kind of money their families possessed. We also lessened the policy's impact on the budget by offering a package of financial aid. Only a portion was an outright reduction of the tuition "sticker-price"; other portions were a low-interest loan and the right to "work-study"—an on-campus job. Nonetheless, the policy was expensive, and we knew we had to place some limits on it.

When this became known in the student newspaper, the customary cries rose up from students: "elitism," "cowardice," "miserliness," and (the favorite term of abuse) "racism." We were suspected of wanting to limit the number of poor students, minority students, the very students whose presence would enrich campus life and make

Wesleyan a truer version of itself. We responded by noting that
Wesleyan's percentage of minority students was as impressively
large as at any comparable institution in the nation. We also
pointed out that more money invested in financial aid would mean
less money for other worthy programs, and we had on hand only
a finite amount of money. This logic, sound though we thought it
to be, made no impression on the students who took the position
that we were people who, supervising some very good policies,
were ourselves morally questionable. A "need-blind" admissions
policy was good, but we were its bad stewards and therefore
required close vigilance. Despite this climate of negative opinion,
we did, at last, set fixed limits on the annual amount of money
directed to financial aid and announced that we would adhere
to those limits. As the 1990s went on, we kept that promise and
thus, in one important way, Wesleyan's budgeting became more
sound.

But money was not the only thing in limited supply at Wesleyan.
The time of the trustees also had to be husbanded. Throughout the
1980s and into the 1990s, a regular and hectic, even rancorous, feature of every trustee meeting was a discussion of the school's investment policies with respect to companies with operations in South
Africa. Like many other schools at the time, Wesleyan subscribed to
the "Sullivan Principles," a code of conduct for human rights and
equal opportunity for companies operating in South Africa that had
been designed in 1977 by the Reverend Leon Sullivan, pastor of the
Zion Baptist Church in Philadelphia. The principles were a means
to persuade U.S. companies with investments in South Africa to
treat their African employees the same as they did their American
counterparts and to "encourage companies to support economic,
social and political justice wherever they do business." For
Wesleyan, this had come to mean disinvestment from virtually every
company working in South Africa; for none met the exceedingly
high demands that Wesleyan, particularly Wesleyan students, placed
on top of the "Sullivan Principles," thinking them inadequate to
challenge the true ugliness of apartheid.

By 1991, Wesleyan had investments in only one company—
Johnson & Johnson—with operations in South Africa. In fact,

the company was doing much good in South Africa, and the Reverend Sullivan found no fault with it. But the students felt they knew better than Sullivan and believed Johnson & Johnson to be just one more instance of the brutality of American capitalism. And hence long and strenuous discussions, pro and con, of Johnson & Johnson consumed much of the time of trustee meetings in 1991 and 1992. I came to believe that these contentious discussions, albeit often philosophically and morally dramatic, amounted to a prodigal misuse of trustee time and energy. Although the trustees could not easily dismiss a conviction that Wesleyan had to maintain fiduciary logic even in the face of South African bigotry, I finally argued at one trustee meeting that the school was not, in the end, primarily meant to be a guiding light about all the evils to which foreign nations had succumbed. That was not our role at all. We were a small liberal arts college in New England. Our purpose? To teach and learn. So I asked, knowing my plea could be characterized as the most craven kind of expediency, that Wesleyan divest itself of all holdings in Johnson & Johnson and thus be rid of its last South African entanglement. I said that the school should never lessen its ambition to be international in its outlook and that it should not, could not, abandon its moral bearing. But we had wrung the topic of South Africa dry in hundreds of hours of discussion and argument. The trustees, brought at last by their own fatigue to see the merits of expediency, struck Johnson & Johnson from the list in 1992. Thus a long and tortured chapter in the ethical life of the institution came to an end.

Both the issues of financial aid and South Africa taught me that it is easy for colleges and universities to lose their way in the thicket of issues that can find a home on the campus. Birnbaum argues, and I agree, that this confusion arises from what is often lost to view on the campus, any campus: an "educational, social, or political consensus on exactly what higher education should be doing, what constituencies it should serve, and how it should serve them. At different times and on different campuses, emphasis has been given to transmitting values, to discovering knowledge, or to improving society."[7] He is right. Without such consensus, the absence of which derives in turn from the fact that actual authority and power are widely dispersed on a campus, the problems of affording financial aid or of responding to apartheid can devour the time and energy of many people. Neither of these issues was, at Wesleyan, devoid of moral charge and significance. But to the degree that Wesleyan focused so much of its energy on them, its interest in education was continually diminished by its high-minded moral responsiveness. That was wrong, and that is why I had to sound my plea, expedient or not, to the trustees. Above all, Wesleyan had to be a place where nothing came in front of teaching, learning, and research. And by tracking how much of its moral energy, some of its financial resources, and a great deal of its time had been spent over the years upon marginal agenda, I saw how the school's identity (the "diverse" school) was enmeshed in its budget, and how its budget in turn was enmeshed in its ethical habits. Those things had to be disentangled. We made a beginning by circumscribing financial aid and saying goodbye to South Africa. We saw that the Institutional Priorities Committee could bring good sense to the academic values of the place. But we had much more work to do.

ENDNOTES

1. Richard Hofstadter and Walter Metzger, *The Development of Academic Freedom in the United States* (New York and London: Columbia University Press, 1955), p. 121.
2. Ibid., p. 120.
3. The Association of American University Professors (AAUP) is a wholly voluntary organization and represents only a tiny fraction (44,000 people, some 2–3 percent) of the 1.6 million men and women holding jobs in post-secondary higher education. It neither governs nor licenses nor polices its members.
4. Rodney T. Hartnett, "College and University Trustees: Their Backgrounds, Roles, and Educational Attitudes," in *The State of the University: Authority and Change*, ed. by Carlos E. Kruytbosch and Sheldon L. Messinger (Beverly Hills: Sage Publications, 1970), p. 63.

5. Kerr, *Uses of the University*, pp. 29–30.

6. Robert Birnbaum, "The Dilemma of Presidential Leadership," in *American Higher Education in the Twenty-First Century*, ed. by Philip G. Altbach, Robert O. Berdahl, and Patricia J. Gumport (Baltimore and London: Johns Hopkins University Press, 1999), p. 329.

7. Ibid., p. 328.

22

Looking at Success; Looking at Failure

At the end of every Wesleyan academic year came Commencement and, with it, a brief moment of blissful reassurance. I enjoyed the presence of many proud parents and relatives and momentarily cheerful faculty colleagues and trustees. The majestic procession of students who, one by one, shook my hand and received their diplomas reminded me of the meaning, through the decades, of the old ceremony. JoAn and I hosted a reception afterwards at the house and greeted the graduates' families. They were grateful for the education of their sons and daughters; we were happy for their gratitude. I heard from mothers and fathers, stepmothers and stepfathers, brothers and sisters, as well as many grandparents, how much the Wesleyan education meant to the new graduates. They told us that Wesleyan had made these young people more prepared, more reflective, more knowledgeable, and even more interesting. Whatever the costs to all involved, the mysterious process of education apparently worked.

At the time, that was all I needed to hear. These young people had come to be educated four years before; now they were leaving with more knowledge than when they entered their freshman year. It was Haverford all over again—youth transformed. Such moments of satisfaction led me to weigh the value of a Wesleyan education against its many costs—the costs to parents concerned about tuition, to faculty members concerned about transmitting complex ideas to young minds, to administrators like me concerned about institutional friction.

By June 1992, I had been president for four years. I knew enough about the school to see that Wesleyan did things the hard way: abrasively and confrontationally. When it underwent a reaccreditation review that year, the team coming from other colleges and universities to assess the school delivered a scathing report: "We were disturbed to encounter in discussions with faculty a widespread attitude characterized by blaming, finger-pointing, distrust, and abrogation of institutional responsibility. We saw evidence of allegiance focused on departments and programs; territorial protectionism; and a mentality of balkanism which interferes with institutional loyalty and vision." What distinguished the institution, they said, is "the long and persistent history of adversarial attitudes and ineffectual attention to university-wide problems, and the extent to which those attitudes and characteristics have become ingrained in the university's culture." Noting that a previous reaccreditation body had reported these same complaints ten years earlier, they admonished the school to correct matters before another ten years passed.

But with the spirit of the 1992 Commencement acting as an anodyne for all that had gone on during the year, I believed that because we had been successful in educating the students, we should bear whatever costs there were. The value of the education was great, the costs be damned. Wesleyan had its way, neither easy nor inexpensive, but its signature. In time, however, I needed to take a closer look at this happy formula. As the Connecticut summer wore on, I tallied, as objectively as possible, how my administrative colleagues and I had enhanced the institution and what the rewards and penalties—emotional and psychological—had been for everyone involved. The improvements—were they likely to last? The victories, however slight—would they prevail? Would the atmosphere of suspicion and "abrogation of institutional responsibility" win out over everything? Were our successes only small and temporary? Did we, in fact, *feel* successful? And, for me, the largest question: what kind of a president was I?

I asked for a formal evaluation from the trustees, but it was slow in coming, awkwardly devised, and, at the end, mild and superficial in its content. I had a hunch that the trustees simply wanted to assume that I was doing a good job and that, if they had to deliver an intensive review of me, it would be only to terminate my presidency. The real review would have somehow to be one I would conduct myself, and I began that summer to construct a means to evaluate myself.

I believe most presidents conduct self-evaluations of one sort or another. Even though they can suffer from all the obvious subjective liabilities, such self-assessments can be more searching than anything distant observers might come up with. They are usually done meditatively, internally. The job is isolated enough that only the president really knows the time and labor it takes, the issues that count, the true quality of the colleagues with whom one works, and the most important stakes for the school. Rightly or wrongly, such self-examinations turn out to be, for most presidents, the only compass they trust. Everything else can seem partial, remote, and shallow.

As part of my self-evaluation, I created a ledger of successes and failures. On the positive side of the ledger, by the fall of 1992 we had secured from the trustees their endorsement of a "University Plan" we had hammered together during more than a year of labor. A rigorously systematic analysis of all the forces and realities comprising the administrative life of the school, it gave us a balanced operating budget for the first time in years. To construct the "Plan," we invited every member of the faculty to give us their ideas. Many greeted this invitation with their customary suspiciousness, but enough of them joined us to give energy to the process. Joanne Creighton's tenacious leadership and her ability to deliver the truth about both the good and the bad of Wesleyan were largely responsible for this leap forward in faculty involvement.

We had programmed expenditure reductions of some $8 million from the operating budget of some $82 million. Of this sum, we scheduled two million dollars to be cut from the academic budget over a five-year period to achieve fiscal equilibrium. We had to eliminate twenty or so faculty positions and saw no way for them to be restored in the future. This cut made even more difficult my plan that we could increase, by brilliant new appointments, the intellectual capital of the place. We also addressed the backlog of deferred maintenance to the physical plant in a systematic manner, and the campus looked better. Other achievements: we became more selective about whom we would let into the freshman class. Because of ceilings we had put in place, we got the financial aid numbers under control. We established a serious academic bookstore near the campus. Because we pushed hard to make Wesleyan international in its curriculum, more students were enrolling in programs overseas. We distributed "Writing across the Curriculum" courses throughout the departments and thus lessened the pressure on the English department to oversee skills in composition. All of these things were to the good.

And we had raised money: some $38 million during those first four years. But this, given our needs, was not a remarkable sum, and I worried that the damage done to the reputation of the school by the firebombing had alienated many older and conservative alumni. Those who gave the $38 million did so for all the reasons that guide most generosity to colleges and universities. Looking at those reasons gave me another way of measuring success and failure. And, as I worked on my ledger, I had to come to terms with the fact that presidents have only a tenuous relationship with most fund-raising.

I learned at Wesleyan that people give out of affection for a past that was once theirs or they imagine was theirs; they give because they believe in something they want the institution to champion; they give out of memory of a friend or child or favorite teacher; they give for selfish reasons, ideological reasons, or coercive reasons. But they give only occasionally because they like the person who asked them for the gift. The professionals who successfully solicit money know how to reckon with the desires, hopes and needs of others. They understand the money is not being given to them personally, but to a cause or a memory or out of deep reservoirs of self-interest. If I was successful with a donor, I understood soon enough not to take credit for the success. I knew I was only one part of a psychological dynamic I could not wholly understand. I observed some generous people enjoy giving without calculation. I watched others whose gifts were the result of exacting studies on the part of their attorneys and financial advisors. Some philanthropy arose from unmediated affection; some arose from affection mediated by consultants. But once Wesleyan received the money, its various origins were lost to view as it became mixed and absorbed in the school's endowment. Large gifts or small, it all helped.

Many people assume that university and college presidents spend most of their time raising money. This was not true in my case, and it is not true of most college and university presidents. Sometimes, when an institution sets forth on the "campaign" trail (what Jim Rosse called "wartime") the president will visit many airports, hotels, restaurants, private homes, and meeting rooms in search of the dollars that, all added up, will reach the campaign goal. But in "peacetime," presidents find themselves, as I found myself, enmeshed in the usual matrix of duties—committees, ceremonies, appointments, rituals of every kind, and the ordinary emergencies of the day—that make impossible a schedule of non-stop fund-raising, a schedule that only fund-raising professionals can keep to. Every school has those professionals—the prospectors, diggers, surveyors, and suave ushers and emissaries of education. Because of the delicacy of their work, they are the only campus employees who need a protective euphemism—they are "development officers." They establish the enabling friendships, design the courtships, and prepare for the climactic events—the "asks"—at which the president, sometimes as much a spectator as a participant, will magically appear if the donor is sufficiently important. As elsewhere in higher education, many others do the work for which the president, given his tribal importance, gets the credit. I had to include this fact in the assessment of my success and failure. What might have been considered "mine" often belonged to someone else; what looked like the possession of another now and again turned out to be something I alone could claim.

In thinking things through during that summer and later in the fall, I was happy to add more items to the positive side of the ledger. I liked the team of administrative colleagues I had put together, and we developed considerable ingenuity in extracting the humor out of situations that otherwise would have been left to fester and at last decay into an ugly residue of discomfort. We knew we were embattled. So we honed our wit, polished our narrative techniques so that we could best describe our favorite campus characters, and learned to cherish the fact that Wesleyan would never fail to present us with the strange, the absurd, the wonderful, and the unique. The oddity of the place would never disappoint. In the middle of one semester, I found on my appointment calendar a meeting with six students, all women. When they entered my office, their demeanor—quiet, deferential, and yet perfectly poised—was striking. I inquired about their reason for wanting to see me. They told me they wanted to establish a new society, one for "women." I immediately wondered what striking innovations in the cause of feminism were at stake. They then told me that they would construct this society, for which they needed my sponsorship, around their right to appear on campus with lipstick and hose. They wanted to wear heels and dresses to class and on campus when they chose. They wanted my assurance that if they appeared in this way, other students, many of whom had fully adopted grunge as their clothing style, would not harass them. I told them I would act as their champion. They then decorously departed.

When my colleagues and I met weekly around a large table in my cavernous and echoing office, decades ago the school's library, we laid out the several problems with which we were dealing and saw which could be tackled collectively. We deferred to each other, keeping the lines of authority straight and not allowing anyone to play us off against each other. We had been able to put an end to the venerable Wesleyan practice that had encouraged faculty members to go from office to office, hopscotching around the administrative matrix, to seek satisfaction of a grievance.

But against these achievements and on the negative side of the ledger, I had to acknowledge that I was neither trusted nor liked by some members of the faculty. The legacy of my inaugural remarks haunted me still, three years after giving them. Those with grudges to hold remained convinced that I wanted to change Wesleyan's mission by defining it as a small college without a profile of research and that I discredited scholarship in favor of teaching (not true but plausible, given my devotion to teaching). Some students were convinced that I had not been wholly sympathetic toward their divestment campaigns against South Africa (true, given what I believed was a willed ignorance on their part about what some companies were doing for good in South Africa), that I had not been happy with the fraternities (true, given their periodic asocial and destructive actions), and that I was no friend to liberal thinking (false). On a small campus, the air does not change often and what is once believed becomes a fixed part of the atmosphere. To nourish enmity for Bill Chace was, for some, all too familiar and easy.

My self-assessment did not stop there. There was more pay dirt to find. Given the complicated nature of the mission of schools like Wesleyan and given the incompatible beliefs within various groups (faculty, students, trustees, and alumni among them) concerning the president's role, what instrument could I use to measure my achievements? I began with certain conclusions I had reached after my four years as president. I knew that the faculty wanted me to exalt their work and free them of institutional obligations, but I believed that many members of the faculty had a stunted sense of loyalty to the school for which they worked; the students wanted me to champion their political idealism and to indulge their various forms of creative immaturity; the trustees wanted me to supervise the school in a businesslike way, but they had only a slender appreciation of the intellectual life to which it was dedicated; and the alumni wanted me to remind them of the glories of their alma mater, but had little understanding of the changes to the institution since they had graduated from it. And since most of the trustees were alumni, they wanted me both to exert executive control over the school and to recreate for them the good place it was when they were students.

How could a proper understanding of success come out of a tangle of all these hopes and desires? Even if Robert Birnbaum is right that "there is no accepted criterion presidents can employ to judge the benefits of one course of action over another" and "no educational, social, or political consensus on exactly what higher education should be doing, what constituencies it should serve, and how it should serve them,"[1] I could not rest easy amid such existential vagueness. I had to lay out explanatory approaches to the subject of presidential success and failure. I needed a useful way to see what I had done and what I had not done. I looked at three different formulas. Each of them, I thought, could prove useful to me, and I imagined they had at times proved useful to other presidents:

1. *If in trouble, blame the institution; if successful, take the credit.*

This approach presumes the difficulty of the job and assigns every failure to the intrinsic obstinacy of the school, while at the same time it identifies oneself as the instrument of any positive development. Either the president cannot succeed because the institution adamantly resists change, or the president can occasionally triumph over institutional inertia. Given Wesleyan, this seemed a promising formula, but it would too easily have let me off the hook. Nonetheless, I learned from Birnbaum that many college and university presidents have successfully employed just this approach. His research shows that these men and women rely on unconscious strategies to reconcile the fact of their failure with their own self-esteem: "they see themselves as successful even as others see them as failing"; and "in a recent study of the performance of thirty-two college presidents, all but one considered themselves successful, even though a quarter of them had lost sufficient constituent support to be identified by the researcher as having been a failure at the job."[2] Perhaps these were the same presidents who identified themselves with positive campus outcomes at a 74 percent rate but identified with campus failures at only a 14 percent rate. While I could see the obvious emotional attractions of this approach, I knew I had to work with something less self-serving.

2. *If in trouble, assert to oneself that the president is, after all, both powerless and irrelevant, and that academic institutions behave in ways unreachable by presidential authority, itself an empty vessel.*

The moral here is: do what you can, it won't amount to much. The classic (and droll) study of the college presidency by Michael D. Cohen and James G. March argues that the presidency is a largely symbolic and more or less ineffectual role occupied by a person whose time is given over to ritualistic events, a figurehead removed from substantive educational matters, a pawn of fate who serves an organization with unclear objectives, and a passive entity whose real connection to either success or failure is much like that of

> the driver of a skidding automobile. The marginal judgments he makes, his skill, and his luck may possibly make some difference to the survival prospects of his riders. As a result, his responsibilities

are heavy. But whether he is convicted of manslaughter or receives a medal for heroism is largely outside his control.[3]

Cohen and March's advice, somber and cynical though it may be, should be required reading for all those presidents buoyed up by an exalted sense of themselves:

> It is probably a mistake for a college president to imagine that what he does in office affects significantly either the long-run position of the institution or his reputation as president. So long as he does not violate some rather obvious restrictions on his behavior, his reputation and his term of office are more likely to be affected by broad social events or by the unpredictable vicissitudes of official responsibility than by his actions.[4]

But Cohen and March were, I thought, far too jaundiced. Even if I were only symbolic, I knew that symbols exert a weighty presence within any human community. And I could remember, with respect, the kind of stoic strength exhibited by Richard Lyman when, during the 1970s, he did everything he could to protect Stanford from attackers of the university coming from both the radical left and the alumni and trustee right. The one wanted to destroy the institution; the other wanted to take it back in time. I thought also of presidents who had become wholly representative of the places they had led—Father Hesburgh of Notre Dame or Clark Kerr of the University of California—and had thereby emerged as both symbolic and substantive figures in the history of American higher education. With examples like that in mind, I found Cohen and March too clever by half. At times, the symbolic becomes real.

Considering myself from afar, I could see that I was at the center of a great many things at Wesleyan and that important events constantly moved around me. Committing myself to countless ceremonies, I served as Wesleyan's ambassador and central representative more consistently than anyone else. Substanceless formality might be part of my daily bread, but I *was* the school for many people. And even if I were to take the situation at its bleakest, I could think about the people at Wesleyan who enjoyed impugning my motives and belittling my actions as itself evidence of my relevance. The institution could not reside entirely outside my control if my presence at it was such a negative factor for them. But this approach was, I thought, much too defensive.

A third approach seemed the fairest.

3. *Concede at the outset: presidential authority is constrained in myriad ways; agreement among the affected parties about what the school is "supposed" to be will never be reached; the faculty is largely composed of free agents who cannot be required to be loyal to the school; history weighs more heavily on a college or university than any quotidian initiative; every president has only an interim moment in the life of the school; a school's reputation changes more slowly than presidential tenure; and no institution can pretend to be free of external pressures and contingencies.*

Having made all these concessions, I could then inspect closely what my own presence on the campus, in fact, amounted to. I knew it would turn out to be modest, formed only of those things I knew were mine more than anyone else's:

- I had set forth a definition of the school. Declaring its teaching to be more important to society than its research, I had argued that its chief clientele was the student body and not the world community of researchers. Some had disliked my position while others assented to it, but only I had been adamant in providing an appropriate definition of the place. People at Wesleyan had to think about what I had said.

- The "University Plan" was a solid achievement, tough, demanding, and true to the circumstances of the place. It was meant to serve for years at Wesleyan as a marker. Although many people took a hand in it, I doubt if it could have come about had I not wanted it to. With it, we had established fiscal solvency and had brought a number of crucial issues—fiscal and curricular—to the fore. The institution would not again be as squishy as it once had been.

- The core administrative staff was made up of strong professionals I had either appointed or kept in office. They were able people, and together we had established a coherent discipline of fiscal life and an effective administrative *esprit de corps*. We liked each other, and our mutual respect provided a positive model for the rest of the institution.

- I had devised ways for the faculty to assume greater proprietary control of their institution. They were at first suspicious about this offering but ultimately grasped what was theirs for the taking. Once they had laid claim to such authority, I was sure that they would not relinquish it. As a result, Wesleyan became stronger and would stay stronger.

- Although I had doubts about how much the trustees knew about the administration's activities, and although I felt sure their criteria for presidential success were hazy, I had their support. When I formally asked them to review our work, they moved slowly, impeded by hesitancy, vagueness, and confusion. Even the most thoughtful of them seemed unsure of the president's role. But, at the end, each review commended what my colleagues and I had accomplished. The trustees knew it was a joint effort, and they respected the group of people I had put together. And I knew the trustees were tough enough to have ended my presidency had I not earned their trust. Our relationship was firm, and that firmness in turn gave strength to Wesleyan.

These, I thought, were the accomplishments of my presidency. With most of them, I had a lot of help. Rare is the president who can point to something that he alone has accomplished. Be that as it may, by the end of the fall in 1992, I had completed this formal look at my record. I had tried to do so without giving in to self-aggrandizement or self-abasement. My verdict, for whatever it might mean: not a bad president, not an excellent one.

I had also come to an understanding of just what the job demanded. Unlike the life of a faculty member, whose best energies are focused on the sharpest and most exacting use of mental power—*thinking* in its most rigorous forms—the brain-work of a president is mainly given over to the routines of duty, strategy, diplomacy, and the politics of managing people. Deep thought, the inventive use of the brain in a disciplined and precise manner, is not the president's chief tool. Stamina, flexibility, cordiality, and common sense count for much more. Presidents have no access to those sustained periods of deep reflection that, for a professor, are the seedbed of new thoughts about the toughest problems of the discipline. Presidents, always busy, must develop (or relearn) the attention span of a child to be successful: five minutes for this emerging matter, seven for that. Just as clinical physicians know that they can allocate only a few moments to each patient in a busy day, presidents understand that they cannot permit any single problem to devour their time, for every problem is "important" if it arrives at the president's desk, and no person with a problem for the president is in the mood to have that problem ignored. The president must fulfill many roles: diplomat and politician, strategist and problem-resolver, but also something of a priest for the small secular world called the campus. The president has the last word, the institutional word, the word from on high. And, like the priest, the president can never afford not to be thinking about the parish and the flock. The job has no days off; the life is the job and the job the life.

The next two years, from the fall of 1992 to the spring of 1994, were to be my last at Wesleyan. Of course I did not know that at the time, nor was I planning to leave. I somehow knew that the academic year 1989–90, with the firebombing and the murder of the student, was the worst Wesleyan and I would ever face. I was ready to be Wesleyan's president for a long time.

ENDNOTES

1. Robert Birnbaum, "The Dilemma of Presidential Leadership," pp. 329 and 328.
2. Ibid., pp. 338–39.
3. Michael D. Cohen and James G. March, *Leadership and Ambiguity: The American College President* (New York: McGraw-Hill, 1974), p. 203.
4. Ibid., p. 203.

23

Learning and Then Leaving

Not all of my hours and days at Wesleyan were given over to the presidency. Every year I stole time from that role to become another person, but a person I once knew well: a professor. Sometimes I taught a course on James Joyce and sometimes freshman English. This innocent theft reminded me what the school meant to so many people. When I entered the classroom, I knew that the students were first puzzled that their teacher was the president, but when I returned their first writing assignments, adorned with the usual kind of corrections and comments in the margin, the fact of my office was no longer relevant to them.

I taught not only because I wanted to be immersed in the school's primary mission, but also because I missed using an important part of my brain when president. The life of a teacher, unlike that of a president, is driven not by responding to appointments and issues but by capturing moments when one can guide young people to places of greater knowledge for them. Presidents develop keen Pavlovian reactions: "challenge" immediately elicits "response." Teachers, on the contrary, learn less instantaneous and more creative methods of using their minds, and they also show younger people how the mind itself is so various. Sometimes the teacher gives answers to questions; at other times questions prompt only further questions. The constant process of classroom interrogation, back and forth, emphasizes the wayward nature of the truth, its elusiveness. Administration has little time for either the elusive or the multiplicity of the ways in which human truth resides, and of course no time at all for art. Teaching at its best moves in harmony with the flexibility of a young person's brain, the speed of its synapses and its imaginative power. The teacher then becomes at one with the student, two people each proceeding toward answers, findings, further discoveries, or even at times blank walls. Presidents, obliged to come up with solutions, cannot afford to stare at blank walls.

One feature of teaching particularly amused me. Some of the Wesleyan students coming to my office with political claims or "demands" also showed up on my class rosters. When they were protesting, the etiquette of our relationship required me to treat their arguments as at least plausible, even if the reasoning was weak and the language inept. But in the classroom, traditional pedagogy had no room for such etiquette. I was free to say shoddy arguments were shoddy and to point to poor reasoning, lack of evidence, and other errors. For me to point out such flaws to protestors would spark accusations of arrogance and unfair play. The classroom also allowed me to prize good reasoning when I found it, as I often did. But to compliment a protesting student on the use of lucid language and convincing proof would elicit complaints of presidential condescension.

To my surprise, the topics I presumed would be provocative when teaching freshman English turned out to be dead keys on the piano. I discovered that race, gender, free speech, inequalities in income among Americans, and sexual orientation were the least stimulating topics I could bring up. Nothing in John Stuart Mill's "On Liberty," James Baldwin's *The Fire Next Time*, Michael Harrington's *The Other America: Poverty in the United States*, or Catharine MacKinnon's *Toward a Feminist Theory of the State* sparked lively class debate, even though I had been sure each of them would. I soon understood that these "hot" topics were hardly new to the students, for they had seen much of them in high school. That is not to say that questions of race or gender or free speech had been rubbed clean of their meaning or volatility to Wesleyan students. Instead, what had happened is that those students had learned to handle such questions much as one uses tongs with hot coals. No one was going to say anything objectionable, naive, or stupid about black people or white people or women or gays or men; no one was going to say something deliberately provocative, even for the sake of lively discussion. These young people, with a mixture of caution and sophistication, had seen how students could make fools of themselves in a classroom led by a teacher who wanted "to get something going." I thought of writing this off to "political correctness," then much in the news as an all-purpose description of college campuses everywhere, and Wesleyan in particular, but decided otherwise. All the students didn't believe all the same things in a uniformly mechanical way. Rather, they had quietly decided, in the interests of self-protection, not to participate in the traditional Socratic drama of behaving unwittingly in classrooms where the teacher could use differences of opinion as a means of illumination through embarrassment. They had no interest in turning the classroom into a version of *The Paper Chase*, with me as John Houseman.

Their diffidence also meant that no one was willing to "represent" a class, a race, or a sexual orientation in discussion. Black students were wary of being "the black voice," and most women were just as uneasy in speaking on behalf of all women. No white student took the job of standing for all white people. To do so would be to fall into just the kind of pedagogical trap the instructor—me—could have put in place. Although it took a while to understand this reluctance, I came to admire it. It was a way for the students to say: although in this class there are obvious differences in race or gender or perhaps even political opinion, we want to be considered, first of all, as individuals; we are not proxies for anything. This attitude ultimately led me to question some of the arguments I had earlier brought forward, when I spoke in public as president, in strong defense of affirmative action.

With utter naïveté, I first thought that the most persuasive argument to make in favor of affirmative action was that it strengthens the teaching process—for white students. It is good to have black, Hispanic, or Asian students in the classroom because, without them, white students gain an unreal picture of life. Students of other racial and ethnic backgrounds often represent startlingly different, even alien, ways of being in the world. Education—again, for white students—is made stronger by the presence of such "otherness." Although the appalling racial parochialism of this line of "reasoning" now embarrasses me, I was not the only white person, or white administrator, to have put it forward.

It simply didn't stand the test of the classroom. It was undercut by the presence of minority students. They were real, and not abstractions to be employed in a pedagogical game. And they did not particularly want to be seen, almost typecast, as minority students. Instead they wanted to be taken, one by one, as the uniquely different young people they were.

Understanding, then, that it would be pedagogical ineptness and moral obtuseness for me to inquire of any young person what he or she as a "minority student" felt about a certain issue, I was left, as both teacher and administrator, with the fact that arguments in favor of affirmative action had to be made on grounds other than "representativeness." I had to come to terms, moreover, with another argument I could not easily turn aside. Every court that has listened to arguments about "affirmative action" or "preferential treatment" has had to pay attention to this argument: what kind of justice takes place when a wholly qualified person is displaced by someone either similarly qualified or less qualified—on the grounds of racial or ethnic difference? How could I defend "affirmative action" if it involved, as I believed it did, that kind of apparent unfairness?

The dilemma is a real one. As a university president, I was caught by a contradiction. So, I imagined, were every one of my presidential colleagues. Educational institutions like Wesleyan, be they colleges or universities, all operate on the basis of two codes: they are both "meritocracies" and "egalitarian communities." The first code celebrates and rewards individual achievement; the second asks everyone to work together for the common good. When the first code is in operation, no preference is given to anything save the power of intellectual accomplishment; when the second is in force, individual distinction is downplayed in favor of community rapport. The first provides the intellectual energy; the second supplies the social lubricant. Both function all the time and both are needed on campuses, particularly by virtue of the fact that students are being taught how, at the same time, to exercise their fullest mental potential and to be citizens in a model commonwealth. I could not imagine any college or university not wanting either code to flourish. But they do not perfectly mesh. All of us were caught between wanting campuses to have brighter and brighter students and wanting all of our graduates to go forward to live in brilliantly healthy civic societies.

What, then, to do? I wanted Wesleyan to be as bright a center of thought as it could be. I also wanted it to be as strong a community as it could be. That meant that, for all the honor the campus gave to academic achievement at the highest level, it also had to reflect the texture and richness of life beyond the campus—the world the students would enter upon graduation and the new "community" of which they would be members. If we permitted campuses to be unreal fabrications sealed off from the rest of the world, we would be doing our students a disservice. Hence I simply could not imagine a respectable university or college in the 1990s returning to the 1950s and recreating campuses without minority students or without the presence of the differences that constitute American life in its fullness. While no student should feel the burden of "representation," I felt even more strongly that neither Wesleyan nor any comparable institution should ever again be homogeneous in the composition of its student body.[1]

In the early 1990s, I could sense, as could many others, that the United States Supreme Court would someday review the entire painful matter and might strike down every form of preferential treatment founded on race. If that were so, I presumed that universities and colleges would nonetheless fashion ways to retain the presence of minority students. They could do no less. And Wesleyan, I knew, would do no less. If "affirmative action" were struck down by state or federal courts, campus after campus would resist a return to homogeneity. Negative court decision or not, there would be no turning back. Despite the difficulties they would encounter, the schools would determine ways to keep a mix of people in the classroom.

The most secure way would be to adopt, even though it is labor-intensive and therefore costly, the method that Haverford used to admit me: read every application, one by one, take into account the grades in secondary schools and both the SAT and the Advanced Placement scores (if any), study the personal statement, offer interviews, and treat each applicant as a person and not a number. At the end, employ judgment. I knew that Wesleyan would be able to continue its tradition of using such a method, just as I knew that more time and money would be needed to do so at many other schools. But added costs could be calculated against real advantages, chief among them being that no student denied admission could plausibly charge that he or she had lost out to someone less qualified. The notion itself of "qualification" would now be understood as a complex human process involving uniquely human judges and uniquely human applicants, not simply test scores. The largest schools—particularly large state universities— would face the greatest costs if this method (sometimes called "holistic") were employed. But those schools are the very ones with the strongest public mandates to produce a class of citizens who understand their responsibility to the larger social well-being. Big state schools are supposed to help the state. And on the matter of racial inclusiveness, help is always needed.[2]

But facing the question of race would not be, I knew, the only duty facing me and other university and college leaders. By the early '90s, it had become clear that the single greatest absence at schools like Wesleyan was not, in fact, going to be racial or ethnic minorities, but rather, students without money. In 2004, the Higher Education Research Institute reported that by 2000, about 55 percent of freshmen at the nation's 250 most selective colleges, public and private, had come from the highest-earning fourth of households, compared with 46 percent in 1985.[3] At Wesleyan, we could feel the change coming by the mid-'90s. We could tell it by the way the cars that students brought to campus changed: BMWs, Lexus SUVs, and even the occasional Range Rover showed up in the student parking lots. And we feared that middle-class students would soon be going the way of poor students, of whom we saw very few indeed.

From the mid-1970s onward, Wesleyan and the other best-known colleges and universities had witnessed reductions in the income of families whose children were applying for admission. Those in the bottom quarter of income suffered only a slight drop, but the middle fifty percent suffered steep reductions. Our director of admissions and the financial aid director told me that in many cases, less wealthy students went to less selective schools, including lower-ranked campuses of (the cheaper) state universities.

Class differences, more than different races and ethnic groups, increasingly defined the composition of the student body. And those differences would be immensely difficult to diminish—on the Wesleyan campus and all others like it. This is among the most important and most difficult problems now facing higher education in America. It asks everyone concerned about the nation's colleges and universities to pose this question: how much do we cherish the idea of the best campuses being accessible to the brightest students who possess the greatest hope and the best intentions—irrespective of the income of their families? Families with wealth have advantages with respect to tutorial training, precollege counseling, and selection of secondary schools simply out of the reach of others. This asymmetry in class privilege will not be solved by any remedy previously tried—financial aid (there isn't enough), government intervention (not with the huge budgetary deficits already facing the nation), or greater loans extended to needy students (the tolerance for indebtedness is not infinite). I believe in the true meritocracy of American higher education; the best American colleges or universities should not become the preserves of the wealthiest families.

The issue of wealth and accessibility did not blind me from seeing that what Wesleyan (and similar schools) were providing to the students was excellent. When I got to know what students could do in the classroom, and when my sometime colleagues—my fellow professors—told me about the successes they too had experienced with the students, I was sure that the rewards to most of the students and their families were worth the tuition and other costs. Of course I could see Wesleyan's price tag increasing at a pace that outstripped, year after year, every national index of inflation. Of course I knew that many parents found the expense almost insupportable, that they were sacrificing, assuming indebtedness, and going without. But when I spoke with them and heard about the pressure our increases had put on their budgets, I urged them to believe that there was no better family investment they could make than in sending their children to places like Wesleyan. I believed that if the liberal arts colleges did not continue to provide a high level of educational excellence, not only would they be unnecessarily expensive, but they would outlive their reason for existence. American education had wisely placed such schools in a special category that has both exalted and limited their function. As the great research universities have grown in power and eminence, as they have taken more and more of the money available from the federal government and other sources, and as they have recruited more of the research teams needed for projects of greater and greater complexity, the liberal arts schools have had to make sure that undergraduate teaching—something the research institutions increasingly have neglected or have handed off to graduate students or part-time secondary faculty—would remain the province of which they were the recognized masters. Their primary purpose—an absolutely vital and necessary one—exists in the small classroom where superb teaching and learning flourish. This is what Wesleyan, and Williams and Amherst and Pomona and Wellesley and Haverford and Carleton and a score of others, could and should proudly offer to the world.

As I traveled around the campus, marveling at what so small a place could do for young people, I knew that there was a special group of students whose presence at the school was worthy of serious reflection on my part: the athletes. To understand them was to understand more of the school's history and, in turn, to reflect on what was happening elsewhere in American higher education. Although Wesleyan played its intercollegiate sports at the Division III level, and therefore had none of the glamour, excitement, and crowds associated with Division I (made up of athletic powerhouses like the University of Southern California, the University of Texas, and Ohio State University), it still fielded some twenty-six teams, both men's and women's. These teams on the little Connecticut campus accounted for about $1 million in annual expenses, about average for a school of Wesleyan's size. Playing at our divisional level, we were prohibited from aggressively recruiting student-athletes, nor could we give them athletic scholarships. The school was far removed from the world of huge stadiums, training palaces, multimillion dollar salaries for coaches, television revenues, and also from the various scandals and embarrassments that have become a traditional part of how the game is played at big universities. Students at Wesleyan were students first and athletes second. Nonetheless, Wesleyan had both football and ice hockey. Those two sports made things different, and that difference revealed to me a wholly new meaning of "diversity" at Wesleyan.

Once, when walking across the campus, I fell into conversation with one of the football players. He was from New Bedford, Massachusetts, the first in his family to attend college, a practicing Roman Catholic, a fraternity member, and a major in political science. Polite and reserved, he first asked me if I really taught a course on James Joyce "on top of being president." I said Yes and he said that he would never take such a course: "too hard." When I asked him about playing football, he told me that it was hard too—hard being both a football player and a student. I said we both did difficult things. He added that the practices in the fall were long and punishing; he was often tired in the evening. And he was mildly dismayed by the fact that so few students came to the games. (At Wesleyan, attendance at football games, made easier by free admission, rarely reached a thousand, even on a lovely fall afternoon, and at least half were people from the town, parents of players, and a few loyal alums.) "I guess we are kind of like freaks here," he said. I responded by saying that, as president, I knew what he felt like and that the school was made up of many different people with interests of every kind. He told me that he had come to Wesleyan because of its strong academic reputation. "But you know, sir, it sometimes is tough as a lineman to look up from the field toward the library on Saturday afternoon and for all the guys on the team to know that more people are in there studying than watching the game; that's real tough." I saw his point, although I also admired the dedication of the students in the library. And then he added: "One more thing, sir. Growing up, I was taught two things: never use curse words in front of women and if you have to settle an argument with another guy, it's OK to use your fists. But here at Wesleyan, it's all different. Half the girls say 'fuck' all the time and the school rules say that if you fight you can get suspended."

It was then that I knew how Wesleyan had been able to field teams in at least two sports—football and ice hockey. The students playing those two sports had to be drawn from a different cross-section of applicants. They were physically tougher, did not come exclusively from the suburbs, had a highly disciplined work ethic, depended on strong principles of male bonding, and often felt separate from (and sometimes inferior to) the other students. Some of them would fight with each other on Saturday nights at the fraternities. And few if any would ever engage in any kind of campus political protest. But other athletes were different, the swimmers, the golfers, and the tennis players: suburban youngsters who never fought with each other and, perhaps, boys and girls together, even said "fuck" now and again. This, then, was a dimension of diversity at Wesleyan that was not much exalted, but diversity it was.

That student from New Bedford graduated from Wesleyan. He performed competently in all his courses. And he left the school with pride in having earned his degree. The diversity he represented made possible the continuation of football, a game rooted in the school's past but now only indifferently supported by its current students. And the presence of football and ice hockey allowed me to see how the school had changed over the decades, with football serving as a marker for the place it once had been. Decades ago, it regularly played Yale, and from 1942 to 1948 it was never defeated or even tied. It had known an athletic glory that was now eclipsed by big-time sports at other, larger, schools.

Those schools had ambitious designs on television licensing, gate revenues, lavish coaching contracts, stadiums, recruitment budgets, and spectacular players who would never graduate[4] or even take a difficult college course. Wesleyan would remain on the sidelines as that vast phenomenon captured the attention of the nation. I thought: lucky Wesleyan. By virtue of its size and its emphasis on study above all else, it had evaded a malady, with

corruptions extending everywhere, that on campus after campus
was disfiguring American academic life.

In the spring of 1993, as we were busy forwarding the various
initiatives of the University Plan, Yale University called. A
spokesman for their presidential search wanted to visit, along with
some colleagues, to "pick your brain" about universities, presidencies, and leadership. The visit would be strictly private, and I was
asked to be as candid as possible with my guests. Agreeing to the
visit, I thought it odd that so great an institution as Yale would
be calling on Wesleyan. But we were "sister" schools, only some
30 miles apart, and hosting the visit seemed the neighborly thing to
do. The six visitors came, asked me many questions, and left.

Several weeks later, the same spokesman called and asked if I
would meet, again privately, with other members of the presidential search committee. Again I said yes, feeling honored that
my advice was still deemed valuable to Yale. After this visit, the
affair took a more serious turn. I was invited to New Haven to
meet with even more search committee members and, after that,
was asked to "be available" for meetings and dinner at a very
swank New York hotel (the dinner was at the ultra-fashionable
Le Cirque) with members of the Yale Corporation. I knew from
newspaper reports that the Yale presidential search was vexed.
Benno Schmidt had abruptly left the university in 1992 after
serving six tumultuous and controversial years as president. The
search had already been widely publicized, and many guesses
had been made about possible candidates. My old Stanford
colleague and friend, David Kennedy, had become a finalist for
the job but withdrew from consideration in the final stages of
the search. David, however, had been a graduate student at Yale.
He was "of Yale." I was not, neither as undergraduate nor as
graduate student. I knew Yale paid great homage to its alumni
lineage and that it had appointed only one non-Yale graduate to
its presidency in the twentieth century. Were I to become Yale's
president, I was sure that my lack of connection to its traditions
would, sooner or later, crop up as a serious deficit at a place so
proud of itself.

And yet I was in some sense apparently being considered a possible candidate for the Yale position. This at once puzzled, amused, and fascinated me. What could they be doing in New Haven? My mind raced back to 1968, when, over the phone, Maynard Mack had offered me an assistant professorship of English at Yale. When I had asked him about tenure at Yale, then and now an iffy proposition, he smoothly responded by saying that "Yale has a place for you." His answer then was every bit as unreassuring as the prospect, as I saw it, of serving as Yale's president. Again I thought: what could Yale be doing? With no antecedents at the place, without a drop of Yale blood in my body, and with the knowledge that the job would be exceptionally difficult (the city of New Haven was at the school's throat, the amount of deferred maintenance on the buildings was reputed to be about a billion dollars, the faculty was restive, the teaching assistants and the maintenance workers wanted to strike, and the campus was surrounded by crime, poverty, and unemployment), I knew that I should bring this odd courtship to an end.

And so at breakfast, in response to a leading question from the head of the corporation about how I would handle certain presidential matters at Yale, I observed that I had not been offered the job and was not at all sure I would accept an offer if one came. That's all it took. The breakfast came to a very quick but polite ending and I was on my way back to Wesleyan. I learned that no one says "No" to Yale (or even intimates it) and has the conversation continue. In a few weeks, a distinguished Yale economist who had done his graduate work at the university, Richard Levin, became the twenty-second president of Yale. That made sense to me; my being considered for the post had not.

I concluded from this Yale episode that presidential searches, no matter how strenuously they are pursued, do not identify a large number of appropriate candidates. The ground is thin when it comes to locating men and women who both can do the work and, more to the point, want to do it. The *Chronicle of Higher Education* reports that the number of applicants for administrative jobs has diminished in recent years. "Five years ago, for example, an institution searching for a president would typically receive 125 to 150 applications," said a managing director at a large search firm. Now, "the average number is between 50 and 70."[5] Perfectly competent people gifted with good sense, an admiration of academic life, a high level of stamina, diplomatic nimbleness, and an ability to remain stoic in the face of absurdity look askance at the job of president. Among them are scholars who wish to remain within their disciplines, senior administrative officers who think the presidency lacks genuine substance, and other perfectly sensible members of the academy who believe the job is impossible to do well. They know that the tenure of the average president is less than seven years; that while the salary and the perquisites are attractive, the job, as Princeton's ex-president Harold Shapiro says, "involves its share of shallow, frivolous, sentimental, and occasionally demeaning activity";[6] and that taking up administrative leadership usually means giving up scholarly leadership. The field is thus left to others.

And perhaps that explains why Emory University in Atlanta called me in the late winter of 1994. They were looking for a new president and, as I inferred, the Rolodexes of "plausible candidates" had turned up my name. I knew almost nothing about the school, other than that it was richly endowed, thanks to its long connection with the Coca-Cola Company. In time, I came to see that understanding this connection was the most efficient way of understanding the institution in its entirety. But that time was a long way off. For the present, I had only a phone call from a search firm in Chicago asking if I could be persuaded to "take a look" at the Emory presidency. At first I said No, then after another call weeks later, I said I would fly to Atlanta, but only as a "consultant" to the presidential search committee. This of course was a fiction to which I was compliant. To be a "consultant" in such matters is to be a candidate. And so, pretending to consult, I went to Atlanta. As I flew South, I thought: might this be a better job for me? Might I have greater success at Emory than I had had at Wesleyan? Would it be a better fit for all concerned? Perhaps in Atlanta and after seeing the school and its people, I would know.

I did not, however, want to leave Wesleyan. The work to which I had committed myself and others was not done. The University

Plan would take years to implement and become a part of how everyone would think about the school. And, despite the fact that being Wesleyan's president was the hardest job I had ever had, some of the peculiarities of the place had begun to grow on me. I could never mistake those particularities—the abrasiveness, the suspiciousness, and the finger-pointing—for charm, but I could see them as a way, Wesleyan's way, of going about the strange business of constructing an intellectual habitat. It is never easy to arrange an institution, and to assemble its people, in homage to the life of the mind. But Wesleyan had—uniquely—done so. It had fused the confrontational and the wayward into the provocatively creative. The contrariness of the place, its habit of being at sixes and sevens with everything including itself, had made it a fertile ground of intellectual imagination. The costs involved in such a difficult enterprise were considerable, and I felt them disproportionately levied on the administration, but such costs were always going to be high if the aim was the development of independent thinkers—faculty and students—who would become steady disturbers of conventional wisdom. The United States would never have enough independent thought, never enough interrogation of the status quo. Wesleyan's people would do their part to help make up for the slack in the national culture.

As Wesleyan's president I could continue to preside over, or witness, or at times suffer, the procedures to which the school had long ago committed itself. My role had become clear: to regulate and augment the fiscal diet on which those procedures had to live, and to make more efficient the machine of planning, money, and facilities supporting the pursuits of the faculty and students. That, I decided, defined the leadership of such a place: to aid those who partially resented my help and to champion those who believed their integrity was endangered by administrative championship. So be it. Wesleyan was a special place and I had been chosen to lead it.

But when I saw Emory, I saw something that Wesleyan could never be. I saw a version of Stanford, a Southern version, a version not as grand nor as startling to the eye, but a version nonetheless: a large, bustling, enterprising, and ambitious place whose diversity (the Wesleyan catchword) was only partly that of race and ethnicity. The diversity of Emory included a law school, a business school, a nursing school, a school of public health, a school of theology, and a constellation of hospitals. Nestled within this complex, and at its heart, was an undergraduate college. This variety created ventilation and the circulation of energy. Small colleges trap the air, leaving everyone to breathe the same thing—old gossip, threadbare rumor, the controversy of the week lingering on to become the controversy of the month or the year. Large universities, with many people and many events, constantly expel stale air. Emory had size. It had promise. It had wealth. And when I saw it and walked the campus, I sensed that it had made its way not through confrontation (thus the genteel South) but through the steady acquisition of talent and means.

I talked to the search committee and was much taken by its chair, also the chairman of Emory's trustees. Bob Strickland was an Atlantan of an old family, a banker, and the leader of the search even though he had contracted cancer and was looking stoically at the end of his life. His demeanor was easy, honest, and direct. He had not graduated from Emory but from Davidson College in North Carolina. His credo was that of a citizen of a city, and he told me that he had devoted himself to Emory because he believed that no city could be great without a great university. Caring about Atlanta, he cared about its leading private educational institution. After the two of us had several conversations that made me think of the ways Southerners might chat about things down at the general store, he said that he had little time left in his life and that he had decided that I should be Emory's president. After that, I could not tell if the search was ever really a search. But every standard procedure seemed to be honored. The committee led me through all the formal steps—interviews, meetings, lunches and dinners, some with JoAn and some without—of a full search.

The process sidestepped a potentially difficult issue: religion. Emory had been founded as a Methodist institution in 1836; this religious identity had over the years become more nominal than real, but the school's most recent president, James T. Laney, was a minister in the United Methodist Church. On the sensitive point of my own "religious faith," the ground had been cleared by a telephone conversation between one member of the search committee—a genial and nimble Methodist bishop—and Wesleyan's Roman Catholic chaplain, who had become a good friend and confidant. The chaplain, Gerry Cohen (Wesleyan *was* different), told the bishop that he considered me a man of moral integrity and steadfast fidelity to everything ecumenical. That was enough for the bishop. Had the search committee asked me if, in fact, I believed in God or had ever had a defining religious moment, I would have been compelled to say No. As an agnostic, I simply have seen no evidence of the existence of God. But thanks to the bishop and the chaplain, that delicate matter never arose.

And then the search was over. I would be Emory's next president. JoAn and I, along with Will, our son, and Katie, our daughter, were invited to Atlanta on the day when the Board of Trustees would ratify my selection. Bob Strickland chaired the meeting, invited me into the room after the vote, and happily introduced me to his colleagues. One of them, a physician, stood next to him because he knew that Bob was a sick man and might not bear up through the meeting. But he did so magnificently. In a few months, however, he was dead.

I had kept Ray Denworth, the new chair of Wesleyan's board, fully informed about the Emory negotiations (just as I had done when Yale made its strange call). A man with worldly experience and wise patience, he encouraged me both to stay at Wesleyan and to investigate Emory. And as a lawyer and a friend, he kept my news to himself. When I told him that I would be going to Emory, he told me he would work hard to bring a successor to Wesleyan who could build on the successes of my presidency. I could not have asked for a more generous or understanding response. I do not think for a moment that he was unaware of the things I had not done well at his alma mater, but I believe he valued the achievements I had brought the school in the six years from 1988 to 1994. He knew the work was hard and the place difficult. He told me he looked forward to attending my inauguration at Emory.

I left Wesleyan with relief and elation. Some hardships and pain would be ended. But I also left it with respect for what it had done and could do. It could set high intellectual standards in the classroom and meet them. It could give students a clear sense of the life of the mind. But I knew, and the school knew, that we were not meant for each other. The contrary style of the place and my own stubborn set of mind could never be in harmony. I wanted it to be friendlier and less prickly; I think it wanted me to be more admiring of its uniqueness. Each too proud, we made our way with one another for six years. When the end came, we both were relieved.

ENDNOTES

1. A recent study finds that eliminating affirmative action at elite schools would lower acceptance rates for African-American and Hispanic applicants by as much as one-half to two-thirds, while white applicants would gain little if these racial and ethnic preferences were removed. The greatest advantage would go to Asian applicants; they would take four out of every five seats created by accepting fewer African-American and Hispanic students. Acceptances for Asian applicants would go up from nearly 18 percent to more than 23 percent. See Thomas J. Espenshade and Chang Y. Chung, "The Opportunity Cost of Admission Preferences at Elite Universities," *Social Science Quarterly* 86:2 (June 2005): 293–305.

2. In fact, the Supreme Court decisions of June 23, 2003 (*Grutter v. Bollinger et al.* and *Gratz et al. v. Bollinger et al.*) allowed the inclusion of race as one of the factors that could be used in admission processes. Affirmative action would be permitted, provided that race would not be the only consideration.

3. As reported by David Leonhardt, "As Wealthy Fill Top Colleges, New Efforts to Level the Field," *New York Times*, April 22, 2004.

4. According to a study conducted in 2005 by the Institute for Diversity and Ethics in Sport at the University of Central Florida, of the 56 Division I-A football teams selected to participate in bowl games for that year, 27 schools or 48 percent did not have even 50 percent graduation rate for their football teams.

5. Paul Pain, "Help Wanted, Please: Applicant Pools for Top Administrative Posts Are Shrinking," *Chronicle of Higher Education*, December 10, 2004, p. A24.

6. Harold Shapiro, "University Presidents—Then and Now," in *Universities and Their Leadership*, ed. by William G. Bowen and Harold Shapiro (Princeton: Princeton University Press, 1998), p. 65.

24

A School with Aspirations

When departing with JoAn from Wesleyan in the summer of 1994, I was pulled aside by an administrative colleague who once lived in Atlanta. "Bill," he said, "keep something in mind: when you leave Atlanta, you're in Georgia." Atlanta is a sprawling and prosperous urban enterprise, a city of banking and law, traffic and commerce. It is the home of Coca-Cola, UPS, Home Depot, and Delta Airlines; its airport is the busiest in the world. Surrounding it is a largely rural, agricultural, and poor state, one bogged down by public schools that are among the feeblest in the nation. Weak states are always envious of strong cities. This difference—urban vs. rural, cosmopolitan vs. provincial—helps to explain Emory's odd presence in Georgia. It is a research university in a state whose intellectual resources are thin.

It is also true that when you leave Emory, you're in Atlanta. As a business city without any historically deep connection to academic activity, it has never known exactly what to make of a research university, even one that turns out to be, with 19,000 employees, the largest private employer in the city and the third in the state. Not understanding Emory, it has never made much of it. This lack of visibility within Atlanta, Georgia, and the South, helped me understand the university's unusual situation. I discovered many things about Emory in my first weeks and months on the campus, but perhaps none more consequential to my new tasks than the fact that the school's ties to the region—never strong—were growing weaker with each passing year.

By virtue of its founding, Emory happened to be in the South, but no longer was it of the South. Its faculty was increasingly national and international; less than a fifth of its undergraduate students came from the state; the graduate student population was not Southern at all. And many of its administrators, including me, had migrated from the North. Separation and distinctiveness had given Emory a disembodied character: its geographical place meaning less and less to the institution while its presiding values— intellectual ambition, selective admissions, high quality research— meaning much more. In addition, Emory had become over the years the single most progressive institution—of *any* kind—in the South. Whereas Duke, one of its few academic rivals in the South, had achieved a bright and favorable visibility in the region thanks to its powerful basketball program, and Georgia Tech, with its famous "Ramblin' Wreck" football and basketball teams, had long secured a place in the hearts of many Atlantans and Georgians, Emory had never played big-time sports. Like Wesleyan, it had always believed in the ideal of the scholar-athlete, with the athlete coming second. Also a Division III school, it was one of the few private research universities in the nation with no football team whatsoever—no players, coaches, schedule, and no stadium. In the South, where football has immense importance, this was strikingly odd. An Emory sweatshirt said it proudly: "Emory Football—Unbeaten Since 1836." But having neither big-time football nor basketball only dimmed Emory's presence in the minds of Atlantans and Georgians.

Talking to people on and off the campus in my first weeks and months there, I learned that Emory was prominent in the area in only one respect: hospital care. Residents of the city, state, and region knew the school because Emory physicians had treated them or family members or friends. What Emory did as an educational and intellectual center, on the other hand, carried little local weight. Its academic luster was recognized instead at other universities around the country and the world, at international symposiums, at places where scholars and academic issues met. Of course this is true of all research universities. Little understood at home, they find their intellectual validation elsewhere. But the South exacerbated this problem for Emory. While the region has been the home of some of the country's best writers, neither Atlanta nor the state has nourished intellectual pursuits. And the region, as its history reveals, has needed its universities—Virginia,

Chapel Hill, Vanderbilt, and others—to ward off an indifference to the life of the mind that at times becomes anti-intellectual hostility.

By the time JoAn and I arrived on the campus in the fall of 1994, the school had entered the fourth phase of its history. Founded by Methodists in the early nineteenth century, it had barely survived the Civil War, and was rescued by a Northern philanthropist hopeful that the defeated South could find a revival through its educational institutions. Entering its second phase at the beginning of the twentieth century, it had as its chancellor Warren Candler, the brother of the entrepreneur Asa Candler, the man who had seen the promise of an invigorating new drink called Coca-Cola. The entrepreneur gave one million dollars of his Coke fortune in 1915 to create a new university and draw little Emory away from its original home in a small town east of Atlanta to the city itself. This move also gave the Methodist Church an educational presence in a major Southern city, a presence it had lost in 1914 when Nashville's Vanderbilt University, under the auspices of Methodism for the first forty years of its existence, severed its ties with the church after a dispute with the bishops over who would appoint university trustees.

Through the first half of the twentieth century Emory was a good regional institution, strong in theology, clinical medicine, and a few of the liberal arts. But little money made for limited horizons. Blocking admission to African-Americans and preventing women from enrolling as residential students for much of that century, it appealed primarily to young Southern men. Thus the setting for its third phase.

In 1953, Emory admitted the first class of residential women. And by the beginning of the 1960s, as the nation changed and as the civil rights revolution got underway, it courageously arranged for the peaceful enrollment of a very small number of blacks. But it continued to be a regional school without the financial means to achieve a prominent national position. That changed dramatically in 1979, when the former, long-time chairman of the Coca-Cola Company, Robert Woodruff, along with his brother George, made a gift of $105 million to Emory. At the time, it was the largest single gift to an educational institution in the nation's history. Its then president and my predecessor, James T. Laney, made the most of this extraordinary benefaction by establishing professorships reserved for only the most eminent of scholars, and scholarships for the very best students in the nation who could be lured to Emory. Its spectacular new endowment base accelerated the research initiatives of the institution, and Emory launched itself into the national academic consciousness.

By 1994, the admissions picture showed more undergraduate women than men on campus and as high a percentage of African-American students as at any private university or college in the nation except the historically black colleges and universities. The surviving memento of its provincial history was the membership of its board of trustees, a group of lawyers, bankers, and businessmen almost all of whom lived in the same well-to-do Atlanta neighborhoods. Not a national board, but an intensely local one, it had only recently opened its ranks to a few women and African-Americans. As a souvenir of the school's by now frail Methodist identity, five places on the board were still held aside for Methodist bishops.

By the fall of my first year, Emory had everything that money could give and hope could imagine. Its impediments were not easy to put aside: the intellectual backwardness of the Deep South and the earlier mediocrity of the institution. But we were coming to a place where those constraints of the past were losing their hold and where prospects for further growth and prestige fueled the conversation of the day. JoAn and I rejoiced that Emory seemed so attractively optimistic. The school, we noted, preserved the warm manners of the South, combining them with a form of political moderation that assumed even better things were on the way. We were everywhere happily greeted and introduced to a campus that appeared, unlike Wesleyan, to welcome leadership and not to think it necessarily malign. Emory College, the undergraduate division, had long maintained a record of distinguished teaching, and good teaching was held in high esteem elsewhere on the campus. The house in which we were to live was a majestic Tudor mansion set down on more than a hundred acres of rolling land complete with a lake, a flowing creek, lovely trees and bird life, and even the rumor of a nocturnal red fox. It had once belonged to a son of Asa Candler, he who had made Coca-Cola a national drink. Once more we were reminded of the tight fit between the university and the soft drink, but only JoAn knew that before coming to Emory, I had drunk about six Cokes in my life (my mother had told me when I was young that the drink would be bad for my teeth). We moved into the house and imagined, in that strange way common to the families of university presidents, that the place was "ours." We had learned at Wesleyan that being president means inhabiting places unlike any one has known before. Emory made this anomalous situation very attractive.

Remembering other lessons of Wesleyan, I knew that the Emory job would present me with its own dangers and bad moments. Our first few happy months did not lull me into thinking that the office of the president at any institution grants either omnipotence or bliss to its occupant. I also had come to understand that the merely symbolic aspects of the job were inescapable. I kept in mind the sardonic words of a Columbia professor of psychology, J. McKeen Cattell, who had observed, "the prestige of the president is due to the growth of the university, not conversely. He is like the icon carried with the Russian army and credited with its victories."[1] I nonetheless set my mind on whatever victories there could be. Immediately liking the chief administrative officers whom I had inherited from my predecessor, I knew that any victories would be joint efforts. What could *we* do, what advancements could *we* make? Someone soon told me about Robert Woodruff's well-known declaration, "There is no limit to what a man can do or where he can go if he doesn't mind who gets the credit," and its homely wisdom helped me. I would lead, but would do so with able colleagues to whom I would give authority, discretion, and my blessing, as well as much of the credit when things went well. As I began my work, the mental compass guiding me was the one that I had sought since my years at Berkeley: an internal instrument responsive to two forces—intellectual curiosity and political awareness. Long ago I learned that this instrument would work best for me on one place only—a campus—and I hoped it would work to keep me aware of dangers to the institution that could sail in like a hurricane Hugo from regions beyond the school. (My Emory inauguration was, by way of contrast, dry, peaceful, and pleasant.)

For a while at Emory, I did not have to worry about money. As I was told during the search process, the school's endowment, some $5 billion, was among the half-dozen largest in the nation. All its books were balanced. Thanks to an indefatigably frugal chief financial officer, the physical plant had no problems of deferred maintenance. The relationship between the far-flung medical enterprise and the rest of the institution seemed healthy. That was reassuring, because, as I learned that first fall in 1994, that enterprise included two hospitals, a clinic, a pediatric facility, a geriatric facility, and the university's historic commitment to staff a huge hospital for indigent patients in downtown Atlanta with physicians, residents, and interns. Since the medical enterprise took up about four-fifths of the annual operating budget of some $1.3 billion, it *had* to remain healthy. Should it turn bad, should it lose the kind of clinical revenue it needed to continue its myriad operations, its problems would swamp the general budget of the university. With such a risk at hand, I took stock of the new medical factors confronting me: a dynamic made up of doctors' fees, reimbursements from insurance carriers, patient volume, the costs of nursing, and the perils of medical malpractice. It was very clear that I was no longer at Wesleyan. I remembered its friendly little infirmary and how an outbreak of mononucleosis on that campus would have constituted a medical nightmare. Instead, I had come to a research university—one with a sprawling health-care operation—and was face to face with all the dangers and complexities that such places have generated over the years on their way to power and prestige.

But such growth, as I soon learned, often turns out to be an irregular affair, one in which the parts of the institution expand at different rates, leaving some of them strong and others weak. Such disparate growth can arise from the ambitions of an academic dean, or from a funding opportunity suddenly presenting itself to a faculty member. Or it might come about as the result of a wealthy philanthropist willing to give to one favorite cause but no other. This was the case at Emory. Owing to the munificence of the Woodruff Foundation, the wealth of which came entirely from the fortunes of Coca-Cola, as well as to the narrow preferences of the leadership of that foundation, Emory's medical dimensions were expanded year after year. But no such fortune had been lavished on the law school, Emory College, or the business school. In comparison, they were underfunded, the little Cinderellas whose prince was yet to arrive.

This disparity among the units of the institution was reflected in other ways too. One of the most difficult problems for a university president is how to generate, and then sustain, the sense that the different units of the institution occupy common ground. What, for example, is Harvard, made up as it is of a number of different schools, each responsible as a "tub on its own bottom" for its separate fiscal integrity and fund-raising? What is the "university" that goes after the name "Harvard"? If an institution with a large health-care center requires that center to be responsible for its own budgetary health and then erects "firewalls" to protect the rest of the university from fiscal emergencies erupting at the hospital, how is that institution the same place for everyone? This is where presidents come in. They must be able to persuade everyone on campus, despite the dissimilarity of their jobs, that they are united in some joint purpose. I soon found out, however, that the Emory units were not sharing common ground with respect to a key feature of academic life, one that carried both real and symbolic significance: faculty appointments. Files proposing the appointment of new members of the faculty would arrive in great numbers in my office and that of the provost, most of them toward the end of the academic year. They would be done well or done poorly; sometimes they would arrive months after the person had, in fact, started work. Some files would include documentation of a detailed and precise sort—carefully written letters of recommendation and full teaching records—while others would provide only skimpy data that seemed to suggest that the entire matter of making a faculty appointment should be no particular business of my office or that of the provost. This, I knew, was not the way things should be. Emory needed a regular system, made up of consistent rules about evidence, that would underscore the fact that each school or unit of the institution would be treated on the same basis as every other and thus all could be thought of as constituents of *one* place. The instrument for this had to be the faculty itself.

So, after a few months in office, I established a high-level committee to consist of nine eminent professors representing the several schools of the university. I would appoint these men and women, but after everyone had gotten used to the committee, the faculty would elect its members. This new group would inspect the file of every faculty member coming forward for a tenured appointment. Its members would advise the provost and me about the merits of the proposed appointments and the degree to which job candidates met quality control. As distinguished members of the faculty themselves, they would represent Emory at its best. But they would also serve to send a message to everyone on the campus that, as large as the university was, it had to adhere to common principles of process and excellence. That I had to form this committee was a reflection of the backwardness I found here and there at Emory, a backwardness that had to be corrected by giving more uniform meaning to the entity called "Emory."

As another consequence of the different rates at which the parts of Emory had grown, the campus had become an architectural hodge-podge. Although the Beaux Arts architect Henry Hornbostel had created the original 1915 design of the campus (when Emory had been moved to its Atlanta location), his plan had lost its authority. Whenever one unit of the institution had found the money to build, it built. Local initiative reigned supreme. Buildings bearing no relationship to one another rose up to become ill-assorted neighbors. And as Emory hired more and more people in the years of its newfound prosperity, it created parking for their cars—here, there, and everywhere. Grassy spaces disappeared and asphalt took their place. Pedestrian walkways were paved over and became roadways. Although I knew nothing about campus planning, I knew that Emory's unattractive visual spectacle in 1994 reflected the problem of its identity. Emory looked confused, and people who worked there or visited the campus felt it *was* confused. The faculty and staff would work better, learn and teach more happily, I thought, if the environment they encountered day after day was coherent.

With the indulgence of the trustees, I secured the services, and then what turned out to be the considerable wisdom, diplomatic skills, and tireless energy, of a first-class campus architect. With his firm, he devised a campus master plan. It envisioned a "walking campus," with a network of buildings and outdoor spaces to bring the university closer together. We took as our object lesson a ghastly parking lot in the middle of the campus, ripped it out, planted grass and trees in its place, and threaded a brick path though this oasis. Although some forty parking places were lost, we gained an attractive suggestion of what the campus could become at its best. The success of this object lesson gave Emory the courage to make similar improvements everywhere. It began its way to aesthetic recovery.

Both of these initiatives, while real enough in themselves, were also emblematic of what had to be done if the university were to secure a sense of itself. And this is what presidents do much of the time: they take what they find, select problems they believe can be solved, and bring together others to focus intently on those solutions. At Emory I learned in short order that the particular problem was much less important than the solution. People like exemplary solutions; they want to believe that success *there* can mean success *here*; problem-solving turns out to be a mimetic art.

I also learned that schools like Emory that have experienced sudden spurts of growth sometimes behave like institutional adolescents. Strong in one place, they are gangly in others. Medical research and clinical care had developed strong musculature at Emory, but many departments in the social sciences and humanities had not. Superb ophthalmology existed at Emory, but the law school and the Economics department fell far short of eminence. Such differences could be found everywhere in the institution. Even the definition of excellence in one's career was understood differentially. Some older faculty, having come to Emory when research demands were not vigorously asserted, had become revered teachers. But now they had offices next to younger colleagues who recognized that newer patterns of national and international professional judgment put a greater premium on research than teaching. Many of those older colleagues had known but one employer—Emory—while their younger colleagues might have known several in their careers. Differences like these often created tension in tenure and promotion decisions as well as conflicts over curriculum. They also showed up in the various ways long-term institutional loyalty was expressed by young and old.

Emory, I learned, shared a good many attributes with a number of other private universities across the country. Along with such schools as Georgetown, Washington University in St. Louis, Notre Dame, Vanderbilt, Rice, the University of Southern California, Tufts, Carnegie-Mellon, Rochester, and Tulane, it was good, but had not achieved the reputation of abiding, long-term excellence. All of these schools had sufficient assets of both money and intellectual capital to imagine themselves as much more distinguished, particularly in the eyes of others, than they were. I saw them as I saw Emory. They were "aspirational" schools. Not in the very top reputational rankings, they were close to it. Yet ahead of them rested, like the immense statues of Easter Island, the apparently unmovable entities of the Ivy League, MIT, Chicago, and Stanford. Most of these schools, older and richer, showed no signs of voluntarily yielding their places as the "best" to anyone else. Public opinion, stimulated by the annual rankings of *U.S. News and World Report*, had made reputation a worthy and important institutional goal. While schools not in the "top ten" would now and again criticize (rightly, I think) the survey, most of them were nervously attentive to it. All of them asked, year after year: how can we "move up"? What can we do to improve on each of the eighteen or so criteria employed by the magazine? The statistical differences were small, yet they seemed to produce dramatic results. Across the country, the presidents and provosts of these "aspirational" schools asked themselves how to alter those numbers. Could one increase alumni giving, pick a more selective class of first-year students by admitting fewer applicants and enrolling more of them, graduate everyone admitted, and keep classes small? Alas, it all seemed painfully difficult. The fundamental problem seemed insoluble: how do you acquire prestige, eminence, and historical superiority—if you never have had it? How do you become a Harvard (1636), a Yale (1701), or a Princeton (1746) if you were founded much later, have fewer famous alumni, have little that is patrician in your culture, and can counter centuries of reputation with only the spunky ambition of the underdog? Even after the administrative staffs at these "aspirational" schools spent countless hours massaging the numbers, the Ivies and the other dominant institutions of the ranking wars remained securely on top.

Emory was (and still is) such an "aspirational" school. As its president, I believed that my job was to transform that aspiration into achievements that would enhance the strength, and thus the reputation, of the institution. At the same time, I was annoyed by the excessive attention paid to the *U.S. News and World Report* rankings. Based on faulty assumptions about what is "best," they were commercial, subjective, and misleading. I believed that for every student, there is a right school—where that young person can gain a good education. But no particular school, no matter how celebrated, is the right one for every young man or woman. Yet so powerful were the annual rankings that each year I was given a "heads-up" by Emory's public relations office hours before the *U.S. News* edition with the survey was published. That was because students would immediately write me e-mails demanding that I "make the school better." After all, their parents paid a great deal of tuition money, and when Emory earned a ranking of below #20 and above #10 (where it usually found itself), they reacted like cheated customers. I wrote back to the complaining students every year, saying something encouraging about Emory and dismissive about the rankings, reminding them that Emory would provide them with a first-rate education if they applied themselves to their work and that, after all, #15 was a good number in light of the fact that the United States had some 3,600 institutions of higher education.

A more reliable measure of Emory's progress came during my second year when the Association of American Universities invited

Emory to join. Then comprising the sixty leading American research universities, public and private, the AAU did not employ opinion polls or any other slippery data before it issued its invitations. Among the things it examined were research volume, the production of Ph.D.s, and the winning of externally funded grants. Owing to the momentum Emory had accumulated in the decade before I arrived, it now became part of the prestigious inner circle of high-powered universities. That was cheerful news indeed, and I knew it would help us in recruiting better and better faculty members, all of whom I hoped would care about teaching (although experience had taught me that good research never guarantees good teaching). As I had learned at Stanford, faculty excellence is the key—the only dependable key—to institutional excellence. Nothing else—money, programs, buildings, or even student quality—counts as much. But a strong faculty is the way to other kinds of strength.

My predecessor Jim Laney, who had sought AAU recognition for years, wanted other things for Emory too. An ambitious and stubbornly determined man, he believed that Emory had to march with the vanguard of American universities. And to be recognized as a leading institution, it could not afford to lag behind with respect to its policies on race and gender. A Southerner himself, he knew the ancient prejudices of the region could retard the growth of the institution. Shortly before I arrived, he had led the trustees of the university through what became the painful process of establishing a new antidiscrimination policy. The sticking point in the policy was the mention of "sexual orientation":

> Emory University does not discriminate in admissions, education programs, or employment on the basis of race, color, religion, sex, sexual orientation, national origin, age, disability, or veteran's status and prohibits such discrimination by its students, faculty, and staff. Students, faculty, and staff are assured of participation in university programs and in use of facilities without such discrimination.

Although the trustees endorsed the policy, not all of them were comfortable with it, and some even warned it could be used to "promote homosexuality." No such motive would have occurred to my predecessor; he was seeking only to bring Emory into conformity with similar positions taken by universities and other organizations across the country. He knew he was fighting a certain kind of bigotry, and he knew it had to be fought.

But the policy almost immediately had dramatic consequences, and these occurred in my first year. A small number of gay and lesbian employees asked that their domestic partners be enrolled in the Emory benefits program, including health care. They observed that married partners—husbands and wives—had such benefits; but that as they themselves could not marry because they were gay or lesbian, they were the victims of discrimination—Emory, they said, was denying its gay employees a university benefit. While I thought their claims were wholly valid in light of the newly established policy, I knew that if the university honored them, some trustees would declare that their worst fears had been realized. In addition, I saw real danger in bringing up the issue at a trustee meeting. I dreaded the thought of this group of Southern businessmen, lawyers, and bankers discussing gay rights. On the other hand, it was not something I could withhold from their attention. They had only nervously accepted the policy; they would not have wanted its consequences hidden from them.

I decided to visit the trustees, one by one, to explain the logic of the claims of the employees. This would also help me learn more about the trustees, people I hardly knew. As things turned out, I got quite an education during this investigation. Several of my visits brought me in touch with men and women, younger rather than older, who not only liked the policy but also favored its full application. Others seemed to require the most articulate defense of the policy I could provide before they accepted its validity and its consequences. Others told me, in polite voices, that they now saw how right they had been in opposing the policy and no amount of persuasion from me could alter their views. One trustee, whose brutal candor in my presence over the years made him oddly endearing to me, said, "Well, Bill, I don't know if we have any queers here in my company, but if we do, I sure as hell hope we don't treat them right." By the end of these interviews,

I had learned much about my employers, the trustees, and had emerged with enough approval of the process on their part that when it came to a vote at their next meeting, it quickly passed (even the brutally candid trustee voted Yes). The victory turned out to be largely symbolic in its impact on the institution; of the 19,000 or so Emory employees, only 44 took advantage of the domestic partners policy. Nonetheless, Emory had taken the right step.

After this moment had passed into school history, I had time to assess Emory's situation and my own. After one full year on campus, I had learned certain things about the school. Its most formidable asset was its endowment; we would put it to work in underwriting future academic enterprises. The Woodruff Foundation, another central asset, had proved immensely generous to Emory in the past and would continue to enrich the school, even though I feared its horizons were limited entirely to medical research and clinical care and that it would not devote any attention to other aspects of the campus. Teaching at Emory was strong both in substance and reputation. Research efforts were growing more ambitious and, in key areas, were well supported. The university was reasonably selective in admissions and would gradually become more so. The administrative staff was good and mutually supportive. The campus was beginning to look better. But Atlanta and the region were not particularly knowledgeable or supportive of what Emory sought to be. I also worried about the ungainly disproportion of money and risk in the clinical health area. If things went awry there, everything else at Emory would be in trouble. Yet another worry: alumni support of the institution was not enthusiastic; annual giving was only modest compared to peer institutions such as Rice and Duke. And I had much to worry about with the trustees. They were insufficiently engaged in what Emory was and what it had to become but were, at the same time, excessively timorous about "hot-button" issues such as gay rights. Most of them were insufficiently generous to the school. Compared to the faculty, the students, the staff, even the alumni, they, the fifth element of the school, were its weakest component.

As I reflected on having been hired as Emory's new president, I tried to imagine what Bob Strickland had in mind when he picked me. I think he wanted Emory to change. And he wanted me to lead that effort. He wanted it to become less provincial and more progressive. He must have known that the effort was not going to be easy. After all, I was going to make my mark as a "liberal" and he knew it. The issue of domestic partners had made that clear. And he must have believed me when I told him over breakfast one morning that if he wanted me to represent my values in how I would lead the university, those values would be liberal ones because the educational process itself is liberal. But Bob Strickland was now gone. I had to remember the trust he had in me. Having identified myself to him, it would now be my job to identity myself, and the school I represented, to the community, both local and national.

This was my second presidency and I now had learned enough to know that a fundamental tension would always exist between the values of the president and those of the men and women who had appointed the president. This tension is part of the presidential role, and while its rougher edges can be smoothed over, it cannot be imagined out of existence. After all, as Harold Shapiro put it after being president at both the University of Michigan and Princeton, "many people wonder why a public or private community should exuberantly support, respect, honor, and treasure a set of activities designed in part to be critical of just those arrangements within which most, if not all, members of the governing board . . . have prospered."[2] The answer for him, as it was for me and every other university president, is that universities exist in large part to interrogate the status quo; their boards exist to keep it going. The president exists precariously in the middle ground between the critical thrust of the institution and the fiduciary duty of the board. The president works as a broker, explaining to the board, when necessary, why this or that faculty member who has done or said something odd, extreme, or embarrassing must be defended. From time to time, he must also explain to the faculty why and how the board has decided to exercise its fiduciary duty—to change the rate at which the earnings on endowment will be paid out, for instance, or to authorize or veto the building of a new library building or laboratory.

The president, however, must never yield on some fundamental points, even when acting at his best as broker. The freedom of a faculty member to be utterly foolish must always be protected (but not the freedom to act destructively, as the Franklin case at Stanford had taught me). In my second year at Emory, I had to explain the right of one of the university's political scientists to publish a book that solemnly and tediously recounted, via something he described as "Scientific Remote Viewing," his encounters with Martians, a race of humanoids he called "the Greys," and with Adam and Eve, Jesus, and the Buddha. The professor had earlier held a faculty chair at the University of California at Los Angeles and was respected as an expert in nonlinear mathematical modeling of elections and other (terrestrial) social phenomena. I found his book absurd; so did his colleagues in political science. The local radio stations had a field day with him and his "encounters." When meeting with the board, it was my role to defend his right to publish his "findings" and to counsel that his fate would best be administered not by punitive sanctions but by the scorn and ridicule that only his professional colleagues could deliver. In time, the political scientists took care of matters and the book disappeared into the oblivion it deserved.

Events like this are rare in a president's life. Much more common are clashes between the values of the institution, as protected by the president, and the opinions of board members who are made anxious by the critical stance universities traditionally take toward the conventional wisdom of the day. A quiet comedy governs these encounters, with the faculty believing that trustees are conventional conservatives, and the trustees believing that the faculty are typical liberals. Each party believes the other enjoys too easy and protected a style of life, and both envy what they think the other has (money in the one case, and the freedom of the campus in the other). Both think the president is a bit too partial to the ideas and values of the other. And the president knows, as I did at Emory, that he can never fully please either party, neither trustee nor faculty member, and will forever remain curiously marginal to both. The job, as people say, is "full-time." It demands complete engagement while, at the same time, requiring a curious detachment from the passions of everyone else. In that middle zone, presidents must find their way. Month by month, lesson after lesson, I was finding mine.

ENDNOTES

1. J. McKeen Cattell, *University Control* (New York: Arno Press, 1977; reprint of original 1913 edition), p. 33.
2. Shapiro, "University Presidents—Then and Now," pp. 67–68.

25

Being a Proprietor

After my first years at Emory, I found it easy at times to believe that I had become the proprietor of a large commercial enterprise. I usually overcame such thoughts by reminding myself that a university is a tax-exempt nonprofit endeavor with learning as its central activity and knowledge its most important "product." Yet considerable evidence now and again suggested otherwise.[1] First of all, Emory—just like a business—needed a great deal of money to sustain its operations, to meet its payroll, keep its utilities running, operate its sophisticated computing networks, and pay down its bond issues. It could turn to only a few sources of income for that money: earnings from its endowment, funded support for research, annual donations from alumni and friends, and tuition payments. The last made up the lion's share (some 70 percent) of Emory's annual education budget. Tuition provided a great harvest of money from parents and others, a harvest we eagerly brought in year after year. While we and other private research universities knew we were increasing tuition at a pace greater than any of the indices normally used to measure inflation, that knowledge did not stop us from turning up the ratchet. We saw the money coming in and we saw it just as quickly going out in payroll, plant maintenance, purchases in equipment, and the like. Just as in a business, our income had to cover all our expenses. We had to have more and more of it. Our creditors were asking for more.

Second, I was prompted to see Emory as a commercial enterprise when I witnessed—daily and in huge buildings near my office—the never-ending flow of patients in our hospitals and clinics. We built new facilities for those patients, sought the best doctors to treat them, hunted for ever-scarce nursing resources, installed state-of-the-art medical equipment, negotiated with insurers, settled malpractice suits, and constantly sought to fill beds with as many sick people as we could while making sure that they did not stay any longer than their insurance permitted. Again, all of this was quite businesslike, vying as we did against genuinely commercial hospitals in Atlanta and the surrounding territory for patients, physicians, and technical staff.

Many of the trustees seemed to be most at home with this side of Emory. I had learned long ago that trustees typically are more comfortable with business enterprises than with intellectual ones. As corporate executives, bankers, and lawyers, they gravitate toward that part of a university most like their own lives. But unlike those who served as Emory's trustees, I worried constantly that the institution had somehow wandered into the world of medicine-as-business and had, with its clinical operations, placed itself in competition with health-care enterprises in Atlanta that had no interest in academic values or principles.

History explains how this happened. Emory had long ago established its two hospitals and its small clinic to provide patients for its medical students. As the years passed, however, the clinical operations expanded, while the teaching needs remained roughly the same. In part, the prospect of increased income for the clinicians drove this growth. More patients meant more physicians, and that meant more employees who could earn greater and greater annual salaries. Most universities with medical schools face the same problem: a volume of patients and a collection of buildings in excess of pedagogical necessity. What resulted at Emory was a business at the heart of an educational enterprise. As I looked at this enterprise, I saw what the trustees saw: income, deficits, ledgers of profit and loss, capital investments, and all the stresses of traditional commerce. But while I worried about what the university as an academic undertaking had thereby become, they did not. They liked what they saw because they understood it. About the rest of the institution their understanding was limited.

There was a third reason to think of Emory as a business: some of the parents and some of their children often behaved like customers. Many families, after paying annual sums approaching

$40,000 for tuition, room and board, and books, viewed the university as they would view any organization from which they purchased services. All of this was a far cry from the attitude of my parents, as well as my own attitude, as I thought back to Haverford. My folks thought I was fortunate to be in college, and they were sure the school was right in all it did (if fault was to be found, it was surely mine). Some Emory parents, on the other hand, saw their tuition payments, on which we relied so heavily, as leverage with which to deal rather sharply with us. One such parent called me to request that his daughter be moved from a dormitory room he considered too small to a larger room, and that a student, any student, on financial aid be relocated to the smaller room. After all, he explained, "I am paying full freight for my daughter and my money is going to help with the financial aid for the other kid." He was right in his understanding of how the money flowed, even if he was deficient in his grasp of how we were determined to treat all students as equals. (We did not move his daughter.)

Another parent, also a "full-freighter," but craftier than the first, called me to ask if he could ask the Internal Revenue Service to consider his tuition payments as a "charitable deduction," since we would be using a portion of them to provide financial aid for some other student. Certainly, I said, but if he did so, he should also inform the IRS that we were making a kind of charitable deduction to him by charging only two-thirds of what his child's education cost us. He asked me to explain, and I told him that most private universities distinguish between the charged "price" of a year's education and the actual "cost" to the institution of educating a student. The schools use donations and endowment earnings to make up the difference. We were thus giving him and other parents a hefty discount, and he was seeing only part of the equation. Thanking me for my information, he told me that, upon reflection, he would not be bringing up his ingenious scheme with the IRS.

The Wesleyan experience had prepared me for the claims, some of them extraordinary, that some parents can make on a school. The "Blodgett Saga" came back to me: the parents of young Blodgett, who received a B+ and not an A− in a Wesleyan course in 1991, had first appealed to the professor in charge for a change in the grade, then to the department chairperson, then to the dean, then the provost, then me, then the chairman of the board of trustees, and, at last, spectacularly enough, Lowell Weicker, the governor of the state. At every door, the Blodgetts were (rightly) rebuffed. The Wesleyan answers were always the same (I don't know how Weicker's office responded): the teacher, in whom sole authority resided, had given the grade and so the B+ had to stand. According to all academic tradition and rules, their son had earned and deserved a B+. Nevertheless, the Blodgetts were determined to prove otherwise, believing as they did that an A− would clearly benefit their son more than a B+. They were exceptional people, but nonetheless revealed the extent to which some parents saw the educational process as just one more system they could "game" by tenaciously fighting it with a grievance.

While I understood the shocking effect college tuition had on the budgets of many families, I sought ways to explain to Emory parents why our costs escalated every year and why we had to pass those increases on to them. I said that they had asked us to provide a first-class education for their children and that we, wanting the same thing for those children, had to pay for what this would cost. To myself, I called this the "climbing wall effect." Parents and students wanted us to do more, add more buildings, make classes smaller with better professors, increase computer power and access, and enrich the menus in the dining areas. A few of them also wanted, in the physical education center, a climbing wall. While we constantly looked for ways to reduce our costs, the demands such "consumers" placed on us were driving up our cost, and thus our price. Were we not to add the wall and do everything else that students and parents wanted us to do, we would fall behind our competitors. The climbing wall was only a part of it. If Duke University had a late-night grill, certainly we should have one. If the University of Virginia was making its campus wireless, our campus should go wireless ASAP. And of course we built the climbing wall.

Added to that competitive spiral was our own desire to reach out to the best professors (who cost much more than walls), to increase the holdings of the library (the cost of books and periodicals soared past any normal inflationary scale), and to improve the appearance of the campus, for the sake of present and prospective students as well as everyone else who lived and worked there. Higher education is people-intensive, and where other enterprises can reduce costs by switching from labor (expensive people) to technology (inexpensive robots), we could not. Who would want the teacher replaced by the DVD or the automated PowerPoint lecture? Nor could we outsource our labor costs to another country; the best teaching at a college or university has to occur on the campus.

Furthermore, we could not abandon, the way a manufacturing company or an insurance firm does, a sideline that is not "generating revenue." Small departments, such as classics or philosophy, are hard to justify if one calculates their costs as a function of their enrollments. But given their centrality to the humanities, and to a liberal education, they must remain permanent parts of every respectable campus. Thus the university is what it is: a proudly venerable institution, traditional in its procedures and customs, remarkably backward-looking in some of the ways it deals with the world of today and the world yet to come, with a central "faculty," that is, the faculty itself, that is always going to be made up of people and never mechanized or turned into fiber-optic cable or shipped overseas. In the end, all these features make places like Emory expensive.

Not only expensive, but largely impractical too. This feature of higher education has always raised questions in the mind of the public. Many Americans have traditionally wanted colleges and universities to settle down to one main task: to solve the country's problems. Land-grant schools were established in nineteenth-century America with that aim—to improve agriculture, to teach engineering, and to show better ways of mining and manufacturing. The argument for such institutions is that education should directly respond to the problems of society, solving things rather than analyzing them. Universities should offer "answers" rather than "understanding." In my nine years at Emory, there was no stronger or more persistent proponent of this attitude to the campus—any campus—than Jimmy Carter.

The former president's relation to Emory and what it stood for was complicated. He and his wife Rosalynn had founded the

Carter Center in 1982 with the blessing of my predecessor and with Emory's willingness to serve as its patron. The buildings of the Center were not on the campus, but some five miles away. Carter was careful enough (and proud enough) to want to protect the integrity of what he and many donors had built, and Emory was careful to respect the independent work undertaken by the Center. The fiscal reality underlying the relationship, however, was one in which all of the Center's endowment was commingled with that of the university, and every employee of the Center, including the former president—who now and again met with classes at Emory—received his or her paycheck from Emory. For this reason, Carter often facetiously referred to me as "my boss."

During the many breakfasts we had together with our wives over the years, I learned that our missions—that of the university and that of the Center—were fundamentally at odds. In part this difference grew out of the strong personality of Carter himself. His extraordinary career—from rural Plains, Georgia, to the White House—was fueled by two powerful engines: his profound Christian piety and his conviction that he was meant by destiny to do great things in the world. The first made him the least venal and materialistic of political leaders; the second made no ambition too large for him to entertain. The naval officer and engineer who could run a peanut farm would also be the man who would become a state senator, a state governor, and at last the 39th president of the United States. He had never found much use for self-doubt.

Armed by the convictions of an engineer and statesman, Carter would now and again question me about the slow and wayward pace at which the university worked, or why it could not ask more of its students to go to parts of the globe where they could deal directly—"hands-on," as he put it—with the problems of peace, hunger, or disease. I wanted to respond by questioning him about the lack of any scholarly findings published by the Center. (I quietly resented his questions; he would have resented mine.)

While accompanying him on his election-monitoring trips to Israel and Peru or, at his invitation, to see him receive the Nobel Peace Prize in 2002, I witnessed how his life made sense. He showed how thinking could yield results, planning could make for action, and that people could achieve wonderful practical victories. But he had little sympathy with research activities that yielded no immediate results. His was an exemplary American career, one in which *accomplishment* would forever trump everything else, even the thought that preceded accomplishment. For him, as for many Americans, thinking people were meant to serve active people. That, I thought, was why the Carter Center showed so little interest in research publications about its own work. What was done was done; it was time for more activity. When I extolled the virtues of thought itself—thinking that bore no direct gain or immediate consequence—his attention wandered. And yet he was proud of his relationship to Emory, and all of Emory was proud that such an extraordinary individual was linked to the university. I had such respect for the man that, now and again, he almost made me think that a university, especially a costly university, should place results ahead of research, results ahead of reflection. Given all I knew about what universities can uniquely do, however, those moments did not last long. To answer Carter properly I needed to quote to him John Henry Cardinal Newman on the purposes of a university:

> The man who has learned to think and to reason and to compare and to discriminate and to analyze, who has refined his taste, and formed his judgment, and sharpened his mental vision, will not indeed at once be a lawyer, or a pleader, or an orator, or a statesman, or a physician, or a good landlord, or a man of business, or a soldier, or an engineer, or a chemist, or a geologist, or an antiquarian, but he will be placed in that state of intellect in which he can take up any one of the sciences or callings.[2]

Getting to know Jimmy Carter deepened my respect not only for him but, more importantly, for the unique invention the research university is. The more he thought it should produce immediate results, the more I knew it should produce the thinking that would lead, yes, to more thinking.

The most delicate campus reality, one that also added considerably to our costs and sometimes made me imagine that I was running a hospital, if not a business, had to do with the psychological care of some of our students. College and university students today require more psychological assistance, and more intense assistance, than they have needed before. According to a 2004 survey by the American College Health Association, almost half of them are so depressed at times that they cannot adequately function in class, and almost one in six meets the criteria for clinical depression. When they check into the psychological counseling centers on campus, as they regularly did at Emory, about one quarter of them are taking psychiatric medications, about three times as many as ten years before.[3] At any given time on the Emory campus, the counseling center reported an average of six students on "suicide watch." The school's psychological counselors, versed in the turmoil and anxiety of students, also knew that post-adolescence is often the time of life at which schizophrenia has its onset. When that happens, college life becomes unbearable for those students and often for those close to them. And the counselors also knew that many students undergoing treatment were contending with issues that came not from their studies but from home: broken families, money worries, excessive parental pressure to succeed, and a host of other realities no campus gates can keep out.

When I learned about the acute distresses with which some students were living, I was stunned by the sadness of their young lives. With difficulty, I became accustomed to the students' problems of eating disorders, alcohol abuse, drug dependency, depression, and exhaustion. Harder to come to terms with were those young lives that seemed blighted from the start. An Emory student was reported absent from all her classes, and her roommate said she had not left her room for weeks. Counselors found her there, curled up in the fetal position. She had not eaten for days. Because she was helplessly weak, the counselors knew that her parents had to come to campus to take her home. But over the phone, her mother responded: "Perhaps you don't understand. She was my problem for seventeen years. She's your problem now."

The American university is unique in the degree to which it proves responsive, often expertly so, to sad realities like this one.

Unlike its European counterparts, where no such solicitude is even imaginable, the American campus tries to attend to student needs (and demands) in all their variety. It provides lodging, food, sophisticated means of communication, entertainment of many kinds, athletic events, career counseling, physical recreation (that climbing wall), medical care, and, for those who need it, psychological and psychiatric intervention. It also teaches. And it is held to account for how it makes all these things available by means of a strenuous competition among universities. Parents study the schools to which their children apply; those children study the schools too. The head of Harvard's student mental health service said, "Since each student has roughly a 50–50 chance of having some symptoms of depression or other problems, I think it has to be part of the consideration in choosing a college."[4] The schools must deliver. But such responsiveness is expensive.

When the counselors described the circumstances some students faced, my mind would turn back to Haverford and the kind of emotional immaturity that overcame me during my first two years there, giving me a way to sympathize with the ordeals endured by some Emory students. What had become different in the passage of forty years or so, however, was the kind of professionals now ready to treat the psychological problems of the students. By way of contrast, Haverford five decades ago had only one psychiatrist on its staff, and his office was open one hour a week for the 454 students. Since he came to campus with his lunch in a box adorned by a decal of Roy Rogers, he was never able to gain our full esteem and confidence (we thought he should look and act more like Sigmund Freud). But all of that was yesteryear. The typical campus mental health center now includes, in addition to psychiatrists, a number of psychologists, social workers, and nurse practitioners. By the 1990s, the numbers of counselors had increased dramatically, as had the number of students needing to see them.

Despite the presence of these professionals, students commit suicide. It happened at least once every year that I was president at Emory. When it occurred, the campus reverberated and many other students, some of them already anxious or depressed, suffered in imaginative sympathy. At these moments I, as president, made the telephone call to the home or visited the parents when they arrived on campus. Time stopped then for everyone, and we would face the waste of a young life and the ending of family dreams. Since so much at a college or university is predicated on the promise of youth, and the way in which a young person is, for the first time, encountering the world without the company of one's parents, the sudden presence of those parents on the campus after a suicide seemed to bring everything to a standstill. And with suicides, no learning seems to have occurred; education has failed; all is lost. It usually took weeks after that kind of death for student life to find its rhythms again.

A suicide can also tell a president about the infinite variety of human response in times of grief. In the spring of 1995, one father, having come to campus to bring home the body of his nineteen-year-old son, who had ingested a concoction of pills and walked into the woods to die, spent his time with me pounding the walls of my office, weeping, and crying out insults against his son: "You stupid son of a bitch, you jerk, you loser, you weak piece of shit! Why did you do this, why did you screw up this whole thing so bad?" At such moments, no president remains a president. He is, as I was then, another father, another man grieving over the loss of a child.

The condition of student mental health exacted emotional costs of every kind—from families, classmates, and the institution. These costs were certainly more important than the financial ones. We worried more about the turmoil some students were facing than the line-item budgetary reality of a large staff of psychological counselors. But those financial costs remained and had to be met the way all costs were met—largely through the ever-dependable tuition income. Hence my recurring worry that I was sitting atop a business and not an educational institution. The students whose families could not pay the full tuition received financial aid. But that aid is not "free." Those on financial aid incurred substantial indebtedness through loans from the institution and the federal government (for those with such loans, the average amount coming due upon graduation from Emory was almost $20,000).

There seemed evidence aplenty that I was operating a commercial enterprise.

But because I wanted to see Emory in light of its high-minded educational mission rather than in the light of the accounting realities embedded in it, I reflected on the quality of moral teaching the school was providing. Or, rather, not providing. I had a suspicion that Emory, just like Berkeley and Stanford, was not teaching its students very much about the ethical standards one might expect of college graduates. The reasons for this failure were easy to understand: too little time to do it, too little understanding of who in particular might provide such moral instruction, too much uncertainty about what rules to follow and what ethical codes to respect. Moral relativism—individual tastes and standards—ruled the day. Yet every study I read revealed that students cheated in myriad ways and that plagiarism was a constant on every campus. They copied from each other; they downloaded papers from the Internet and presented the work as their own; they colluded on lab reports. Most of the professors knew this was going on. So did most of the students.

Despite my own grim awareness that any such project might ultimately be written off as quixotic, I established a committee to look into those kinds of violation of academic honor on the Emory campus. How much was there, what was being done about it, and how might we improve the process to deal with it? I asked the dean of student life and the head of Emory's ethics center to chair the committee; to work with students, faculty members, and administrative personnel appointed to the group; to report to me and to the campus in general on their findings; and to make recommendations about what the university could do to end this kind of dishonesty.

After months of hearings, the circulation of questionnaires, and the visit to the campus of colleagues from other universities, the committee finished its work and told me, with somber regret, that while cheating of various kinds could be found everywhere on the campus, it was not able to recommend any changes in our means to deal with it. A quixotic venture indeed. The committee had discovered what I feared it would discover: professors in general were unwilling to do anything different about a problem they knew was real but which they thought insuperable. Even though the campus had the apparatus to conduct formal hearings into charges of cheating, many professors thought the process was too lengthy, too stressful, and likely to issue in penalties either too severe or too weak. Other professors were simply too preoccupied with their research to take the time to file charges; suspecting that cheating had occurred, they wrote it off as the minor collateral damage of the day. Yet others simply preferred to bypass the invocation of any hearing and, on their own, to give the offending student a failing grade. And some preferred to believe that, in the end, the moral responsibility as well as the moral consequences lay with the student who had cheated: people who cheat cheat only themselves. The community itself should stand aside, just as they would stand aside.

The committee's dismaying results confirmed what I feared: large research universities are inept in forming ethical standards and processes affecting students. "Citizenship" is not a meaningful educational goal at such places, and the topic is formally addressed only on those occasions, such as commencement speeches and welcoming remarks to parents, where its force is rhetorical and not practical. Those who should be the key players in the endeavor of civic and moral education—the faculty—have differing beliefs and attitudes about it. Some of them are too busy to care, others do not trust the formal hearings at which students can be brought to account, and others fear parents bringing lawsuits against them if they challenge the honesty of student work. The consequences, at Emory and elsewhere, are a mishmash of neglect, a few formal sanctions, and private justice randomly dispensed. I was once again reminded of how great a distance I had traveled since those days long ago at Haverford, with its strict honor code.

I was also reminded, painfully, of my own limited power as president to act. I now knew, from the committee and my own observations, that a sizable number of students were failing to abide by proper ethical standards and that many members of the faculty were negligent or cynical. But I could not close the gap between my knowledge and the action I wanted Emory to take. In large measure, presidents ask others to act. In this instance, I had asked the faculty to act, and it responded, like Melville's Bartleby the Scrivener, that it would "prefer not to." In the end, nothing was done, and I look back on this episode with shame. My hope that the ethical mission of the institution would clearly differentiate it from a commercial enterprise was given little support from this lesson about the moral mission of the campus.

By the late 1990s, another ethical dilemma arose. University presidents and many others had become aware that the American research university was showing some signs of becoming a commercial operation through the expansion of an avenue that had opened up a few decades earlier—the connections faculty members could establish with profit-making companies, particularly pharmaceutical firms, biotech operations, and computer enterprises. Venture capitalists, getting wind of what an innovative chemist had come up with in the lab, could underwrite the scientist's research on condition that part of the profits resulting from the patentable ideas or products deriving from that research flowed back to the investors. By means of a profit-sharing formula, the university and the scientist made money too. Some fortunes had already been built in this way; others seemed possible. By the late 1990s, three Emory scientists—Dennis Liotta, Raymond Schinazi, and Woo-Baeg Choi—had seen their work result in a antiviral "cocktail" valuable in the worldwide struggle against AIDS. The drugs they helped to create, Emtriva and Truvada, were approved by the Food and Drug Administration and were made available, at production cost, in dozens of developing countries through the pharmaceutical company Gilead. After a period of intense legal wrangling, in which Emory lawyers and outside experts supported the scientists, they had become multimillionaires and the university had seen some tens of millions of dollars per year begin to flow into its treasury. Money like that gets the attention of everyone. It also prompts some people to fear that the research imperatives of the university are being bent in the direction of the dollar and that crass motives are fouling the cherished purity of scientific investigation.

I saw no way to stop these kinds of scientific enterprises, some of them both immensely beneficial and immensely profitable; nor did I believe they should be stopped. It is impossible to dictate the limits beyond which a scientist's investigations should not go, provided that he or she has met clear rules concerning the use of human subjects and has been fully responsive to other basic considerations. I was also happy about how we would use the school's share of this annual new revenue; we directed all of it to support scientific research in general on the campus. We established, moreover, definitive rules about the relationships that off-campus companies could have with Emory faculty, and we redrew the profit-sharing formula to enhance the university's interest. More than that I did not think we could do.

Nonetheless, I worried about the imbalance that profitable research creates between members of the faculty. In sanctioning certain kinds of research in the natural sciences and the medical school, research that could generate great amounts of money for the researcher and for Emory, we knew that a few professors were occupying privileged positions. But what about the others? There was no way to imagine that either the professor of Argentine history or the philosopher writing about Hegel would ever come up with a profit-making idea. That kind of difference between faculty members could work to undermine the notion of a "community of scholars."

While I think this problem will never become an emergency on any campus, including Emory's, owing to the small number of million-dollar schemes, it is real. Money does give orientation to research in a few academic areas, and it can divide the faculty. The impression that the university is "for sale" or that it is a "kept" enterprise can also injure the reputation of the academic pursuit in general. It can contribute to the belief among attentive American citizens that the university, incapable of rising above its own parochial concerns and financial self-interest, should lose its tax-exempt status. These twin concerns—is the academy being commercialized, and are fissures being created within the faculty?—will intensify as entrepreneurs see more clearly the profits to be made and the advantages of working with some researchers and not with others. Emory and all other research universities will have to exercise continuing vigilance to protect their institutional integrity. Moreover, some entrepreneurs will want to write contracts with professors that limit access on the part of all others to the research. They will not care about the traditional niceties of open disclosure or academic freedom. This conflict between private revenue and pure research will test universities and their presidents. On this point, the presidents will have to be very tough in remembering what their institutions are: nonprofit and educational.[5]

From the very start of my Emory presidency, I learned that one area of university life would give me no worry at all, financial or otherwise: intercollegiate athletics. Emory belongs to the University Athletic Association, whose members—Brandeis, the University of Chicago, Carnegie Mellon, Case Western Reserve, New York University, the University of Rochester, Washington University in St. Louis, and Emory—have pledged to put scholarly life before the pursuit of sport. They have become accustomed to the logical result: a complete local and national obscurity enshrouding their games. In my nine years at Emory, the Atlanta newspapers never reported a single score from any contest on the campus but gave close attention to every football and basketball game at nearby Georgia Tech—a Division I school. No Emory game ever caused a crowd to gather. And yet some of the students who played intercollegiate sports at Emory could have played at the Division I level had they wanted. Instead, correctly perceiving that athletic demands at Division I would jeopardize their academic pursuits, they enrolled at Emory. Their presence was spectacular. Student-athletes at Emory performed better in the classroom, with higher grade-point averages and more academic honors, than students not participating in college sports. What made this wonderful result possible? Perhaps their physical conditioning, their observance of rigorous schedules, their coaches, or perhaps the fact that Emory preserved the ideal of the healthy and accomplished student-athlete. Whatever the causes, the results were splendid.

As I got to know some of those students and their successes, I tried to imagine the impossible: a landscape of American higher education from which the most prominent features of Division I athletics were removed. Gone were the immense stadiums, the skyboxes, the acres of parking spaces for fans, the skewed admission standards for the athletes, the consequent presence of a number of young men and women who are students in name only and whose likelihood of ever graduating with a meaningful degree is slim,[6] the long training hours and the travel schedules that make hours of study hard for the athletes to come by, the segregation at some schools of the athletes from the other students by virtue of their special diets and exercise regimens, and the large coaching staffs with their swollen salaries and lucrative perquisites. If all these things were gone and no memory of them remained, would anyone, I wonder, seek to create them? Since they are all inimical to the spirit of intellectual life and academic pursuits, would it even occur to anyone to think they were meant to be an integral part of the American university? What university president, aware of what the Knight Commission calls a "disgraceful environment" and a "sellout" to commercialism, would want to bring "ugly disciplinary incidents, outrageous academic fraud, dismal graduation rates, and uncontrolled expenditures" to the campus?[7] Whenever I met with my presidential colleagues, many of whom were the custodians of huge athletic departments, I noticed that they treated the subject of big-time sports with the same embarrassed helplessness that surrounded the topics of, say, grade inflation or student cheating. Their phlegmatic attitude was close to surrender. They seemed to be saying: who can do much about these things; who can fight against what the Knight Commission has called "the big business of big-time sports"?

Yet all my presidential colleagues know this fact: no European or even Canadian university has big-time athletics or would want them. They are an accident of our nation's history, the result of an innocent pastime for college students now run wild and rampant, fueled by television, the power of spectacle, and the love of crowds for frenzied ritual. Despite the pleasures afforded to the fans, the costs of such distortion are great to the schools and even to many of the athletes. In their study of intercollegiate sports, William G. Bowen and James L. Shulman have shown how student-athletes in high-powered programs are often confined within a university subculture in which superior intellectual performance, rather than valued, is scorned.[8] Education's primary thrust passes them by. In his several books on big-time sports, Murray Sperber has run to ground the myth that winning sports teams bring money into the general university coffers. He has shown, as has the Knight Commission, that fans of winning teams contribute substantially to athletics, but give nothing to other university programs. And even with such fan support, the games, with few exceptions, wind up as a drain on general university funds.[9]

All of this meant little on the Emory campus. Intercollegiate athletics seemed to exist in ways unique to itself. Another study by Bowen and Sarah A. Levin investigated Division III schools that offer no athletic scholarships and pursue no dreams of national glory. At most of these schools, unlike Emory, the athletes were more likely to end up in the bottom third of their college class, performing worse than the students who played no college sports. Even more troubling is the evidence that the athletes elsewhere did even less well academically than predicted by their test scores and high school grades.[10] But what Bowen and Levin discovered at Emory was the exact opposite: the athletes did better than the other students. Indeed, the situation seemed as good as it could get, and Bowen and Levin congratulated us for such an accomplishment.

With a record of success like this, few students, faculty members, or trustees ever asked me to explore the possibility of Emory becoming a Division I institution. I think they were quietly grateful for what the university had. Thanks to the accidents of its history (was it the Methodist ministers at the turn of the century who worried about gambling at sporting events?), Emory did not have to carry the burden of expense, time, and scandal that now so often marks big-time college athletics. And for me, not having this immensely expensive folly to think about, I was free to worry about the other ways in which the university could be considered a commercial enterprise and I its proprietor.

ENDNOTES

1. My walks around the Emory campus told me that most of the people
I saw working for the university were not, in fact, teaching at all. Those
people made up the bulk of the Emory payroll—some 68 percent of it.
Other schools showed the same thing. Employees who are *not* teachers
comprise 75 percent of Harvard's total payroll, 80 percent at Princeton,
and a whopping 85 percent at Vanderbilt. Professors, that is, constitute
only a minority of university workers; the majority is made up of administrators of various sorts, fund-raisers, maintenance and clerical personnel,
and myriad technical and support staff. See the "2003 Fall Staff Survey"
conducted by the Integrated Postsecondary Education Data System
(IPEDS) of the National Center for Education Statistics, http://nces.ed.gov/
ipedspas.
2. John Henry Cardinal Newman, *The Idea of a University* (New Haven &
London: Yale University Press, 1996; originally published in 1852),
p. 118.
3. See the *National Survey of Counseling Center Directors*, conducted
annually by Dr. Robert P. Gallagher of the University of Pittsburgh, as
reported by Mary Duenwald, "The Dorms May Be Great, but How's the
Counseling?" *New York Times*, October 26, 2004, section F, p. 1.
4. Ibid.
5. A first-rate study of the many issues involved in this problem is:
Donald G. Stein, ed., *Buying In or Selling Out: The Commercialization
of the American Research University* (Piscataway, NJ: Rutgers University
Press, 2004). In it more than a dozen experts look at the many complexities involving academic life and commercial possibilities.
6. The National Collegiate Athletic Association disclosed in early 2005
that almost one half of the top-level college football and men's basketball teams would likely graduate less than half of their athletes. See
Chronicle of Higher Education, March 11, 2005, p. A40.
7. *A Call to Action: Reconnecting College Sports and Higher Education:
Report of the Knight Foundation Commission on Intercollegiate Athletics*,
June 2001, pp. 11, 20, and 13.
8. James L. Shulman and William G. Bowen, *The Game of Life: College
Sports and Educational Values* (Princeton: Princeton University Press,
2002).

9. Murray Sperber, *College Sports Inc.: The Athletic Department vs the University* (New York: Henry Holt and Co., 1990), pp. 4 and 2.

10. William G. Bowen and Sarah A. Levin, in collaboration with James L. Schulman, Colin G. Campbell, Susanne C. Pichler, and Martin A. Kurzweil, *Reclaiming the Game: College Sports and Educational Values* (Princeton: Princeton University Press, 2003).

26

Real Power and Imaginary Power

By 2000, I was making almost half a million dollars a year. My salary was greater than that of anyone else at Emory, save several clinical physicians and those who oversaw the affairs of the health sciences. It was three or four times as great as it would have been had I remained a professor of English. Moreover, JoAn and I lived, free of any cost to us, in that large and imposing house. When we entertained, which was about three times a week, we had cooks, servers, and people to prepare and clean up. Since we ate so often at university functions, our grocery bills were small.

In addition, my office was superbly maintained by a smart, efficient, and witty woman who kept my schedule clean and problem-free. Another woman, keen-eyed and discreet, was paid by the university to come by our house once a week to go over its budgets. Unlike some of my presidential colleagues, I had neither chauffeur nor house manager, and preferred that situation. Instead, I drove myself in a car furnished by the university. But had I asked any time for a driver, one would have been assigned to me. When I flew on airplanes, I often sat in first class.

No one else at Emory lived as we did. Our circumstances were both appropriate to the presidency and absurd. Appropriate because they settled on me, by tradition, certain symbolic characteristics that were essentially princely. As president, I was to be "separate," shorn of mundane cares, cosseted, and thus free to exercise important guiding functions. When I spoke, I alone was to speak for all of Emory. From my hand came the power to confer degrees at graduation and to open a new building by cutting the ribbon. I also acted for the institution in thanking this person or celebrating that one. No important philanthropic gift came to Emory without my knowledge, and many came at my initiative.

In official processions, I was either the first or the last, but always prominent. I was the only one mentioned by name when the trustee bishops prayed for the sake of Emory. My parking hangtag was numbered "1." It was hard to take all of this seriously, and occasionally I marveled at the absurdity of the role. It was always a relief when old friends—from Haverford, Berkeley, or Stanford—showed up and I could reclaim our pre-presidential style. They were pleased to remind me who I once had been, and in their presence I removed the mask that presidents wear.

Our circumstances were appropriate because institutions like modern research universities, with built-in disintegrative potential, need traditional symbols and atavistic presences to keep them moving forward in a stable fashion. But the circumstances were absurd because the symbolic power so generously conferred on me had no true relationship to my actual power. University presidents, as it took me several years and two presidencies to discover, must always live with the uneasy knowledge that a strange fiction hedges their lives. That fiction has to do with their authority. Sooner or later they see that it is mitigated by rules and traditions, held hostage by the power of others, and constantly undercut by the simple fact that the most important agents of a university—the faculty—enjoy the rights of tenure, particularly the right and freedom to do largely as they please.

When presidents announce that the institution is to move in a certain direction, they must be sure that others have carefully prepared the chosen path and that it is close to other paths traveled before. On occasion, presidents can, if they wish, proclaim a "vision" for the school, but that vision must already have been purged of elements that would prove offensive to any large number of faculty, alumni, or trustees. They are hobbled leaders. Their lordly lives and the material advantages lavished on them do not mirror the limitations of the clout they have. Their power is both real and imaginary.

The story of failed presidents makes up, in fact, a small but important part of American academic history. In some cases, the story is simply one of inadequacy and poor preparation. Such was the situation when Kenneth Pitzer came to Stanford during the Vietnam War protests and stayed only 630 days. In other cases, the person who fails is the holder of a vision well in advance of the time when the institution is able to embrace it. The story of Henry Tappan, who presided over the University of Michigan from 1852 to 1863, is an early example of this kind of failure. Tappan believed the future of American higher education would reside in how well it could accommodate itself to the German model of pure research and graduate training. Contemptuous of practical education and taken with the belief that only an intellectual elite could move the university away from a concern with everyday knowledge, he wanted Michigan's public schools to be led by exceptionally trained graduates of the university. But Michigan was not ready for his ideas, and the university's Regents, after seeing those ideas belittled, dismissed him. Having given Michigan more than a decade of service, he spent the rest of his life in Europe.[1] Two decades later, Johns Hopkins University adopted the Germanic model, placed graduate education at the center of things, and transformed higher education in this country by declaring that it would be much more than what the traditional college could be. Tappan was right, but his timing was bad.

Four recent attempts by presidents to change their respective institutions, and the dramatic failure of those attempts, have continued this melancholy history. In the late 1990s, Hugo Sonnenschein, president of the University of Chicago, proclaimed that the institution had to be transformed. An economist by training, he noted the relatively weak endowment of the school, its mediocre record in attracting the very best undergraduate students (against competition in the Ivy League and with places like Stanford and MIT), and the reputation of Chicago as a "grind" school. So he proposed to transform the old "Common Core" curriculum, which had evolved from the school's "Great Books" course of the 1930s. He also sought to reduce the number of required courses in the humanities, sciences, and social sciences from 21 to 15 and to remove a long-standing foreign language requirement. The core courses would now make up only one-third, rather than half, of a student's required classes. Planning to expand the size of the undergraduate student body by about 20 percent, to 4,500, he intimated that Chicago would henceforth be "smart but fun."

Chicago was not ready at all for his vision of things. In short order, a group of concerned students, alumni, and faculty, including Nobel laureate Saul Bellow, wrote a letter to Sonnenschein telling him to cease what he was doing. The core curriculum should remain as it was because it was the soul of the Chicago experience. They also said that to make academic decisions "on the basis of marketing is itself a crime against the mind." Some alumni announced that they would no longer contribute to the school if the new plan were put in place. Many students cried "foul." It did not take long for the mounting pressure to force Sonnenschein to resign, and so he did, after seven years in office. So much for his presidential plans to effect change.

In 2001 at Tulane University, president Scott Cowan, viewing with alarm the fact that his school's Division I athletic program constantly lost games and hemorrhaged money, asked the trustees to undertake a thorough investigation of the place of football at the institution and to see if Tulane might move from Division I to less expensive and more appropriate Division III. After many months of research and fact-finding, an eight-member ad hoc trustee committee voted 7–1 to abandon football and seek membership in Division III. But no sooner had this news become public than an onslaught of community protest, organized in part by members of the Tulane athletic department, broke forth. Many New Orleans citizens and the local media proclaimed their desire that the "Green Wave" go on forever as a Division I school, even though the football team, playing in the New Orleans Superdome, hosted poorly attended games and every year drained some seven to eight million dollars from the school's treasury. President Cowan knew that football would never enhance the intellectual reputation of the school but only weaken it, and that Tulane, suffering from a weak endowment (some $600 million), could ill afford to absorb loss after loss to its budget. And he knew that by going to Division III, Tulane would no longer have to bear the burden of hundreds of athletic scholarships and many other athletic expenses. As president, he knew what had to be done. But as a president with

strong survival instincts, he knew that his "vision" would have to
yield to the realities of the day. Those realities ultimately included
a trustee vote to override the ad hoc committee's recommendations. Tulane's athletic program would continue at the Division I
level. President Cowan, unlike President Sonnenschein, scrapped
his visionary plan to change sports at the university. He also kept
his job.

At Cornell University, Jeffrey S. Lehman ended his presidency in
2005 after only two years on the job and, in so doing, stunned faculty, alumni, and students. Brought to the campus after a distinguished career as dean of the University of Michigan Law School,
he was the first Cornell alumnus to serve as its president. Decisive,
strong, and apparently possessed of a clear idea of the direction in
which the school should go, he encountered a board of trustees
with its own settled notions for Cornell. As the chairman of the
presidential search committee when Mr. Lehman was hired put it,
"He and the board came to separate conclusions as to the strategy
for achieving Cornell's long-term vision . . . there were differences
of viewpoint as to how to achieve that vision, not just with the
chairman but with other board members."[2] Lehman departed and
the board remained.

Perhaps the single most dramatic crash of a university president
was that of Larry Summers at Harvard in 2006. A gifted economist, and former Secretary of the Treasury under Bill Clinton, he
was selected by those governing the university as a strong leader
who would assert his authority over the many entrenched academic fiefdoms that make up Harvard. Going right to work, his
solid achievements included establishing an institute on stem-cell
research, increasing faculty size and expanding Harvard's campus.
But he also used his "bully pulpit" to express opinions on a number of controversial issues—the innate scientific ability of women,
institutional divestment from Israel owing to its policies with
respect to Palestinians, and the scholarly value of the work of
individual Harvard professors (most prominently Cornel West).
His authority to put forth his vision of the university was not in
question; but the manner in which he did so—brusquely, without
nuance, and with an executive's taste for "command and

control"—led him to disaster. Amid a rancorous turnover among deans, he suffered a no-confidence vote from Harvard's Faculty of Arts and Sciences in 2005. Facing a similar vote in 2006, he announced his resignation. To his supporters, Summers was perceived as an inspired change from college presidents who devote themselves to fund raising. To his detractors, he was considered a bully. In the end, Summers' "vision" proved no match for the strength of his faculty adversaries. He had the shortest stint of any Harvard president since Cornelius Felton died in 1862 after two years in office.

Presidential "visions" often wind up as only modest forays into the densely thicketed landscape of faculty prerogatives, trustee caution, alumni intransigence, and student apathy. They are snuffed out by compromise and fatigue. And yet the added irony is that while presidents might not get to see their "visions" realized, they do control other matters. They are those that only presidents— because they are presidents—are given. They are particularly the problems that local newspapers are fond of covering: student unrest, faculty misbehavior, scandals revealing the foolishness of intellectuals, and anything involving sex. This truth came home to me with particular force in my third year at Emory.

In late June, 1997, I was informed that the dean of Oxford College, Emory's two-year satellite campus, had denied the use of the chapel there to two men, one of them an Emory employee, for a same-sex commitment ceremony. The employee complained that his rights under the university's nondiscriminatory policy were thereby abridged. If weddings could be performed in the chapel, then he could be united there with his partner. Believing he was correct, I immediately apologized to him and overturned the dean's decision. Within a few days, the foundation on which Emory rested began to feel tremors both large and small. The local press assumed its customary predatory interest in a matter it deemed sensational. While no one on the campus seemed upset, members of the United Methodist Church, particularly the leadership of the North Georgia Conference, began to voice their objections to my decision. They said that church policy specifically proscribed both the use of Methodist churches for "ceremonies that celebrate homosexual unions" and the right of Methodist clergy to officiate over such events. Led by the Methodist bishops who were university trustees, they further claimed that Emory University "is a United Methodist university owned by the Southeastern Jurisdiction of the United Methodist Church" and therefore had to abide by Methodist regulations concerning homosexuality. They asked me to reverse my decision and scheduled a private meeting with Bradley Currey, chair of the trustees, and me, with the clear implication that if I did not change my mind, they would demand that the trustees overrule me. Other Methodists urged my firing, and the mail I received at the time told me a great deal about how the Bible can be interpreted, if one is so inclined, to see homosexuality as a monstrous sin. I knew that I had made a crucial decision, one only a president could have made, and that my presidential authority was now at stake. While I never thought I would be dismissed, as Hugo Sonnenschein had been, I was unsure how the matter would be settled.

The resolution was typical of how, at times, presidential determination can be backed by institutional fortitude. I charged the dean of the chapel at Emory, Susan Henry-Crowe, to join her counterpart at little Oxford College, to undertake a series of visits, consultations, and meditative sessions with their fellow Methodists, members of the board of trustees, and myriad others with the aim of seeking a resolution of "the chapel issue." They proved indefatigable and shrewd, their work exemplifying the kind of patience needed in situations where a slow pace and methodical manner can work wonders in undermining the passion of one's adversaries and the limited attention span of the press. Neither of them believed, any more than did the board or I, the remarkable claim that the church "owned" the university. Emory's duly constituted board of trustees had from the beginning assumed total fiduciary responsibility for the institution. Administrative officers had supervised its affairs on a daily basis for decades. The United Methodist Church had managed nothing at Emory, and its annual donations to the University were a pittance (though individual church members had given considerable sums to the school). Equally weak was the belief that I was championing "gay marriage." A same-sex union is not, legally, a marriage. I knew that; I was championing a correct reading of university policy.

After months of controversy, the community had enough, and the trustees met to put the issue behind them. Without serious dissent, they decided to permit same-sex unions in the chapels only under two special circumstances: that the ceremony be performed by a minister or rabbi from one of the various denominations, Protestant or Jewish, that allowed such unions, and that the minister or rabbi be a known presence on campus. By regulation, no Methodist could perform such a ceremony, but ministers representing Unitarians or the United Church of Christ, or a rabbi representing the Reform wing of Judaism, could. By implication, the trustees also wound up condoning same-sex unions anywhere else on the campus—under a tree, by a nearby stream, or in any classroom. But in those circumstances, the ceremony would have as much legal validity as a same-sex union anywhere else in the state of Georgia: none. Before they were done, the trustees also voted full confidence in me. Thus the matter came to an end. Brad Currey, who never could have imagined that he would have to mix in gay matters when he became chairman of the trustees, showed superb courage and steadfastness throughout this peculiar chapter of Emory's life.

What I learned from this experience is that only a president could provoke such a controversy; only the backing of the president could end it. As I found out, presidential authority is odd in its expression and odder still in its validation. It is hard to make it work, but work it can. And when it functions, it needs support. It is best employed sparingly—to focus on key issues. And the president should select issues on which to fight where he can be fairly sure that he must win and will win. Gay rights was such an issue at Emory. As a Southern school in the Bible Belt, Emory had to divorce itself, clearly and emphatically, from the surrounding atmosphere of bigotry and ignorance. It did so and now need never look back. (I also note that the issue, as important as it was to the institution, had nothing to do with the life of the mind. Most of the faculty rightly took no interest in it, nor did most students. Presidents now and again have to explore distant and strange territories remote from education.)

This experience also reminded me in yet another way that while much of what presidents do is ceremonial and totemic, they represent something profoundly substantive. Their worlds are much shaped by symbols, but they are surrounded by two activities—teaching and research—that are thoroughly real. Presidents must understand these activities and do all they can to exalt and support them. My own teaching, which was part of my yearly calendar at both Wesleyan and Emory, was a steady reminder to me of the power of the classroom. What I learned there as a teacher inspired me as a president. To teach is to meet everything that young minds can bring to that arena: expectation, curiosity, preconceptions, resistance, and hope. That is why I returned every year to teach (and studies show that about one in five of my presidential colleagues did likewise).

At its best, teaching is unlike any other experience in life. It asks the teacher to take at face value everything the students said or implied when they filled out their applications for admission—that they want to be challenged, that they know the material is difficult, and that they will show their full capacity to be intellectually responsive. Given those conditions, the teacher who enters the classroom has tacitly accepted a parallel responsibility: to honor the commitment the school made in all of its colorful brochures—that the teacher will stimulate, provoke, and challenge aspiring students. Out of these two agreements, the classroom exchange assumes a moral identity. It is a wager about hope. The principal parties each seek to bring forth the better sides of their natures. Each has gone further in optimism than customarily occurs in life, and thus they acknowledge the classroom as a place suggesting a suspension of customary—and often negative—expectations. If they can sustain this suspension, with both teacher and student demanding the best of each other, they can achieve memorable results.

Of course some classroom results are memorable because they are charmingly odd. Every other year at Emory I would teach my class on James Joyce, with special emphasis given to *Ulysses*. I would tell the students that they would have to work very hard to understand the book but that I would always be there for them—as instructor, explainer, and "coach." I would urge them on, giving them reading strategies, consoling them when the difficulties seemed insuperable, and promising them that all their efforts would prove rewarding. We would read the great book *together*. Nevertheless, now and again, while all of us were throwing all our intellectual resources into the reading, a student overwhelmed by the magnitude of the project could say something that would momentarily render our efforts absurd. This happened one day when I asked the class what the chief difficulty of the book seemed to be. The over-whelmed student plaintively said: "The words."

Some students are never overwhelmed. One student at Emory stands in my mind for all the hopes and dreams of the students I came to know in forty years. Danielle Sered entered Emory in 1995, shortly after I did, and in four years had accomplished so much that she became one of the university's nominees for a Rhodes Scholarship. It happened that in 1999, her senior year, I accepted an invitation to chair the regional Rhodes committee that, interviewing the finalists from seven southern states, would name a number of winners. I had not taught Danielle Sered, but had heard a good deal about her extraordinary achievements. Coming from a broken and poor family, she had taken out sub-stantial loans to keep herself in school. Her father, taking little interest in her academic career, offered her no financial support. She supported herself by working twenty or more hours per week as a waitress or work-study clerical employee. Nonetheless, she made every year count and left an indelible mark on the memories of her teachers. She published essays and poems in national liter-ary and collegiate magazines; her critical essay on the work of an Irish poet won a national prize. She was elected to Phi Beta Kappa. She founded a program teaching conflict resolution, prej-udice reduction, and sex education through the arts in Atlanta city schools and juvenile detention centers. She launched the Emory Women's Alliance, a network of mentors and support for female Emory faculty, staff, and students, and helped to develop a cam-pus theater company that performed plays in local schools.

When interviewed by the Rhodes committee, she wore a dress purchased for her by one of Emory's administrators, a colleague who knew how little money for clothing Danielle had. In her new garment, she was poised, self-possessed, and alert. Questioned by everyone but me (I had to remain neutral), she was resourceful and serious. I was amazed by her fluency and her ease with questions meant to be challenging that, in her hands, became opportunities to quote poetry, allude to critics, and remind us all of the sumptuousness of English literature. It was a performance glistening with a young person's astonishing talent.

When we convened to make the final decisions, I fought to keep silent. The committee could only name, from the fourteen finalists, four Rhodes Scholars. One member opened the deliberations by saying "I suppose there's no point in talking about Ms. Sered." For one long moment, his pronouncement stood in the air for me, cryptic with its own suspense. Then another member said, "I concur. She was simply stunning, spectacular. Let's go on. We now have to select three others." I could not have been happier for Danielle Sered or prouder for Emory. She went to Oxford and sustained the same creativity and intellectual engagement there that she showed at Emory. When glorious things happen, they reveal everything a university can be.

The research activities of a university can be no less gratifying. When I arrived at Emory in August 1994, the university's Yerkes Regional Primate Research Center lacked both direction and energy. But by the end of that academic year, we had recruited a research psychiatrist, Thomas Insel, from the National Institute of Mental Health, to become its director. He went to work immediately to make Yerkes a leading center in the effort to develop a vaccine for HIV/AIDS. He announced that he would focus half of the funding coming to Yerkes on that effort. To that end, he lured Harriet Robinson to Yerkes from the University of Massachusetts in 1997. She brought both energy and an entirely radical way of thinking about vaccines. Knowing that vaccine production is a matter of protein synthesis, she asked if cells could not be "taught" to produce the specific vaccine by giving them ready-made DNA to generate the desired protein. For years other scientists denigrated her approach on the grounds that the DNA in question would not be taken up by enough cells to yield an immune response. But in time, DNA vaccines began to seem plausible and Robinson's research methods and results gained favor. By 2001, they had become so important that one of her papers in *Science* was, for several months, the most cited article in immunology. Her vaccine tested well with monkeys at Yerkes and was approved by the Food and Drug Administration for human trials that began in early 2003. With AIDS having killed more than twenty-two million people since 1981, and with forty million others infected, she knew that the stakes of the struggle were very high, as was the global competition to produce a vaccine that would be both inexpensive and dependable.

In time, perhaps a pharmacological firm will market and distribute the results of this research. Harriet Robinson shares a financial interest in one such firm. But at the foundation of her work is the support and encouragement that only a university could have given her. Since the thinking and creativity germane to such research entails considerable risk, Emory and Yerkes have to reckon with the possibility that their investment, along with that of the federal government, might yield no useful results. On the other hand, Robinson's work might bring to the world a vaccine that could prevent massive death. Such is the nature of academic invention—risky, indeterminate in its results for years, and highly dependent on key individuals and the ways they are recruited and supported.

To speed invention means, for the president, appointing the right academic officers and the right fiscal experts. If, in the end, a university is no better than its faculty, the best faculty will not accept appointments, nor will they remain, unless the deans are smart, energetic, and ambitious. Nor will that faculty do its best work unless it is well paid and well supported. I once asked Emory's dean of admissions what I should do if I suddenly found myself with 25 million new dollars for the university. He said the school should invest the money in new faculty. I agreed with him, but commented that presidents don't appoint faculty: department chairs, deans, and provosts do. That means those officers must be shrewd in assessing intellectual promise. Recognizing this fact, I spent a good part of my time as president in supervising the appointment process that would put the best people in charge of Emory's nine academic divisions—the deans. Since those deans themselves had to be well led, I also had to be sure about the quality of the person to whom they would directly report—the provost. In my nine Emory years, I (along with the customary search committees) appointed a dozen deans and two provosts—Rebecca Chopp, a distinguished theologian and later the president of Colgate University, and Howard Hunter, formerly the graceful and patient dean of Emory Law School and now the president of Singapore Management University—as well as a chief fiscal officer, the legal counsel for the university, and other key administrators. In hoping they all would have strong and successful records, I was again reminded that presidents are not without power, but they can use it only at specific moments within fixed structures of understanding and agreement. As I kept on learning, presidential power is a sometime thing.

Whenever the deans and the provost and I discussed faculty quality, and whenever we tried to imagine what the "perfect" new faculty member would bring to the campus, the answer always came down to one indispensable attribute: a quality of mind, such as that possessed by Harriet Robinson, that could transform the given discipline itself. Of course we saw the value of other positive attributes: most importantly, strong and inspiring teaching combined with a good sense of civic responsibility to the institution. But we saw genuine intellectual excellence as a virtue surpassing all others. We also knew it was rare. Most faculty members, as good as they are, do no more than further the life of a discipline and give it sustenance over time. They supply the brains and devotion on which that discipline rides through the years. And that is service enough to constitute an honorable career. But now and again, someone will understand the inner life of the field and will see how, if it is truly to prove productive for a new generation of scholars, it will have to take on a new shape. These are the colleagues who create new paradigms for the discipline while shattering the old ones. Every field has such people. They come, however, only infrequently: Amos Tversky in psychology, Fernand Braudel in history, Meyer Abrams in literary history, James Watson and Francis Crick in chemistry, Noam Chomsky in linguistics, Amartya Sen in economics, Niels Bohr in physics, Benoit Mandelbrot in mathematics, Barbara McClintock in physiology, and so on.

Simply to conjure with such names, as we occasionally did, was to remind ourselves what the presence of such creative minds can do for a discipline and a university. It trumps money, location, age of the school, and even the reputation of good teaching. When it is present, however, it helps with the money and can augment the kind of prestige that lures other distinguished researchers and, in turn, excellent teachers, to the campus. There is nothing more valuable than the kind of accelerated push toward excellence that Emory was beginning in my time. But we knew that Emory's situation was like that of most American research institutions: we all had a great distance to go. For my part, I was happy with the knowledge of how far we had come. I also believed I was carrying out the mandate given me by Bob Strickland.

As I now and again reflected on my salary, a considerable part of which we yearly distributed to various charities but whose size invariably embarrassed me, I thought of the relative cost to recruit the very best faculty. My mind went back to Haverford and how that school negotiated the delicate relationship between faculty and presidential compensation. Four decades ago, Haverford pegged the president's salary as no more than $250 greater than that of the highest-paid professor. The president was important, but only modestly so. As the years went on, all universities and colleges had ramped up presidential compensation to the point that some of my national colleagues in 2002 were drawing close to a million dollars a year.[3] How had this happened?

One of the two engines of change was the mistaken but nonetheless ever-popular notion that the president is not so much an intellectual and moral leader as a CEO, and should be defined by trustees in terms appropriate to the world of business. The other force prompting the escalation was the competitive ratchet: no school wished to leave its president in the category of "worst-paid," or even modestly paid, for that could reflect badly on the school's financial standing and could make people believe that it was an "also-ran." Annual surveys of presidential salaries allowed each board of trustees to monitor its president's place on the national ladder and to set a suitable salary increase. As every school jock-eyed to do better than the average, the entire cohort ascended higher and higher. My presidential colleagues were hardly unaware of this competitive pressure, and, using it to their advantage, some adapted to it with remarkable skill. Few could directly command salary increases, but many found themselves in agreement with the notion that the school would be damaged were it to "fall behind." This collusive ratcheting upwards, particularly at a time when faculty salaries lagged and tuition rose, invited sharp criticism. Robert H. Atwell, a former president of the American Council on Education, expressed the worries of many critics who saw how the life of the mind was aping the life of commerce: "Just because corporate America is engaging in excessive greed is no reason for public universities or private ones to go down that same road. . . . It is a bad trend, and it's getting out of hand."[4]

My reaction to the situation mixed curiosity with embarrassment. Wanting to know what the trustees thought of me, I asked Brad Currey, a man of considerable integrity and moral bearing, for annual reviews of my performance. These discussions were informal and brief. "Bill," he would say, "I like what you have done and so do the other trustees." And that was that. No more discussion. He knew what other presidents made; Emory was not going to lose its place. He would then tell the treasurer what the new number for me for the coming year was. I would find it out when I opened my pay envelope. Although he had not gone to Emory (Princeton was his alma mater), as board chairman he had the same deep civic consciousness as his predecessor Bob Strickland. He wanted Emory to flourish because he wanted the city of Atlanta to flourish. I was not unhappy to think that he believed Emory's president should also prosper.

No matter how they are compensated, some presidents are haunted, as I was, by the knowledge that I have earlier described in this book: they work in an atmosphere dominated by the strenuous exercise of the human mind at its best but they do not engage in intellectual work at all. Presidents do not think the same way that their most eminent faculty colleagues do. They can't. Presidents must reckon with the problems of the day, shipping some of those problems off to other administrators and living with the ones no one else can cope with. They are forever to confront, respond, mitigate, and resolve. That kind of work creates in presidential life the sense of continual motion. This perpetual busyness is not to be confused, however, with the kind of rigorous intellectual inventiveness undertaken by the best of the president's professorial colleagues.

Although my Emory presidency did not focus on raising money, and I was more on the campus worrying about its welfare than traveling the country in search of philanthropic support, I often observed what the institution lacked and only a generous donation could establish. Among the absences was a first-rate performing arts center. I knew, as did many others, that such an absence was embarrassing. So I began to try to raise the money for that building, only again and again to be frustrated by the apparent lack of interest on the part of the business-minded trustees as well as every potential donor we approached. In addition, Emory's strongest philanthropic supporter—the Woodruff Foundation—not only continued to confine its contributions to the medical side of the house but also made it clear that it would not support a performing arts center that might compete with the Woodruff Arts Center in downtown Atlanta.

Just as I was beginning to think that such a center at Emory would never get built and that donors and trustees would forever see the arts as mere trifles, an event occurred that reminded me of how mysterious and chancy fund-raising is. At a dinner in New York City, one of many we hosted to bring Emory to the attention of alumni and parents, I again described the extraordinary need we had for such a center. It would provide a platform for the creative work of our students and faculty and could also be a venue for great performers from elsewhere in the world. Not a bauble, but a focal point of imaginative energy. It would recognize and celebrate just how much of what human beings do best is not limited to the linear, the systematic, and the provable. The campus, I said, should provide experiences that spoke to all dimensions of the brain and spirit.

Two days after the dinner, one of the guests called me, and asked simply: "Would eight million dollars help?" The caller was Marvin Schwartz, whose wife and daughter were Emory alumnae. An extraordinarily successful investment broker in New York, he had heard my message. Combining a formidably keen analytical mind with a love of what human creativity can be, Schwartz changed Emory history with that call. After it, we could go to other donors and urge them to follow his lead. With his call, he created momentum. In time, and at the urging of one particularly devoted and insistent trustee, all of the other trustees were at last convinced (some still reluctantly) that one hundred percent giving on their part was a part of board responsibility. And in the course of the next few years, the center, now a jewel of the campus, was built. We had known next to nothing about Marvin Schwartz before that dinner. He had known little about us. But the chemistry suddenly formed between donor and institution made all the difference.

Other donors acted more mysteriously. In 1997, one of them, after being asked for $3.5 million to help the business school, told me that he would be willing to give $3.6 million but not $3.5. Momentarily imagining how my response might compete with his for pure oddity, I fantasized turning him down. But of course I said that Emory would be honored by his generosity. (I suspect that his accountant had given him the number.) On another occasion, a donor cut me off in mid-sentence, saying he wished to hear nothing more from me and that his check, drawn exactly to the amount I had named for his donation ($1.5 million), would be in the mail the next day, and it was. Had I told him more about how good Emory was, perhaps he would have decreased his gift accordingly.

Fundraising is a process that depends on a large army of campus mercenaries, formidable (but always incomplete) research and intelligence, patience, and the recognition that not only is "donor strangeness" part of the external environment, but that "sales" will forever have to confront "customer resistance." In the case of Emory, the institution's endowment wealth always posed an impediment to giving. Why give, as many potential donors preached to me, when the university's endowment is so large? How could a gift of, say, ten thousand dollars make much of a difference to an institution sitting on an endowment of more than four billion dollars? And when the Woodruff Foundation was giving so much (in my nine years at Emory, it gave more than $700 million to Emory, all funneled into the health sciences), an individual donor could not be blamed for thinking his contribution a mere pittance. In the face of such resistance, I would argue that any gifts, large or small, could be made not to the endowment but to a specific part of the university. There they could carry substantial consequences. Sometimes my answer proved convincing; sometimes it was not. Emory looked rich, very rich, and I had to live with that fact while pointing out to potential donors that parts of it were quite poor.

With the building of the performing arts center, and with my recognition that, after some eight years of my presidency, Emory had experienced the greatest period of new construction in its history, I began to think that I had completed my job at the school. The Emory everybody now could see was different than the Emory I had entered in 1994. Some $800 million of construction had dramatically changed the landscape. The new structures included not only the Schwartz Center for the Performing Arts, but also a cancer institute, a new residential center for students, a biomedical research building, and a major renovation of the library. We had added some 1.3 million square feet of new space and another 53,000 square feet of renovated space for teaching, research, and residential living. Emory was thus rivaling every university in the nation for the scope of its investment in such facilities.

I could feel good about other accomplishments too. In 1996, when I appointed the new head of the vast health sciences operation at Emory, I told him that it would be wonderful if his division

could double its research funding in five years from its level of
$132 million. By 2001, the total had reached $278 million, and by
2003, $319 million. Having appointed ambitious deans and pro-
ductive scientists, we could expect that research volume would
grow even more rapidly.

The record elsewhere was bright. In forming a partnership with
Georgia Tech, we had created a doctoral program in biomedical
engineering. As an alliance between a private institution and a
public one, the partnership might seem unlikely. But it came about
because it linked a school that did no engineering with one that
did no medicine. It now stands a good chance of enduring over
time. And in another area that meant a great deal to me as an
English professor, we had developed one of the strongest collections of twentieth-century literary material in the world. People
would come to Emory to study Seamus Heaney, Ted Hughes,
Anthony Hecht, Lady Gregory, the poets of Northern Ireland, and
a score of African-American writers and artists. Moreover, for
Emory's reputation in general, the news was good. Undergraduate
admissions had become much more selective. In some areas—
cancer research, physics, religious studies, public health, business,
law, and psychology, among others—the determination to make
stronger faculty appointments was paying dividends. Thanks to
the generosity of one ambitious donor, the campus had taken on
a much richer international character; more and more distinguished students, scholars, and visitors were coming to Emory,
and more Emory students were studying overseas.

A decade is about as long as anyone can serve as president of an
American research university. A few people go longer and remain
productive and helpful to the institution, but in other instances
such long tenure is stultifying. The American Council on
Education reports that presidents serve, on average, about six to
seven years.[5] Every two years, almost a third of them leave office.[6]
The reasons for such short terms are many. Energy flags, the
president repeats certain ideas without being able to give them
new force, and the constant friction between the president and
resistant faculty or trustees takes its toll on everyone. The situation
is better at private schools than at public ones. The latter often

heap on presidents problems not of their own making and over which they have little control: a losing football team, a refractory state legislature, reduced tax revenues for education, or a public momentarily outraged by the conduct of a faculty member. Private institutions can be more tenderhearted, but as I learned at Wesleyan, the quality of mercy does not droppeth everywhere as the gentle rain from heaven.

Public or private, the job of being president is wholly consuming, never-ending, and, while intensely interesting, is also simply intense. Few people indeed have been put into the world who can take on the identity of a university as their own, but that is what presidents must do. Inevitably, however, the gap between the identity of the solitary human being and the identity of the institution opens up and, after that, only becomes larger. It is then time to leave.

My departure as Emory's president came about this way. In 2002, I asked the new chair of the board, Ben Johnson, a leading Atlanta lawyer who succeeded Bradley Currey, how he would assess my achievements. Adopting his customary opaque and funereal manner (which served as protective camouflage for his privately cultivated liberalism), he limited himself to remarking that I had done "well." He then observed that I would soon be 65 years old. It is easy to make sense of some laconic statements. I concluded that he felt Emory could do better with a new president. Presidents are often asked, at the end of their terms of office, if they have "jumped" or have been "pushed." Ready to leave, I jumped once I knew the push was on its way. We agreed that the coming academic year, 2003–04, my ninth as president of Emory, should be my last. I said I would like to return to the campus, after some time off, as an English professor. Johnson accepted my plan. We shook hands, and, with that, I knew my life as an administrator would soon come to an end.

ENDNOTES

1. See Arthur Levine, "Succeeding as a Leader; Failing as a President," *Change*, January/February, 1998, p. 43.

2. Julianne Basinger, "In a Surprise, Cornell Chief Steps Down," *Chronicle of Higher Education* June 24, 2005, p. A1.

3. The American Association of University Professors reports that, in 2004–05, the ratio of the salaries of presidents to average full professors at public doctoral institutions was 3.02 at the median and 5.07 at the maximum; at private doctoral institutions, the median was 3.27 and the maximum was 6.72. At some schools, then, the president was deemed almost seven times as valuable as the average full professor. See the AAUP website: http://www.aaup.org/research/Index.htm.

4. As quoted in Julianne Basinger, "High Pay, Hard Questions," *Chronicle of Higher Education*, November 9, 2004. In the 2004 fiscal year one university president received $1.33 million in total compensation from his institution, and he made an additional $275,000 by serving on five corporate boards. See Audrey Williams June, "College Presidents Break into the Million-Dollar Club," *Chronicle of Higher Education*, November 18, 2005, pp. B12–B14.

5. See *The American College President* (Washington, DC: American Council on Education, 2002). This report, found at http://www.acenet. edu, says: "The average length of service as president remained steady at 6.3 years in 1986 and 6.6 years in 2001."

6. *Presidents Make a Difference: Strengthening Leadership in Colleges and Universities* (Washington, DC: Association of Governing Boards of Colleges and Universities, 1984), p. xii.

27

"A King of Infinite Space"

On September 23, 2003, nine years and one month after JoAn and I came to Emory, I gave a formal farewell to the presidency, and the university said goodbye to us, at least for a while. The trustees awarded me a sabbatical year to mark the time before I would come back to teach in the English department. JoAn could put behind her forever a role that was wholly stimulating and at times exciting, but also ambiguous, demanding, and uncompensated. For her, no more afternoon teas and no more amiable and gracious pleasantries to compose the entire substance of many a long evening. I would depart from a position I had enjoyed and from which I had learned a great deal about many aspects of private higher education, but whose minor glories and unremitting pressures served to drive a wedge between who I was as a person and who I was as an official.

I would always look back on the Emory presidency as a distinctive honor. But for a long time I had known that being president is a way of adding to one's life a great many acquaintances while only rarely adding new friends. And friendship was something I increasingly missed. As I thought about its elusiveness, a passage from *Ulysses* came to mind. In it, Joyce describes the way his hero Leopold Bloom's life had developed: "the progressive extension of the field of individual development and experience was regressively accompanied by a restriction of the converse domain of interindividual relations." A charmingly convoluted way of putting it, but true indeed about being a Jew in Dublin in 1904 and true also about being a university president. Over the years, I had not enjoyed feeling apart from things, even when I knew I was at the center of them.

September 23 was a day of pleasure untouched by any second guesses about the decision to step away from the presidency.

Seamus Heaney, whom we had known since 1975, came from Ireland and filled the house at the Schwartz Center for the Performing Arts with an afternoon poetry reading in our honor. The Nobel laureate took the occasion to announce that he would be consigning his entire literary correspondence and personal papers to the Emory library. No announcement, this one coming from a wonderful poet and good friend for more than twenty-five years, could have given me more pleasure. His decision would help make the university a central location of materials relating to twentieth-century poetry. In the evening, we hosted a buffet dinner and dance to which we invited not only most of our acquaintances but all of our friends. To everyone's relief, not a single speech was given.

And then it was over. We went away for a year to a small house in Mystic, Connecticut, to read, walk our two dogs, learn some Italian, and look at falling snow. Committee meetings, personnel decisions, and what Yeats calls the "management of men" would forever be a part of the world of our memories, but no longer a part of the world around us. In that sabbatical period, I began writing this book.

In its introduction, I said that "none of the rooms where the work of a college or university is done is now a secret to me," and I remarked that they had made up my world. Being in and out of those rooms for half a century, with one year off for bad behavior, has made me a champion of higher education. I preface my advocacy with the usual acknowledgments about the flaws that can always be found when any human institution is under scrutiny: inefficiency, redundancy of effort, parochialism, venality, and self-satisfaction. Critics can always find some professors or administrators to be craven in this regard or slovenly in that. So be it. I believe, however, that higher education in this country has done immeasurably greater good than harm and that it is among this country's greatest achievements. I hope that its future will include a central legacy of its past—its success as a social escalator moving young people to stations in life unavailable to their parents. I also hope that it will continue its role as a lubricating agent in freeing up the movement among different racial and ethnic groups in this country, for that will reinforce a key element of the American democratic dynamic. But against these hopes is my concern, one shared by many who have "followed the money," that high tuition costs and burdensome post-graduation debts will restrict the best of higher education to a narrow sector of America's families.

Because some of what it does is arcane, much of it old-fashioned, and all of it expensive in labor and time, it will attract, as any successful yet uncommon human enterprise inevitably does, a cavalcade of critics. Lively minds will continue to derive much satisfaction in creating caricatures of the campus and its residents. If they did not secretly admire it so much, their denigration would have less force. Tom Wolfe's grotesquely cartoonish picture of the university as a zone of uninhibited sexual coupling and boorish beer-guzzling might strike some readers as plausible until they put aside *I Am Charlotte Simmons* and visit an actual campus. Similarly, the belief that all colleges and universities are arenas closed off to free thought because they are dominated by liberal political correctness will enjoy a long life among right-wing commentators—who, aware of quality, nevertheless will seek admission for their own children to just such places. Those children will encounter a complicated variety of thinking and belief on the part of professors who enjoy disagreeing with everyone about everything—including politics. They will also find that politics is simply absent from most classrooms. Chemistry, ancient history, mathematics, Slavic linguistics, Homeric poetry, computer science, statistics, microbiology, and countless other disciplines—the bulk of the curriculum—are innocent of ideology. The waters of ideology lap in but a few areas—English is one, as, by their very nature are women's studies, gay and lesbian studies, and ethnic studies. But the claim that the nation's universities and colleges are hothouses of political conformity cannot withstand close scrutiny. On the other hand, those who believe that the American university is on its way to becoming one more corporate institution obsessed with marketing, advertising, and the licensing of patents will have to ignore the many archaic procedures and practices that permeate the modern university and make it strikingly different from a business.

Some critics will complain that the university is not fulfilling its role as a moral academy devoted to the inculcation of specific values. Given its lamentable record in only fitfully honoring that responsibility, I conclude, with mixed regret and relief, that it should no longer try to do so. The morality it teaches, which must be seen as the best it can do, will come by indirection and example: teachers devoted to exactitude of thought and honesty of finding, libraries retentive of all learning and belief, and researchers determined to test, again and again, what is "obvious and settled" knowledge.

Other kinds of criticism will also enjoy a long life. Some legislators and conservative columnists will forever believe that much of the enterprise, in addition to being too expensive, is useless. On some days they will argue that its funding should be slashed, but on other days, they will solemnly note how much higher education has done for civic well-being. Some trustees will continue to have trouble in admiring, much less comprehending, the academic work of the institutions they are nominally overseeing. Some students will wish the process of education were over more quickly and satisfying jobs more at hand. And some professors will dream of an academy cleansed at last of administrative busybodies.

Some criticisms carry much more weight than these familiar grousings. The cost of education is indeed too high. Colleges and universities have become too expensive for many families, even those benefiting from financial aid, and while it is true that the consumer demands of some of those families have helped drive up the costs, the institutions have proved too compliant in yielding to those demands. The costs must come down by reducing some shopping-mall comforts of the campus. They are not meant to be "Club Eds." They must distinguish themselves from the conventional entertainments and commercial amusements of American life. If they do, in the end they will lose none of their attractiveness and will retain their special place in American culture. They are meant to be havens of thought, not pleasure resorts.

The admission procedures at colleges and universities should be geared more to the person who applies than to the numbers— SAT or ACT scores and grades—he or she can supply. This—a fundamental change—will be expensive and labor-intensive, but treating applicants as faceless units only encourages those admitted to treat the institution as a service and they themselves as customers. One by one the applications should be read, the young person considered as someone who may or may not be a good fit with the institution, and a match made between the potential of the actual applicant and the specific quality of the college or university.

Another fundamental change, and one to help reduce costs—my fellow presidents will consider this a form of heresy to be practiced only by someone no longer in office—should come by rethinking the levels of compensation provided to senior administrators. A realistic appraisal of the limits of their power—of what they can and cannot do—should bring their compensation down closer to that of the faculty. As things now stand, some presidents are paid more than $1 million per year, vastly more than any professor (save a few in clinical medicine) could imagine earning. Presidents should not be likened to business executives, for they are not. They should be seen, and see themselves, as men and women who are on campus to support the productive lives of the scholars, researchers, and students who are at the center of what the institution is all about. Presidents are not what academic life is all about. Most senior administrators would, in fact, not be good at business, nor should they be. They should love the peculiarities of learning and want, without excessive salaries, to help it along.

But they will continue to face tough assignments. One of the biggest is to recognize that at many schools they have allowed the growth of a cancer—big-time intercollegiate athletics—to infect the intellectual and moral ethic of genuine higher education.[1] Senior administrators must return the original spirit of "student athletics" to the campus by starving big-time sports of money and glamour. This will be exceedingly difficult to do, given, as I argue, that presidents possess limited power. But they should each use the share of power they have, unite it with that of their colleagues, and mount the bully pulpit available to them. That pulpit is today largely vacant. From it, university presidents can examine the ruin the cancer has already caused and face down those who will cry that big-time sports are crucial to the life of American higher education. They are not. They must be permanently disentangled from the life of learning. Only the presidents—speaking with one voice—can do this. First they must persuade their trustees, and then the public. They will have little trouble persuading most members of the faculty.

Even as schools outlive criticism and misunderstanding, faculty members and administrators will have to accept the fact that not everything in academia is now flourishing as it should. The field I know best—the study of English and American literature—will need a resurgence of toughmindedness to find its right place again in the academy. It has lost its way and now appears less a discipline with a coherent body of knowledge than a jumping-off point for other forms of investigation and pursuits having little to do with the literature of either England or the United States. Why is this important? Because as English departments go, so go many other departments in the humanities. And at the heart of what many people want to find in the university is the human wisdom once believed to reside within the humanities. Shakespeare does matter. A recovery effort, based on dedicated and intimate teaching in the humanities, should locate that wisdom again. Such a project must begin with a devotion to the books themselves, the ones that have lasted, and not with the elaborate theoretical apparatus secondary to those books or with distantly related topics.

Nor is the research effort now rightly understood on all campuses. Research should not lead to monetary profits, but to further learning. Nowhere is this truer than within medical centers. At large research universities such as Emory, the preeminence and fiscal weight of the health sciences, buttressed as they are by hospitals and patients and clinical money, cannot be permitted to overwhelm and jeopardize other areas of investigation. But medical centers, like certain forces of nature, have no self-limiting instincts. Therefore presidents, trustees, and others should enforce restrictions on their growth. Universities should have medical schools for one reason only: to teach medicine and to develop a deeper understanding of disease and health. In turn, they need patients to show medical students how disease occurs and how to treat it. After that come the hospitals. But those hospitals with those patients should exist solely for the sake of that teaching and that research. To maintain hospitals as competitive corporate ventures that do not train young doctors or do not produce research is to lead medical centers astray. Nothing at a university should become a business for its own sake.

In general, colleges and universities should concern themselves less with how they differ from each other and should seek ways to combine their resources, linking strength here with strength there. Every academic bond that Emory created with its neighbor Georgia Tech strengthened both schools; we found out that we could do some things together that we never could have done alone. On the other hand, the desire to produce a particular "vision" for each school in the nation or to concoct for each a "brand," and then to ballyhoo some minor difference among institutions that are, in fact, very much like each other, is a childish undertaking that should be laid aside. It wastes energy in the pursuit of phantoms. Tradition, inescapable in higher education, makes most colleges and universities more similar to each other than different.

The facts of the matter are stubbornly simple: every first-rate institution has, at its heart, an undergraduate college. Surrounding that college are professional and graduate schools and, in some cases, institutes and centers. Laboratories and libraries and computing centers support that venerable structure. What makes some schools better than other schools is one thing only: the quality of the faculty. Strong faculties attract others of their kind. Then the best students come. Then reputations change. Everything else is secondary. But changed reputations occur only slowly. They will not come about from the boosterish notion that schools should emphasize minor differences among themselves to titillate consumer demand. The British philosopher Richard Jenkyns is right in saying that it is foolish to want universities to produce "mission statements" other than ones that say: "We teach, study and write, and try to do these things as well as we can."[2] His plea, and mine, is for modesty and honesty in how universities represent themselves to the public.

They should, moreover, seek better ways of bringing themselves to the attention of that public than through attempts to raise money. Some universities and colleges have now become better known by virtue of their fund-raising campaigns than through their intellectual and educational activities. Such schools not only seek more and more money, but they also compete with each other to crank up the largest possible philanthropic goals. Because quality costs money, the first ambition is understandable. But because higher education should not construe itself as a money-gathering rivalry, the second is not. Moreover, those who are asked for money should ask if the ambitious campaigns they are told about are rooted in genuine educational needs or are the product of internal empire-building not unlike congressional "pork-barreling." One should give to a university or college only after one is convinced that the money will directly enhance the academic substance of the institution and not because the campaign goal is stunningly large.

The higher education that I have seen in the last fifty years has emerged to define much of our economy and our culture. In that half-century, it has created the largest storehouse of intellectual learning and mastery, spread out across the widest array of disciplines, in world history. A monumental resource like that attracts attention of every kind, some of it bad but most of it good. On the domestic front, it has become a dominant force in how many families budget their income and plan their futures. For navigating the world that teenagers see ahead of them, a college degree has become as important as a driver's license. Those young people deem success with the SAT or ACT to be the passport to future security. The campus has in turn become for them at once the destination, the prize, and the guarantee. Their parents recognize this importance and have learned to budget their resources accordingly. They should not be short-changed in what they have paid in tuition, but they should also understand that their child in attendance at a college or university is not a customer but a student. And students are not in school to demand ephemeral things; they are there to learn about important matters.

Those young people will be present on campuses that have come to monopolize the discourse in almost every intellectual field. They can walk into libraries that store much of the world's learning. This is a spectacular privilege. And they will see, if they are attentive, that the "campus" has now become the central metaphor for learning everywhere. Almost all the men and women who work and think outside the campus gates— residents of think tanks and of foundations, independent jour- nalists, and analysts in governmental agencies—were all trained at universities and tend to imitate, if not replicate, the academic lessons they learned there. It is hard in America to get away from the memory of the classroom, the lab, or the seminar. We are all seminarians now. And what corporation or business is today not proud to call its headquarters a "campus"? In both substance and figurative language, the American university shapes our thinking about thinking, wherever that activity takes place.

But I know it will change. That change will be slow because the institution of higher education is old, because its customs and rituals are deeply embedded in the minds of those who inhabit its campuses, and because the nation's colleges and uni- versities are among the small number of places where tradition, always at risk in America, still enjoys some prestige. Nonetheless, the numbers of young (and not so young) people who want and need an education will grow by the thousands in the years to come and colleges and universities will respond, forever awk- wardly, to their demands. Perhaps higher education, driven by market pressures, will be segmented, as James J. Duderstadt has imagined, into three groups: highly selective, expensive, and high-cost institutions that will continue to offer campus-based education to traditional age groups (e.g., Haverford, Berkeley, Stanford, and Emory); institutions that will enroll enormous numbers of students in low-cost but traditional programs (e.g., regional universities and community colleges); and proprietary institutions that will offer a broad range of educational services in cost-effective, customer-focused business models (e.g., the University of Phoenix).[3]

In that case, the six schools you have read about in this book will be seen for what they have always been: parts of a special and privileged entity in American culture. Among them, Haverford is its most perfect exemplar, a form of education wholly centered on the individual and his or her moral and intellectual development. Berkeley and Stanford represent the highest achievements of the "university" in all of its potential as a generator of research. But all of these places, including Stillman College, Wesleyan University, and Emory University, small and large, have been slow in forming, expensive to maintain, and driven by imperatives not always understood or admired by the public at large. They now will have to take their places in the company of other entities providing higher education for more people, and they will have to learn to exist as parts of a much larger fabric. They will still enjoy prestige, but their share of the larger world of higher education—in student and alumni numbers, in classroom and laboratory space, and in total employment of faculty and staff—will diminish year by year.

Nor will higher education itself ever be dominant in the life of this country. Universities and colleges make up only a tiny fraction of the immense panorama of modern American life. Higher education is not everything. But for me, it has been almost everything. Within its embrace, I have played, for a while, my part, a small one. Yet my surroundings—Haverford, Berkeley, Stillman, Stanford, Wesleyan, and Emory—have always looked big to me. Like Hamlet, but without his bad dreams, I have for fifty years—those one hundred semesters—been "bounded in a nutshell," inside higher education and always on a campus, and yet have counted myself "a king of infinite space." In providing me such a large and rich world to inhabit, the university has constantly been a reminder of the promise of youth, the excitement of learning, and the sanctity of teaching. In this book, I have thanked the people who helped me in my education. In closing, I thank the institutions—resilient, of many faces, and forever changing while always deferring to tradition—that sustained me and will sustain the teaching and learning of tomorrow.

ENDNOTES

1. Like cancer itself, the budgetary growth of big-time athletics within the body of universities grows faster than almost anything else. A new NCAA subcommittee on fiscal responsibility, which sees that "current trends are not sustainable," and that presidents must act to stave off "a looming crisis," reports that, "for the 2001–03 period, athletics operating expenditures in each subdivision of Division I grew more than three times as fast as total university operating expenditures." See NCAA Presidential Task Force, "White Paper No. 1 (Draft)," October 10, 2005.

2. Richard Jenkyns, "Mother Tongue," *Prospect Magazine*, January 2005, http://www.prospect-magazine.co.uk.

3. James J. Duderstadt, *A University for the 21st Century* (Ann Arbor: University of Michigan Press, 2000), p. 303.

INDEX